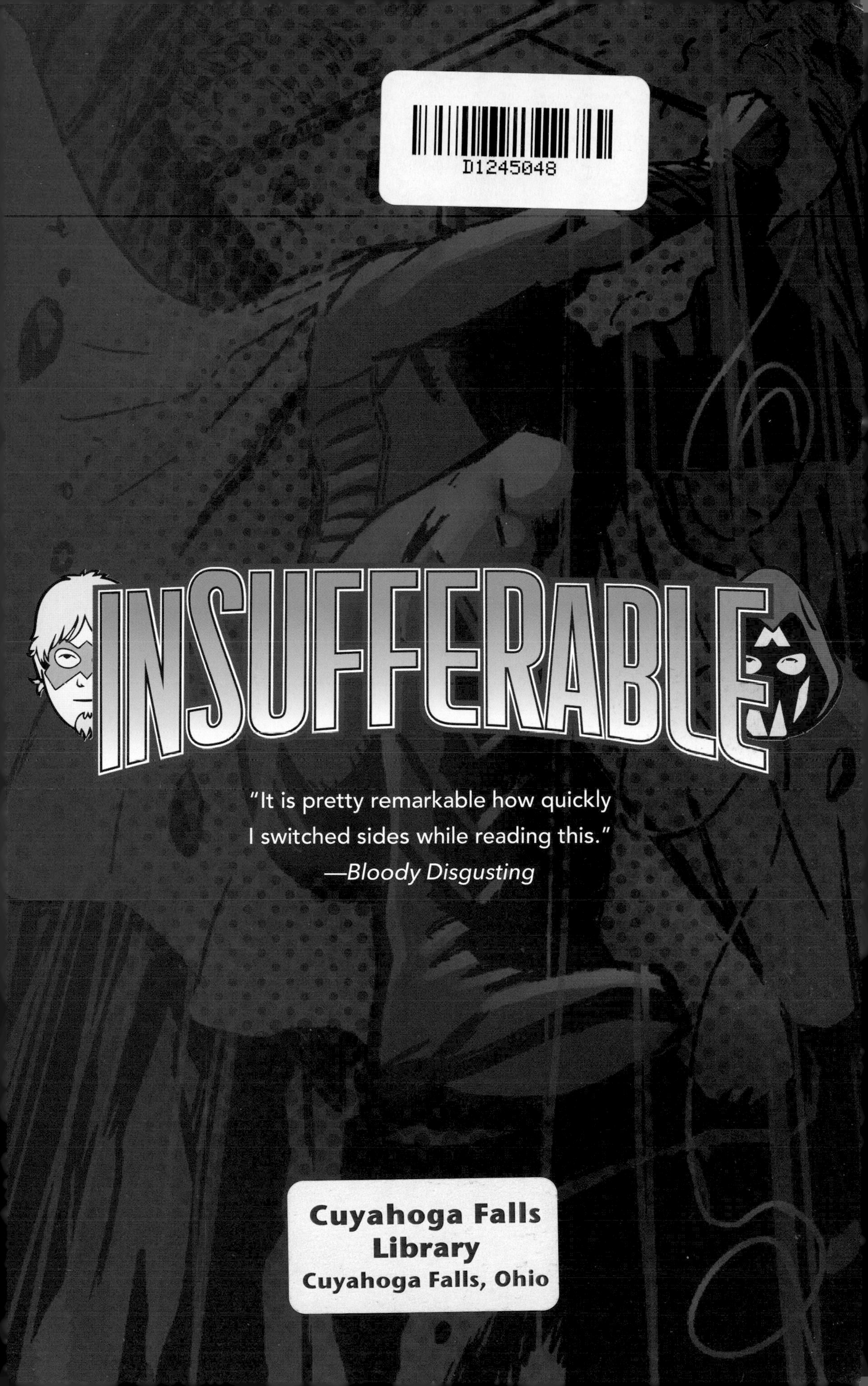

INSUFFERABLE

"It is pretty remarkable how quickly I switched sides while reading this."
—*Bloody Disgusting*

Become our fan on Facebook facebook.com/idwpublishing
Follow us on Twitter @idwpublishing
Subscribe to us on YouTube youtube.com/idwpublishing
See what's new on Tumblr tumblr.idwpublishing.com
Check us out on Instagram instagram.com/idwpublishing

978-1-63140-511-2   19 18 17 16   1 2 3 4

COVER BY
PETER KRAUSE

COLLECTION EDITS BY
JUSTIN EISINGER
AND ALONZO SIMON

COLLECTION DESIGN BY
CHRIS MOWRY

Originally published as INSUFFERABLE issues #1–4.

Ted Adams, CEO & Publisher
Greg Goldstein, President & COO
Robbie Robbins, EVP/Sr. Graphic Artist
Chris Ryall, Chief Creative Officer/Editor-in-Chief
Matthew Ruzicka, CPA, Chief Financial Officer
Dirk Wood, VP of Marketing
Lorelei Bunjes, VP of Digital Services
Jeff Webber, VP of Licensing, Digital and Subsidiary Rights
Jerry Bennington, VP of New Product Development

For international rights, please
contact licensing@idwpublishing.com

INSUFFERABLE CREATED BY
MARK WAID AND PETER KRAUSE

WRITER / STORYTELLERS / ARTIST
MARK WAID
& PETER KRAUSE

COLORIST
NOLAN WOODARD

LETTERER
TROY PETERI

SERIES EDITOR
MICHAEL BENEDETTO

INTRODUCTION

There are certain human behaviors that, despite the best work of my long-suffering therapist, set me off disproportionately to the gravity of their sin. If you want to test this, watch my face the next time the customer in front of me waits until all his or her purchases are rung up and totaled before s/he thinks to start rummaging around for a wallet, or clock my blood pressure when I see some guy obliviously lingering at the bottom of an escalator like he's grown roots.

I'm not proud of having pet peeves; to quote my therapist, "Why be mad?" And he's right. And he's getting through my concrete skull, slowly. These days, the main thing that I just can't seem to let pass gracefully is arrogance. I loathe the arrogant. I believe humility, grace, and empathy to be some of the more socially positive traits of the human race, and nothing eats at me quite like hearing some loudmouth brag about how talented or clever or gifted he is and/or, worse, gas on with active disdain or contempt for those who made his path possible. If you ever stick me in a room where it's just me, Kanye, and Donald Trump, I'm the one guaranteed to end up on Death Row.

Maybe this is because I was raised by two relatively humble families (the Waids and, honestly, the Kents). Maybe it's because years of mainlining American superheroes into my veins has unfortunately and irrevocably skewed the value I place on selflessness. Maybe I'm just too sensitive. I dunno. What I do know is that the comics industry has a surprisingly low asshole-to-sweetheart ratio compared to other entertainment fields, well... sometimes....

INSUFFERABLE was originally based on two former-friend creators I know. I was reading an interview with one of them and, as he blathered relentlessly on about what a visionary he was and how tiny the rest of us were, I remembered the phrase "Why be mad?" and instead expressed my frustrations creatively through the language I know best: comics. I'd do an ongoing series, I decided, about two former crimefighting partners where the junior one grew up to be an ungrateful lout and the senior one would lose hair and gain wrinkles, choking back his resentment.

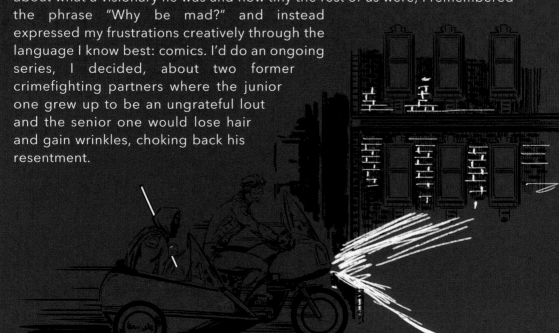

And if I'd left it there, INSUFFERABLE would never have gotten off the ground.

My mistake was in initially trying to make it far more darkly comedic than dramatic. In time, I remembered—yes, I have to re-learn this stuff *every day*, thank you—that an idea is not a series and jokes are not characters. The set-up as I'd envisioned it wouldn't sustain unless our players had some actual depth and motivations that we could, if not admire, at least relate to. A story is only a story if (a) it's about someone(s) who wants something and (b) something's in his/her/their way. On top of that, it's a story worth telling only if (c) the reader has reasons to care about (a) and (b).

This is where artist Peter Krause came in. Peter gave life to my series IRREDEEMABLE over at BOOM! Studios a few years ago and immediately—*immediately*—became a partner and collaborator of unparalleled value. Since IRREDEEMABLE, we'd been scheming to find something to co-create from the ground up, and this was it. I shared the bare-bones concept of INSUFFERABLE with Pete and, in our conversations, the characters gained dimension, I think in no small part because Pete's been a father and mentor himself, so he was able to shed some light on some of Nocturnus' finer points. And when Pete delivered his preliminary character sketches, they got real. He even came up with the names Nocturnus and Galahad, further shortening the time until the day finally comes when he realizes I need him a lot more than he needs me.

Colorist Nolan Woodard and letterer/designer Troy Peteri completed the creative team, and Pete and I are forever indebted to them both. If you're looking to hire, I'm happy to forward any job offers to them through **mark.waid+insufferable@gmail.com**; they know I'll let them roam as far as they like so long as they always come home. We launched INSUFFERABLE three years ago as a weekly comic on my **Thrillbent.com** digital comics website, and it's lived a lovely little pixelated life there, but the fine folks at IDW have partnered with us to reformat it for print for the first time, and we're all spiffing it up and tweaking and fine-tuning the material for re-presentation—meaning that even if you've read this on Thrillbent, there'll be some surprises coming your way.

And hang onto that email address, we're likewise happy to answer your (civil) questions, so feel free to write. If you like what we've done, tell your friends; we appreciate the support.

—Mark Waid

CHAPTER ONE

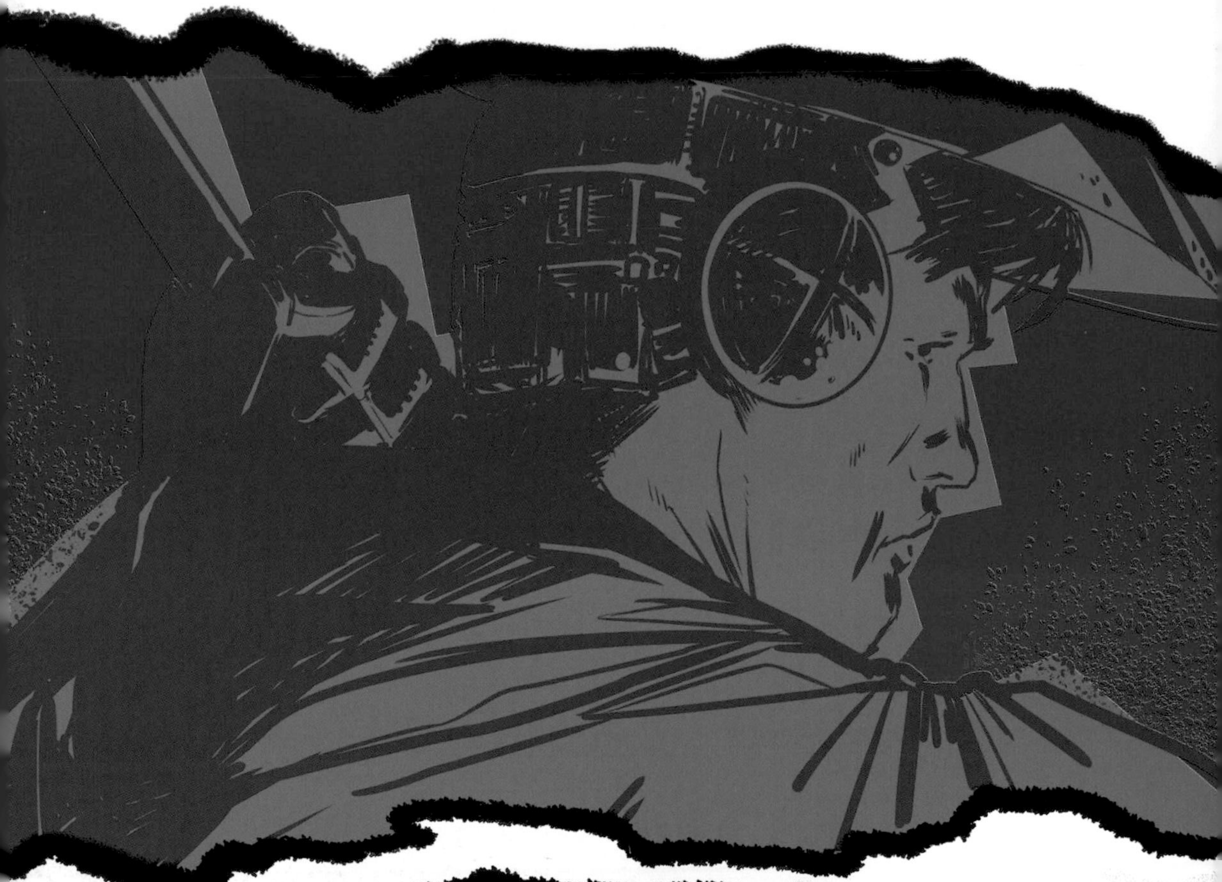

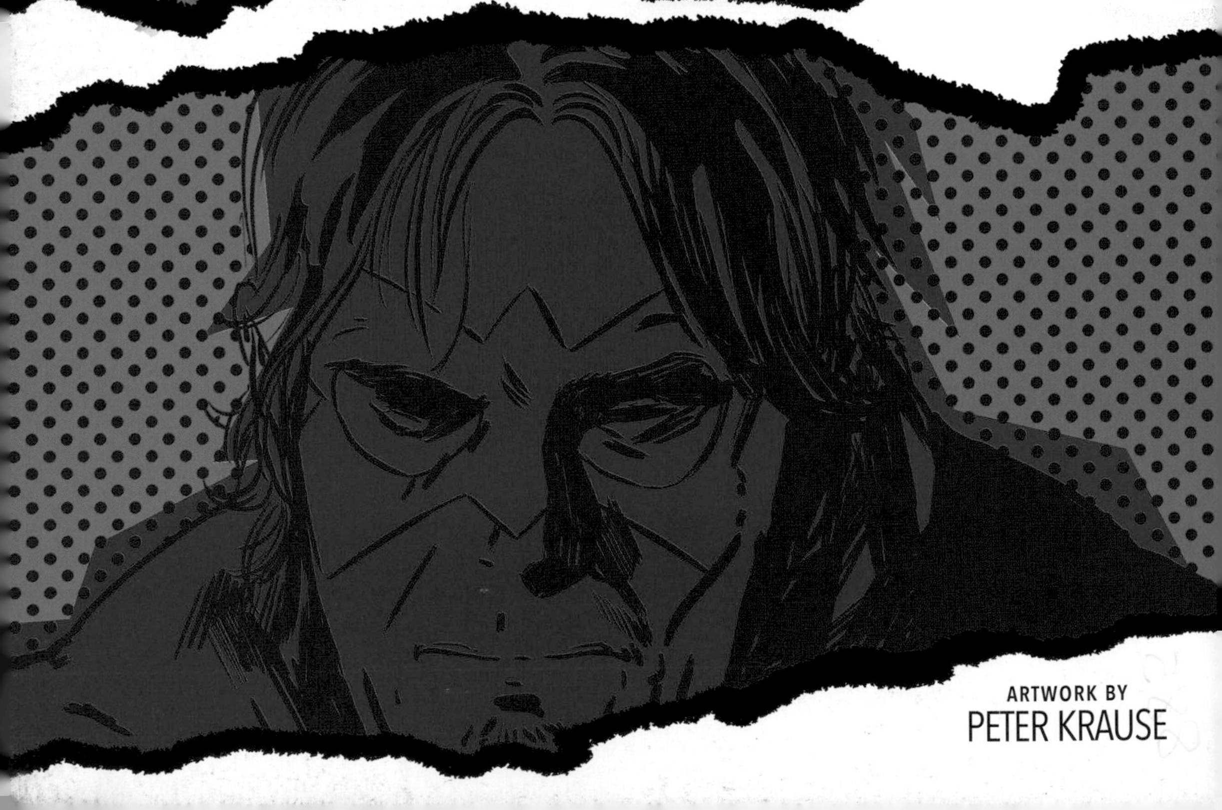

ARTWORK BY
PETER KRAUSE

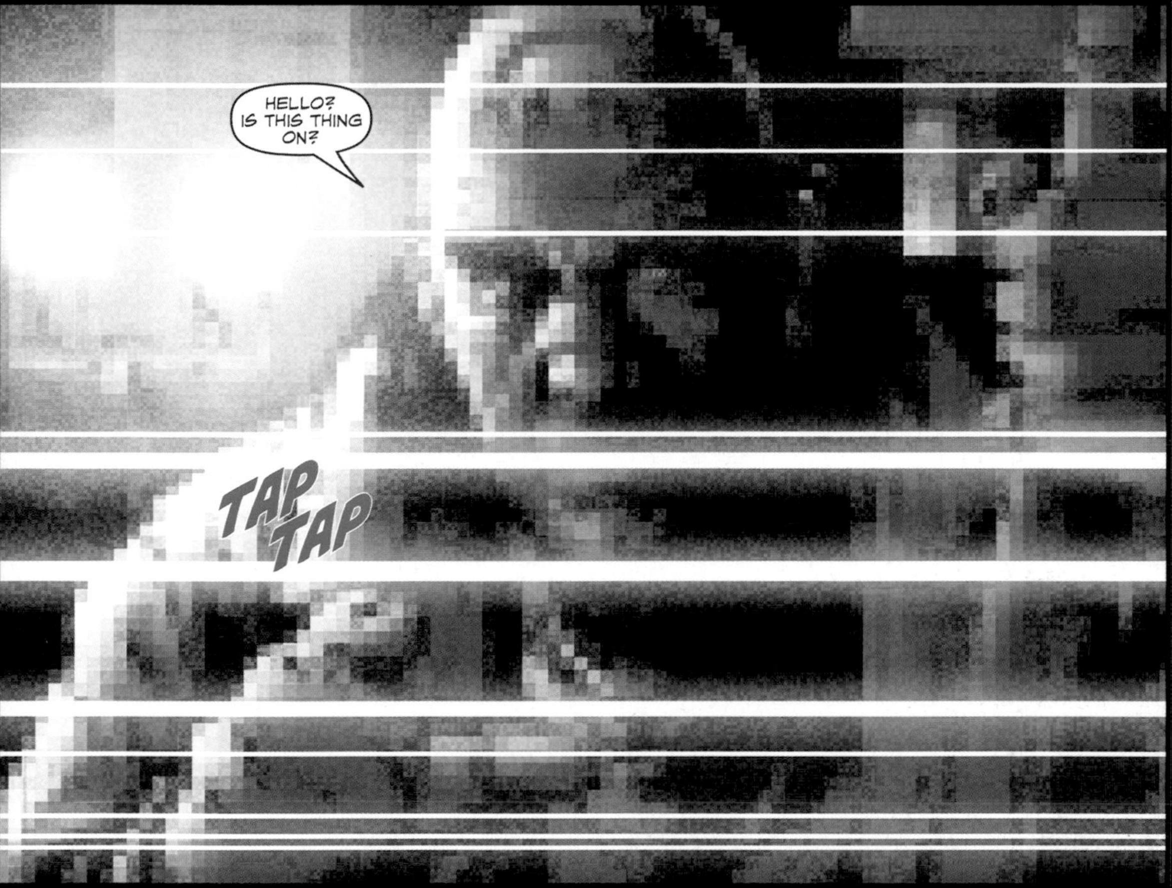
HELLO? IS THIS THING ON?
TAP TAP

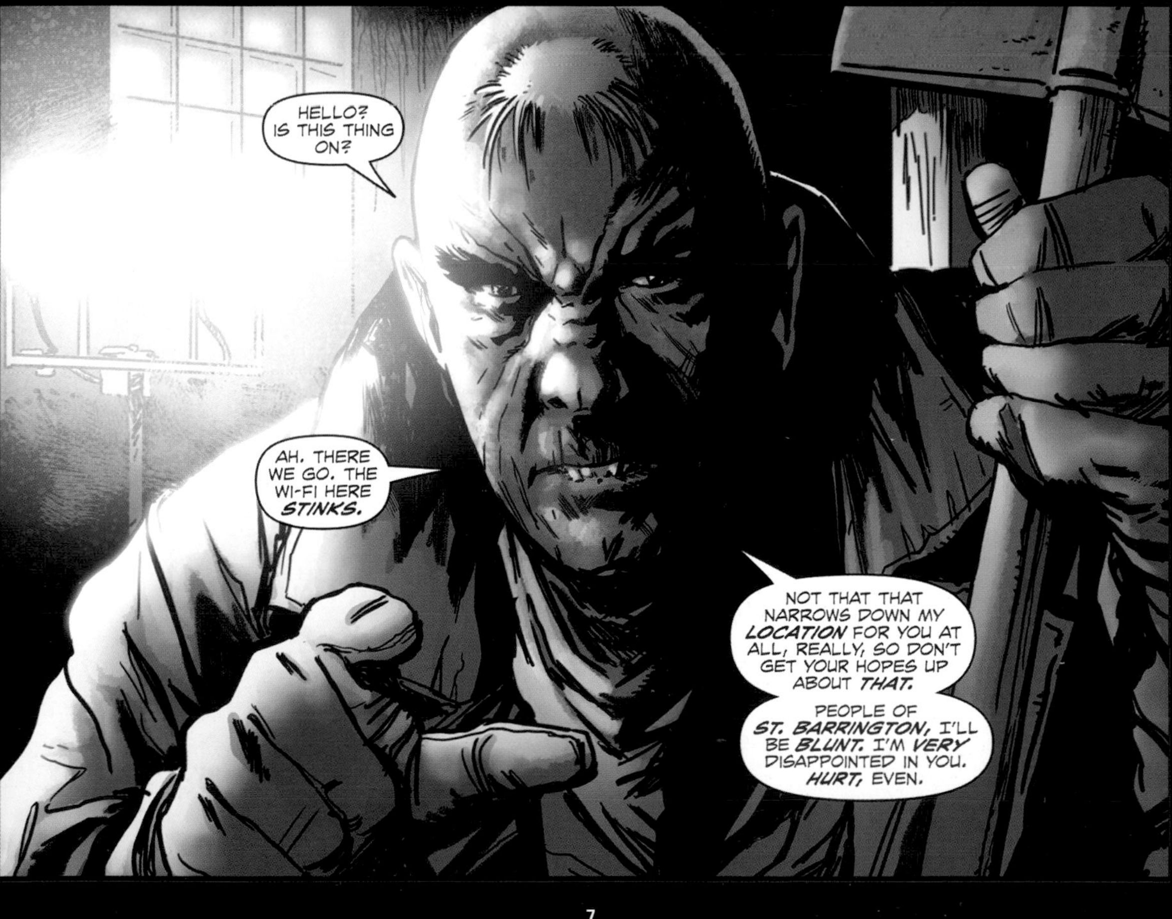
HELLO? IS THIS THING ON?
AH. THERE WE GO. THE WI-FI HERE STINKS.
NOT THAT THAT NARROWS DOWN MY LOCATION FOR YOU AT ALL, REALLY, SO DON'T GET YOUR HOPES UP ABOUT THAT.
PEOPLE OF ST. BARRINGTON, I'LL BE BLUNT. I'M VERY DISAPPOINTED IN YOU. HURT, EVEN.

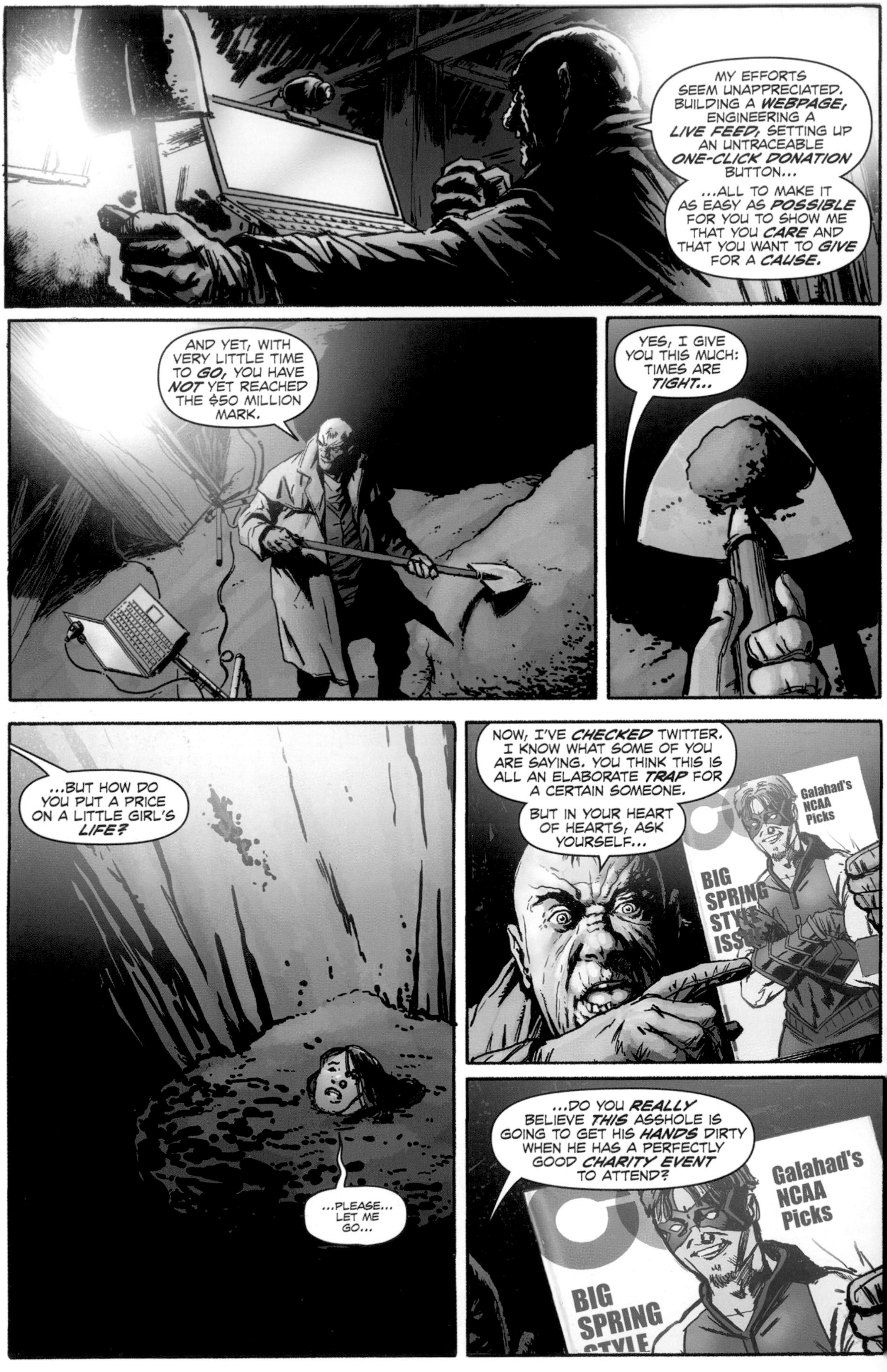
MY EFFORTS SEEM UNAPPRECIATED. BUILDING A WEBPAGE, ENGINEERING A LIVE FEED, SETTING UP AN UNTRACEABLE ONE-CLICK DONATION BUTTON...
...ALL TO MAKE IT AS EASY AS POSSIBLE FOR YOU TO SHOW ME THAT YOU CARE AND THAT YOU WANT TO GIVE FOR A CAUSE.
AND YET, WITH VERY LITTLE TIME TO GO, YOU HAVE NOT YET REACHED THE $50 MILLION MARK.
YES, I GIVE YOU THIS MUCH: TIMES ARE TIGHT...
...BUT HOW DO YOU PUT A PRICE ON A LITTLE GIRL'S LIFE?
...PLEASE... LET ME GO...
NOW, I'VE CHECKED TWITTER. I KNOW WHAT SOME OF YOU ARE SAYING. YOU THINK THIS IS ALL AN ELABORATE TRAP FOR A CERTAIN SOMEONE.
BUT IN YOUR HEART OF HEARTS, ASK YOURSELF...
Galahad's NCAA Picks
BIG SPRING
...DO YOU REALLY BELIEVE THIS ASSHOLE IS GOING TO GET HIS HANDS DIRTY WHEN HE HAS A PERFECTLY GOOD CHARITY EVENT TO ATTEND?
Galahad's NCAA Picks
BIG SPRING

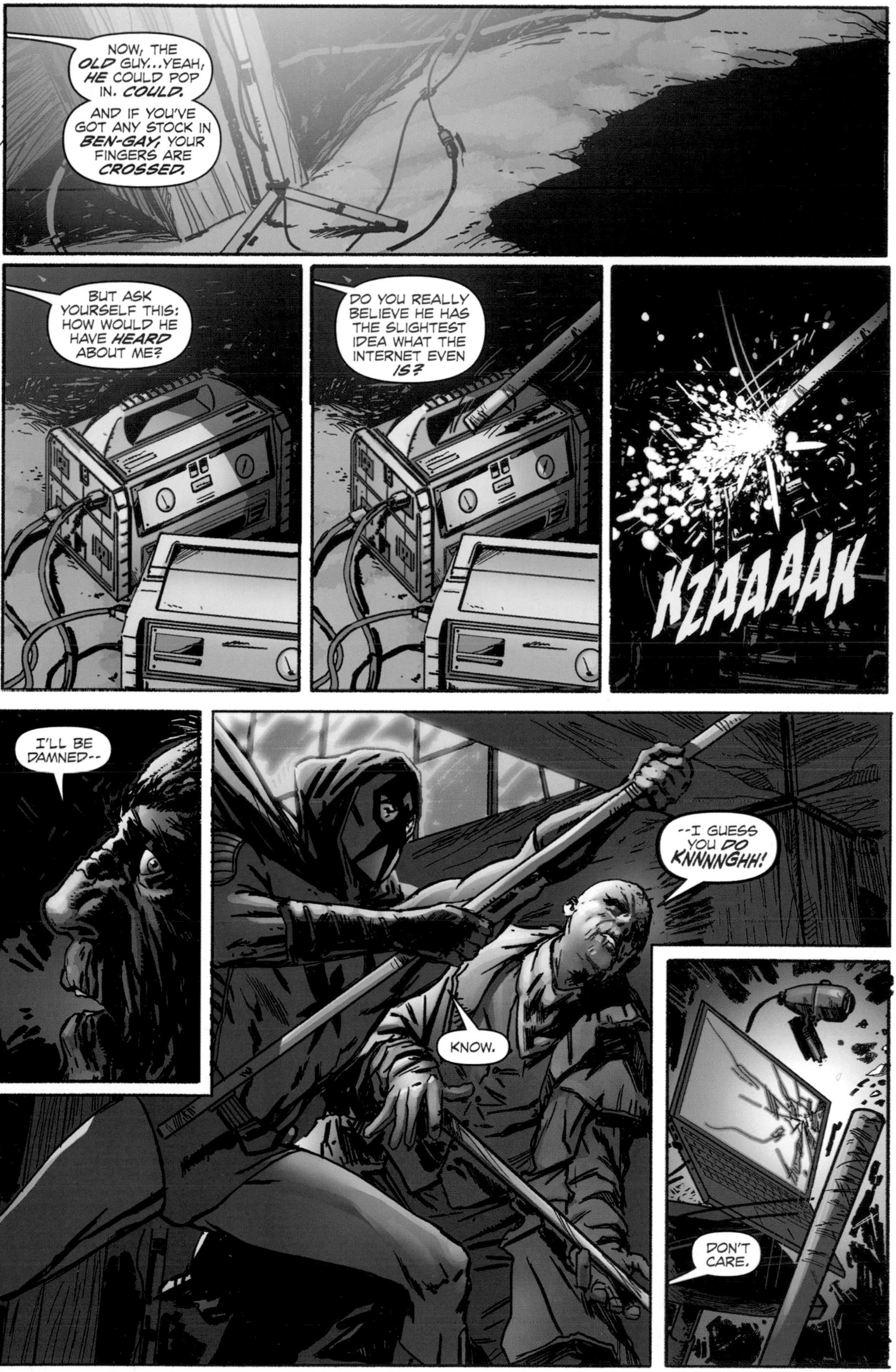
NOW, THE OLD GUY...YEAH, HE COULD POP IN. COULD.
AND IF YOU'VE GOT ANY STOCK IN BEN-GAY, YOUR FINGERS ARE CROSSED.
BUT ASK YOURSELF THIS: HOW WOULD HE HAVE HEARD ABOUT ME?
DO YOU REALLY BELIEVE HE HAS THE SLIGHTEST IDEA WHAT THE INTERNET EVEN IS?
KZAAAAK
I'LL BE DAMNED--
--I GUESS YOU DO KNNNNGHH!
KNOW.
DON'T CARE.

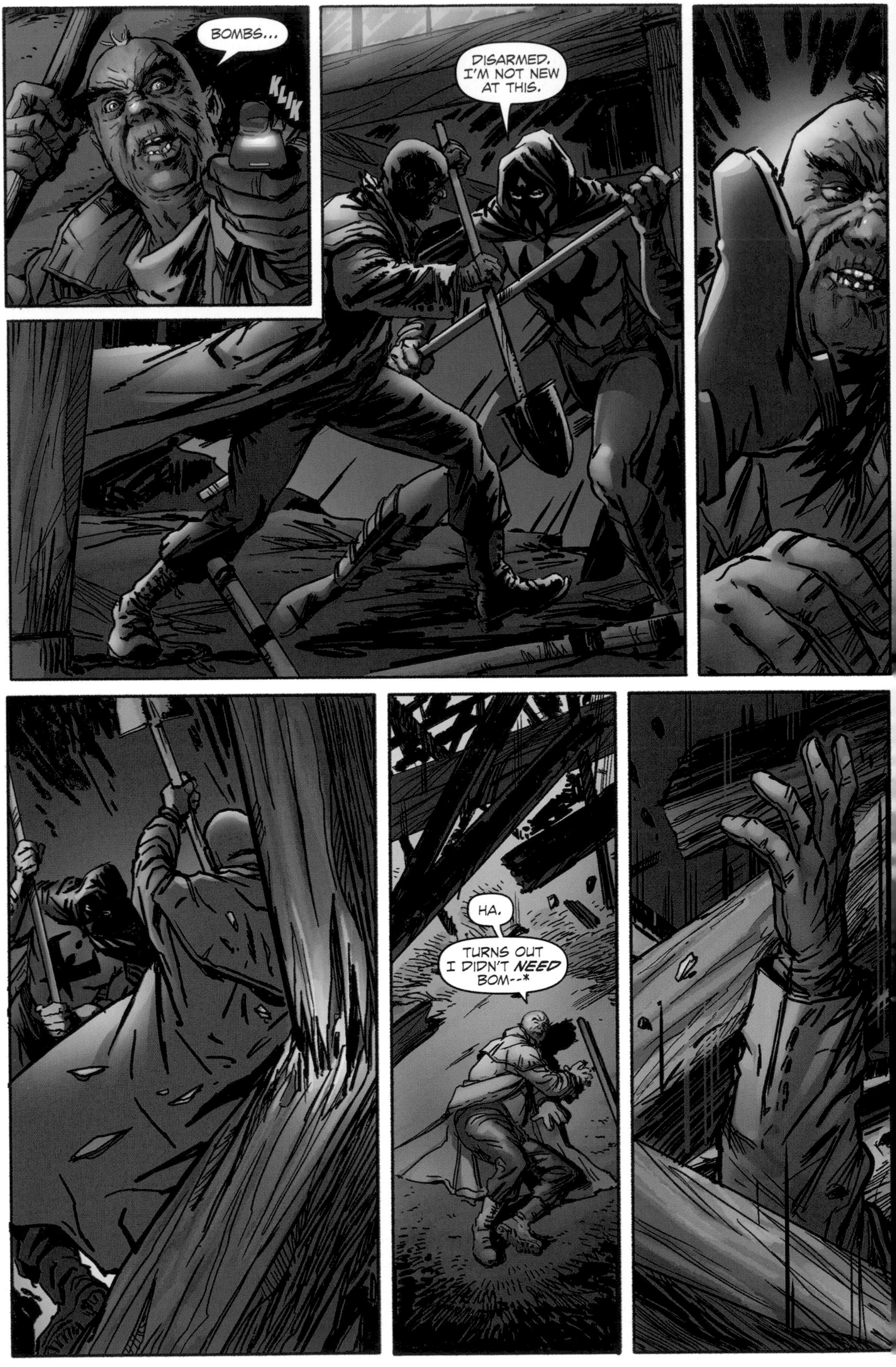
BOMBS...
KLIK
DISARMED. I'M NOT NEW AT THIS.
HA.
TURNS OUT I DIDN'T *NEED* BOM--*

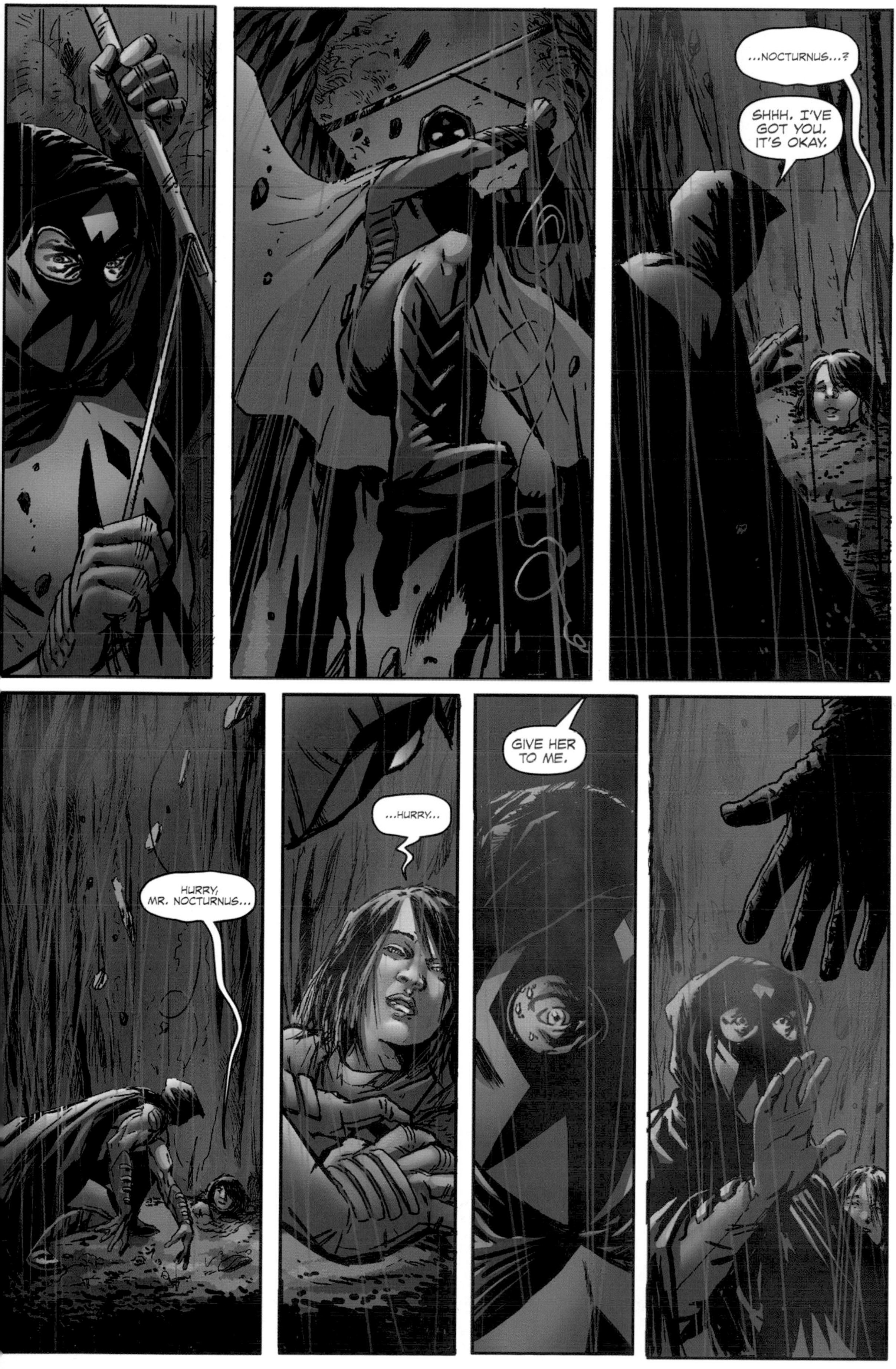
...NOCTURNUS...?
SHHH. I'VE GOT YOU. IT'S OKAY.
HURRY, MR. NOCTURNUS...
...HURRY...
GIVE HER TO ME.

I DON'T NEED YOUR HELP.

DON'T START, OLD MAN. NOT NOW.

THIS RAT-TRAP IS RAINING *ROOF.*

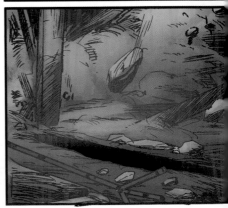

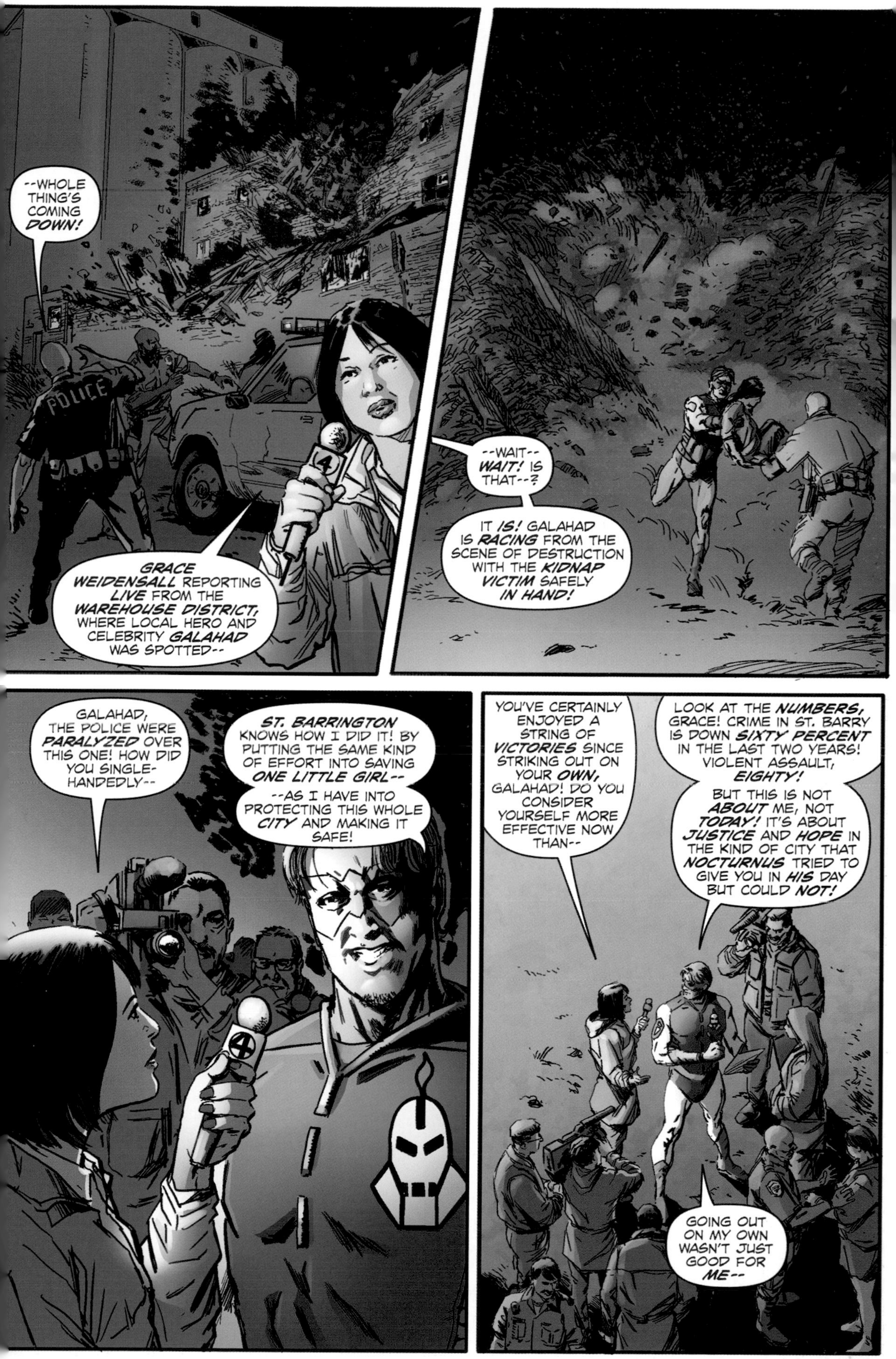
--WHOLE THING'S COMING *DOWN!*
GRACE WEIDENSALL REPORTING *LIVE* FROM THE *WAREHOUSE DISTRICT,* WHERE LOCAL HERO AND CELEBRITY *GALAHAD* WAS SPOTTED--
--WAIT-- *WAIT!* IS THAT--?
IT *IS!* GALAHAD IS *RACING* FROM THE SCENE OF DESTRUCTION WITH THE *KIDNAP VICTIM* SAFELY *IN HAND!*
GALAHAD, THE POLICE WERE *PARALYZED* OVER THIS ONE! HOW DID YOU SINGLE-HANDEDLY--
ST. BARRINGTON KNOWS HOW I DID IT! BY PUTTING THE SAME KIND OF EFFORT INTO SAVING *ONE LITTLE GIRL--*
--AS I HAVE INTO PROTECTING THIS WHOLE *CITY* AND MAKING IT SAFE!
YOU'VE CERTAINLY ENJOYED A STRING OF *VICTORIES* SINCE STRIKING OUT ON YOUR *OWN,* GALAHAD! DO YOU CONSIDER YOURSELF MORE EFFECTIVE NOW THAN--
LOOK AT THE *NUMBERS,* GRACE! CRIME IN ST. BARRY IS DOWN *SIXTY PERCENT* IN THE LAST TWO YEARS! VIOLENT ASSAULT, *EIGHTY!*
BUT THIS IS NOT *ABOUT* ME, NOT *TODAY!* IT'S ABOUT *JUSTICE* AND *HOPE* IN THE KIND OF CITY THAT *NOCTURNUS* TRIED TO GIVE YOU IN *HIS* DAY BUT COULD *NOT!*
GOING OUT ON MY OWN WASN'T JUST GOOD FOR *ME--*

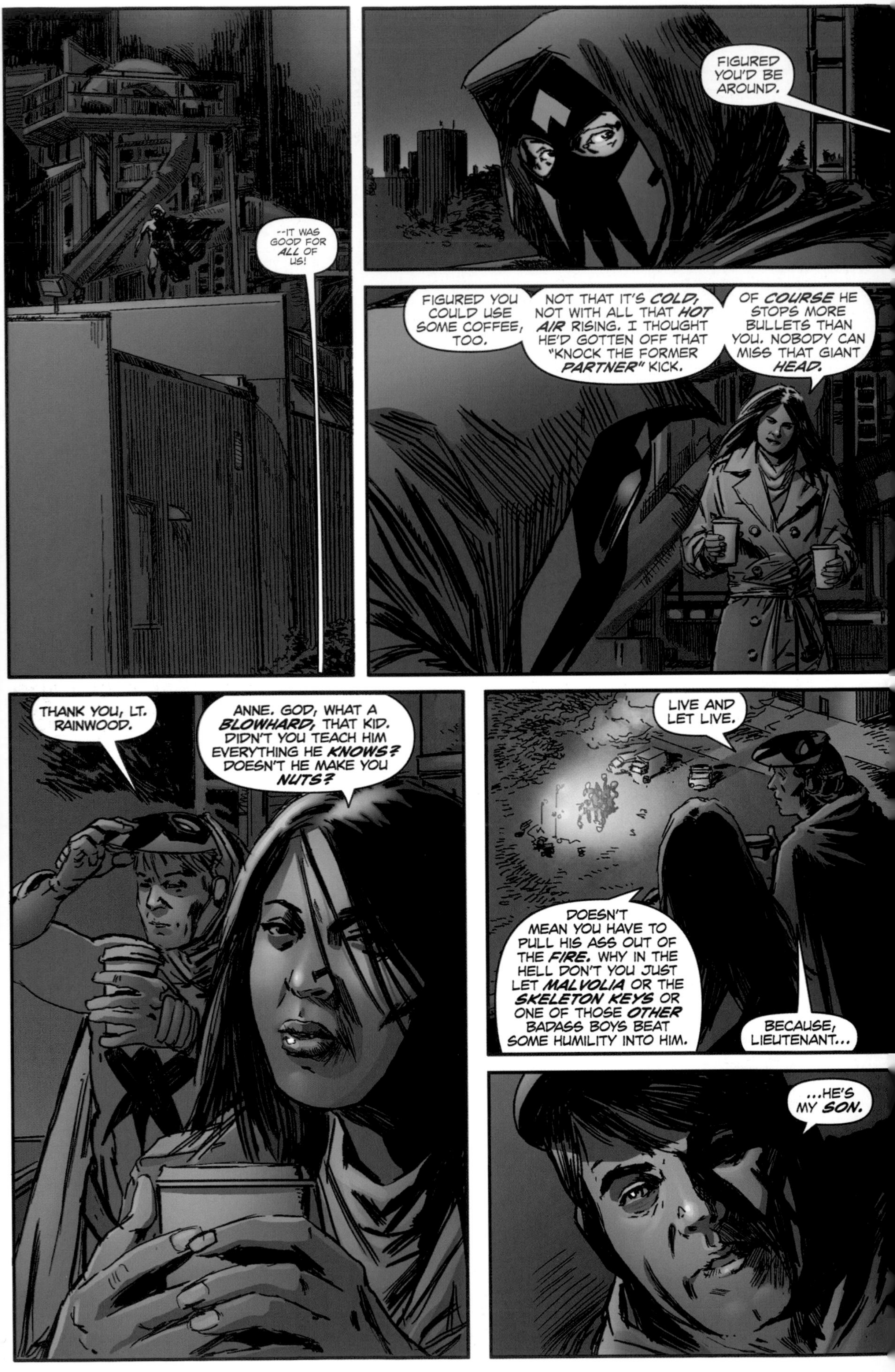
--IT WAS GOOD FOR ALL OF US!
FIGURED YOU'D BE AROUND.
FIGURED YOU COULD USE SOME COFFEE, TOO.
NOT THAT IT'S COLD, NOT WITH ALL THAT HOT AIR RISING. I THOUGHT HE'D GOTTEN OFF THAT "KNOCK THE FORMER PARTNER" KICK.
OF COURSE HE STOPS MORE BULLETS THAN YOU. NOBODY CAN MISS THAT GIANT HEAD.
THANK YOU, LT. RAINWOOD.
ANNE. GOD, WHAT A BLOWHARD, THAT KID. DIDN'T YOU TEACH HIM EVERYTHING HE KNOWS? DOESN'T HE MAKE YOU NUTS?
LIVE AND LET LIVE.
DOESN'T MEAN YOU HAVE TO PULL HIS ASS OUT OF THE FIRE. WHY IN THE HELL DON'T YOU JUST LET MALVOLIA OR THE SKELETON KEYS OR ONE OF THOSE OTHER BADASS BOYS BEAT SOME HUMILITY INTO HIM.
BECAUSE, LIEUTENANT...
...HE'S MY SON.

GALAHAD'S YOUR *SON?* LIKE, *BLOOD RELATIVE?* THAT'S NOT JUST AN URBAN MYTH?

IT MADE HEADLINES BEFORE YOU CAME TO TOWN.

YOU WANT TO TALK ABOUT IT?

NO POINT. DON'T LIVE IN THE PAST, LIEUTENANT.

YOU NEED A RIDE?

"I HAVE TRANSPORTATION."

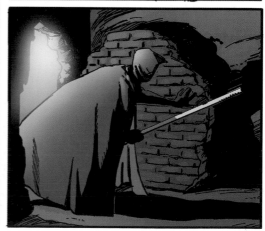

CHK-KLIK

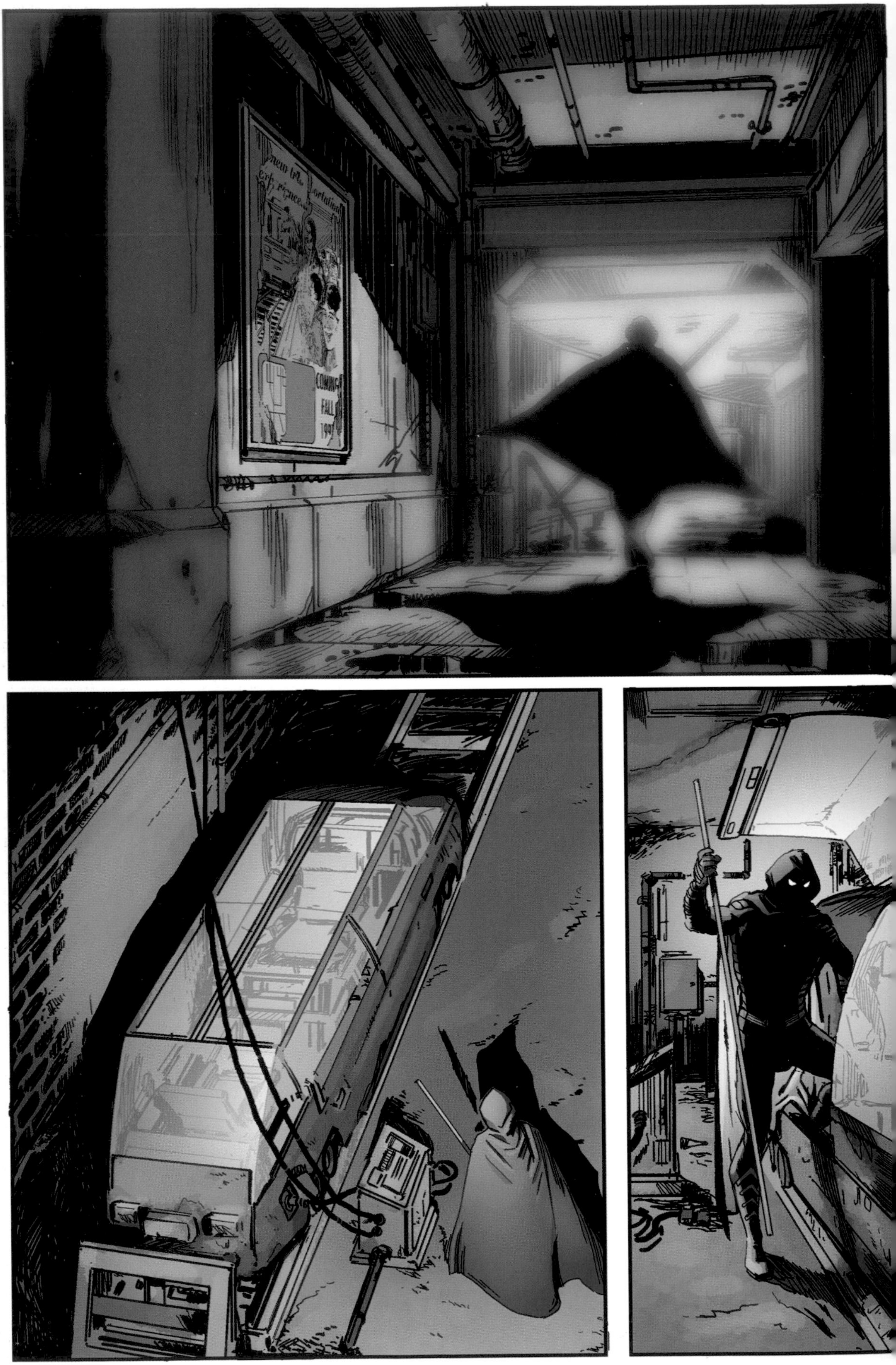
COMING
FALL

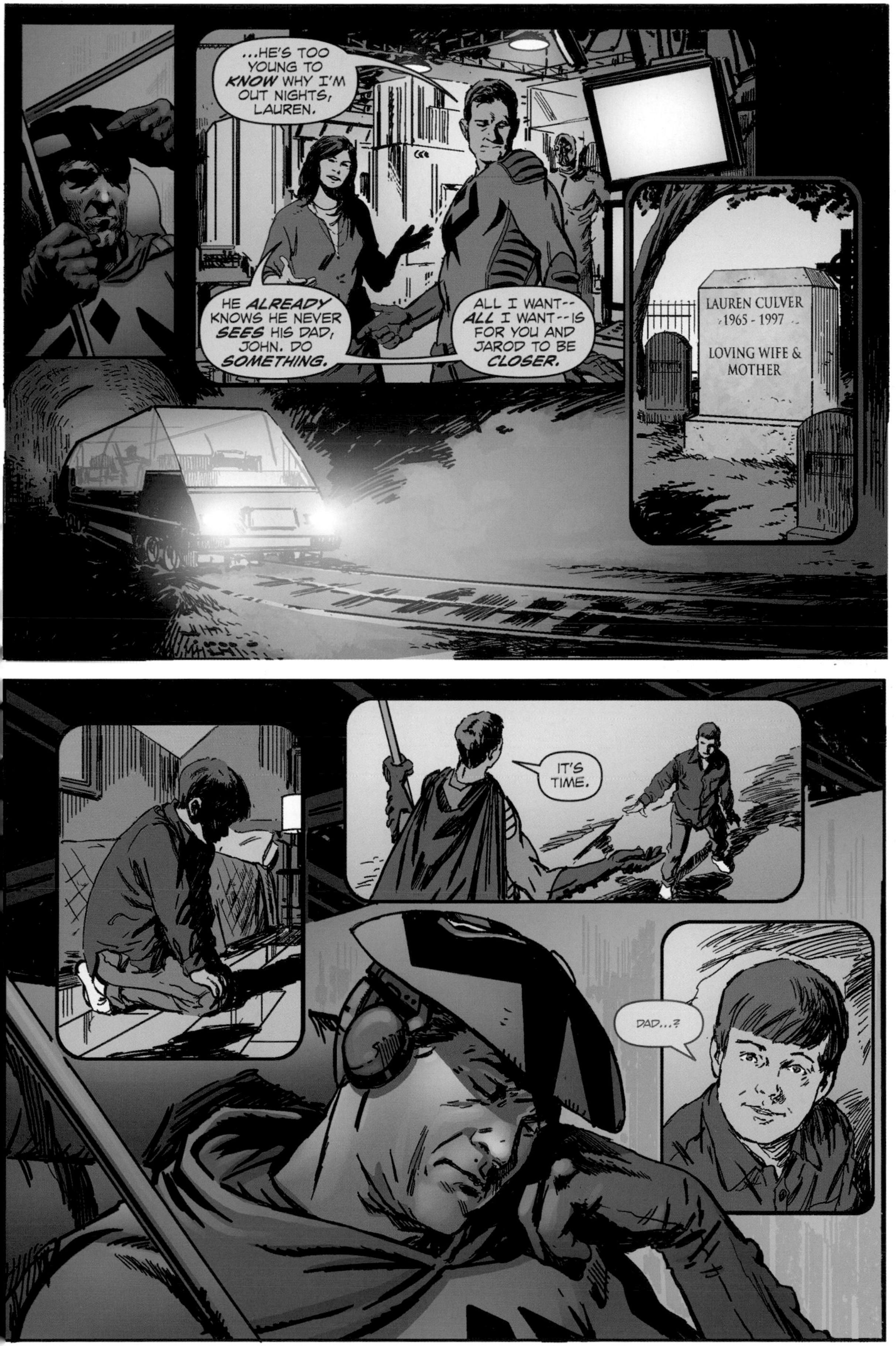
...HE'S TOO YOUNG TO KNOW WHY I'M OUT NIGHTS, LAUREN.
HE ALREADY KNOWS HE NEVER SEES HIS DAD, JOHN. DO SOMETHING.
ALL I WANT-- ALL I WANT--IS FOR YOU AND JAROD TO BE CLOSER.
LAUREN CULVER 1965 - 1997
LOVING WIFE & MOTHER
IT'S TIME.
DAD...?

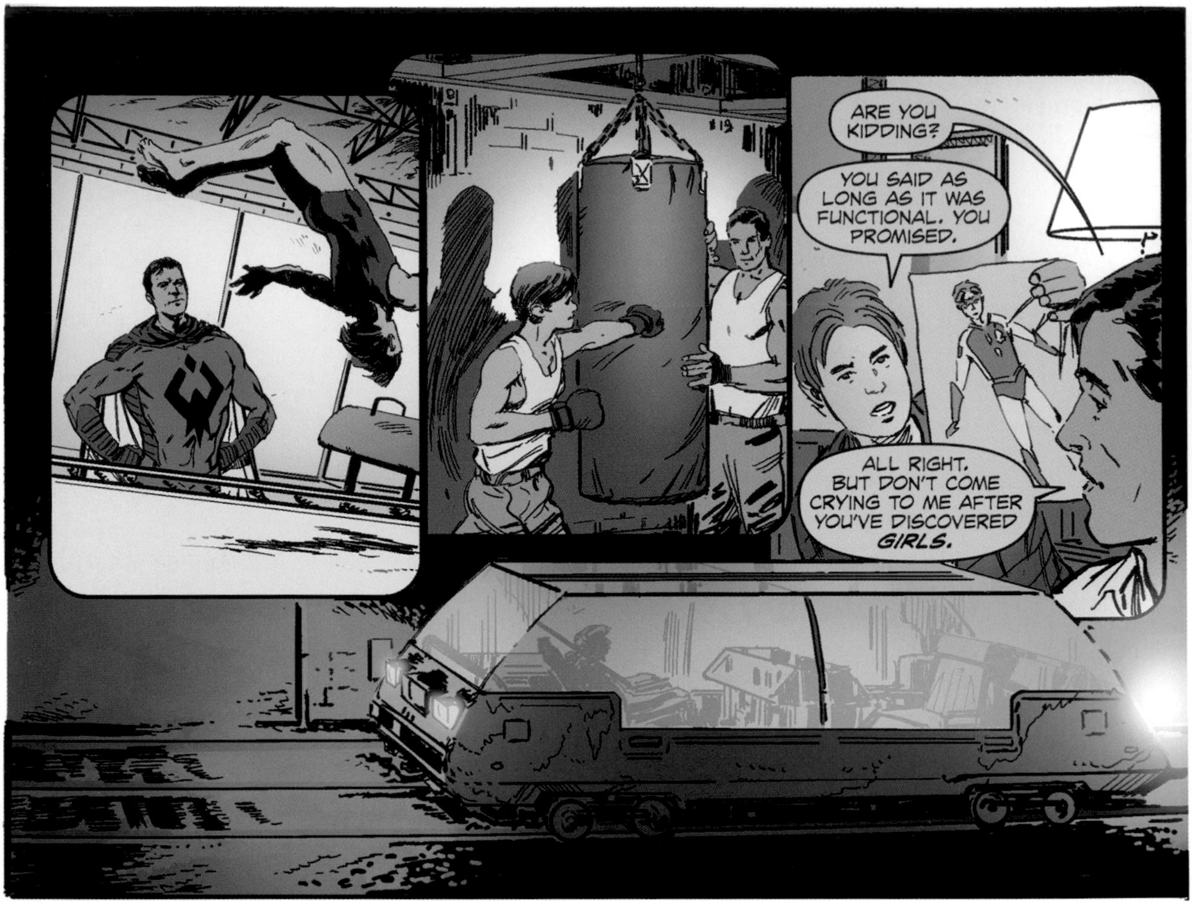
ARE YOU KIDDING?
YOU SAID AS LONG AS IT WAS FUNCTIONAL. YOU PROMISED.
ALL RIGHT. BUT DON'T COME CRYING TO ME AFTER YOU'VE DISCOVERED *GIRLS*.

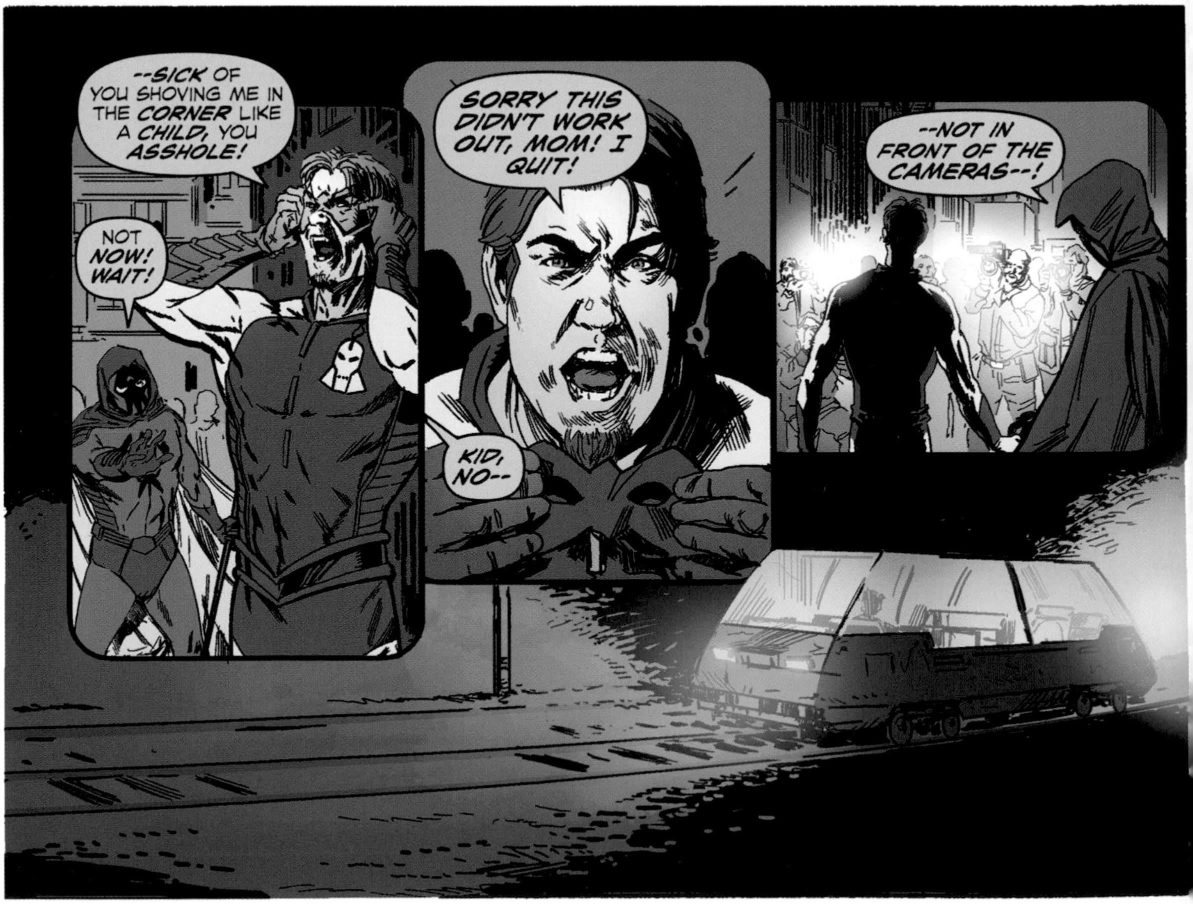
--*SICK* OF YOU SHOVING ME IN THE *CORNER* LIKE A *CHILD*, YOU *ASSHOLE!*
NOT *NOW!* *WAIT!*
SORRY THIS DIDN'T WORK OUT, MOM! I QUIT!
KID, NO--
--NOT IN FRONT OF THE CAMERAS--!

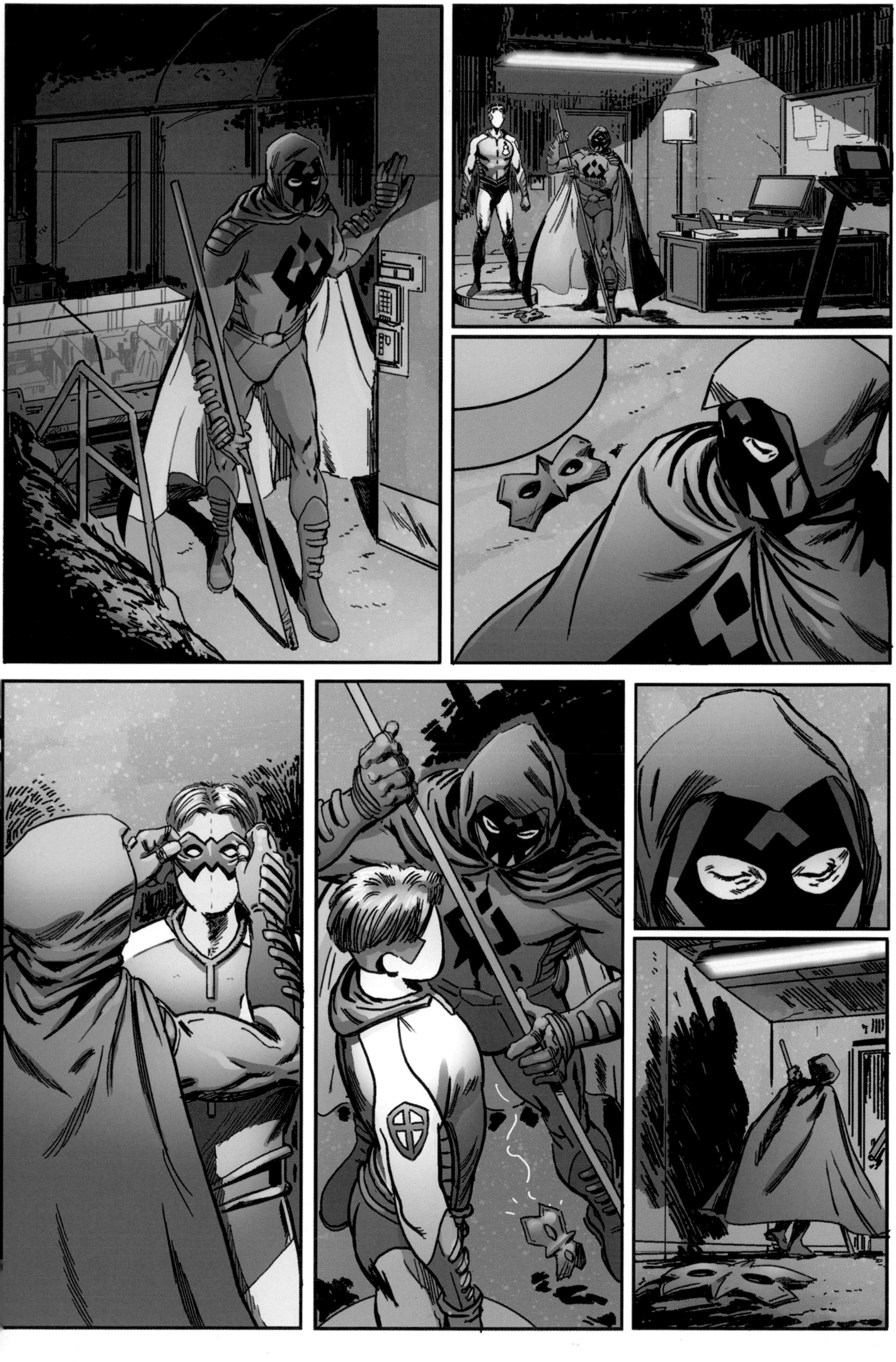

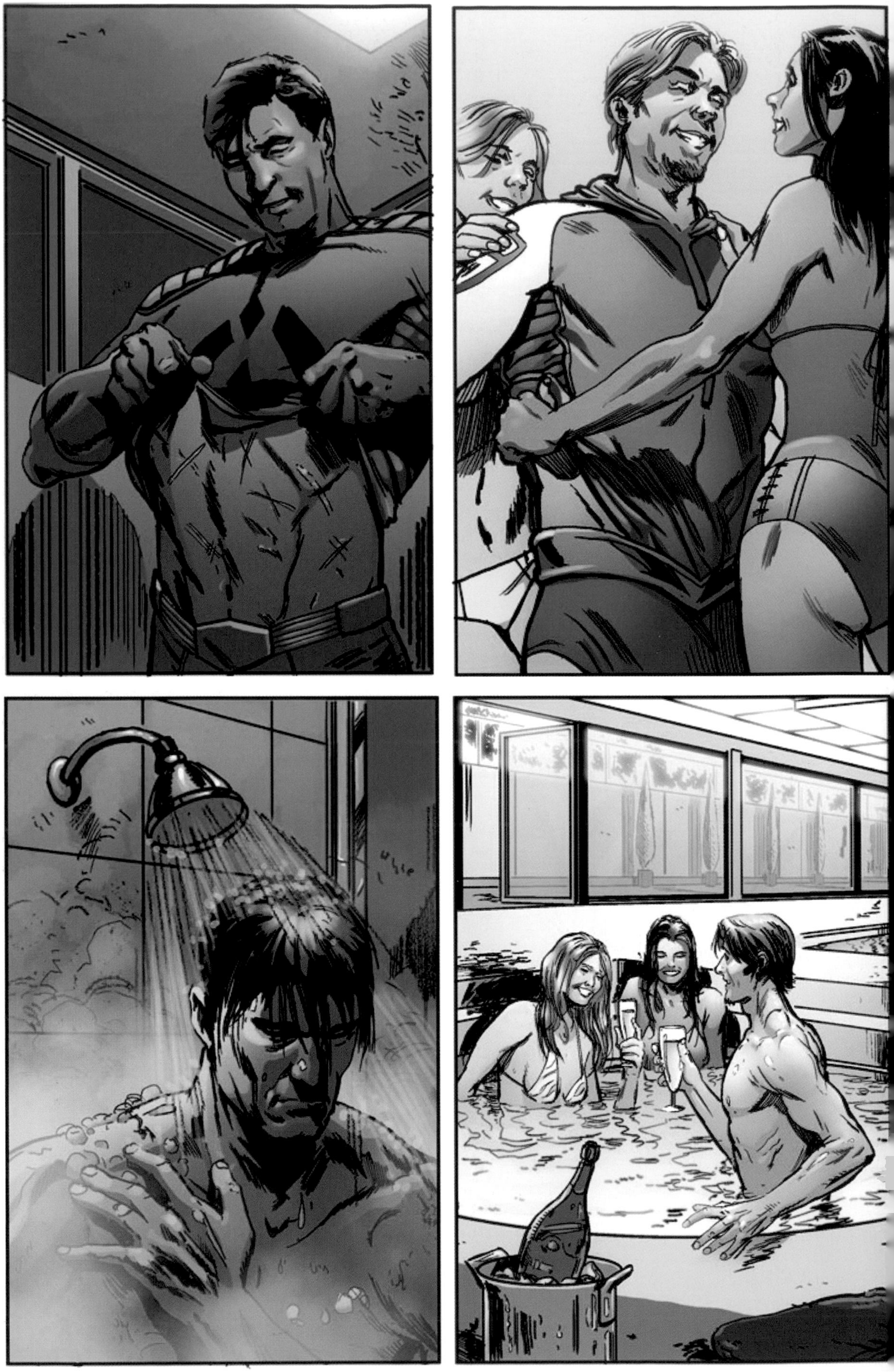

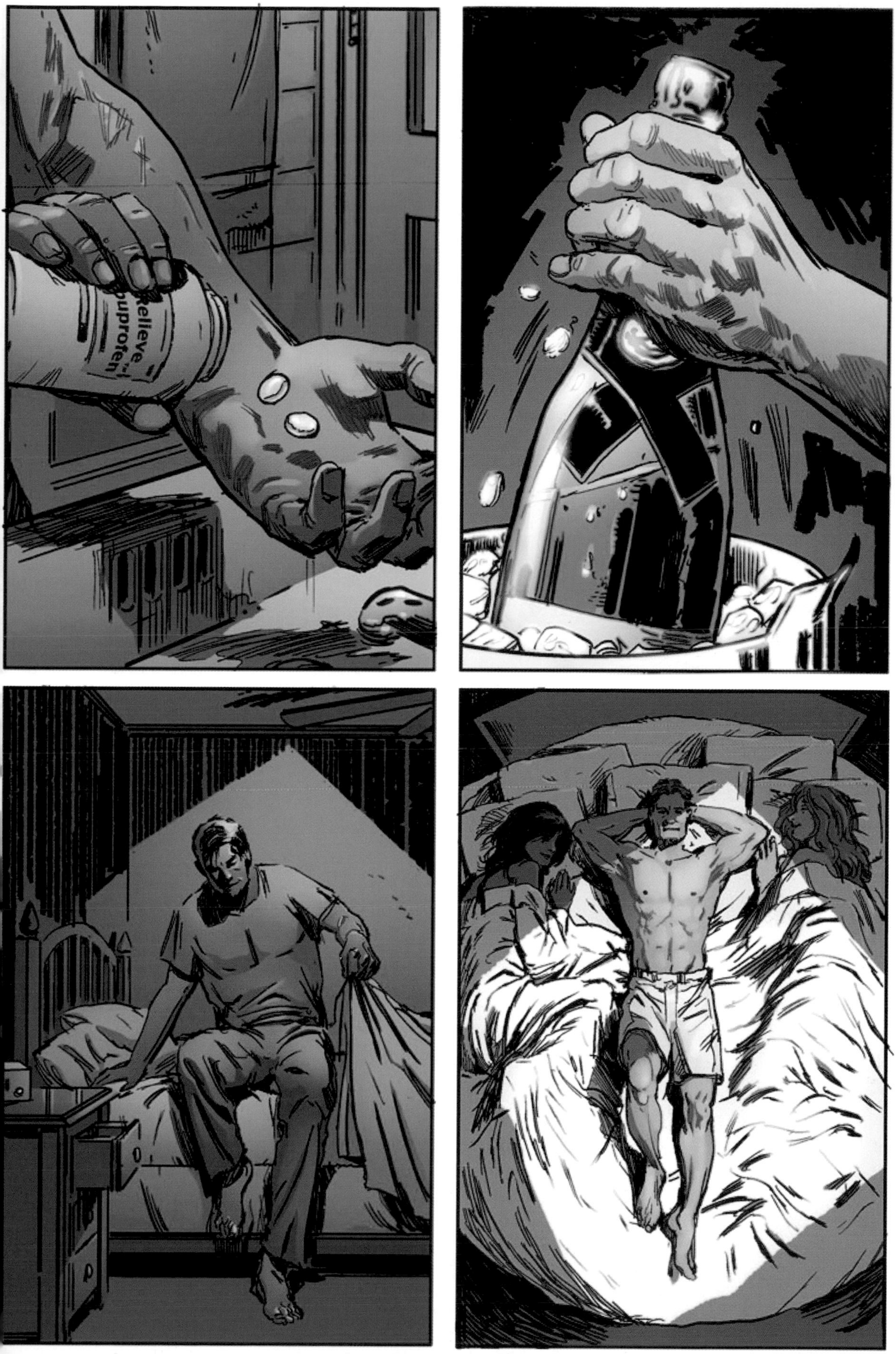

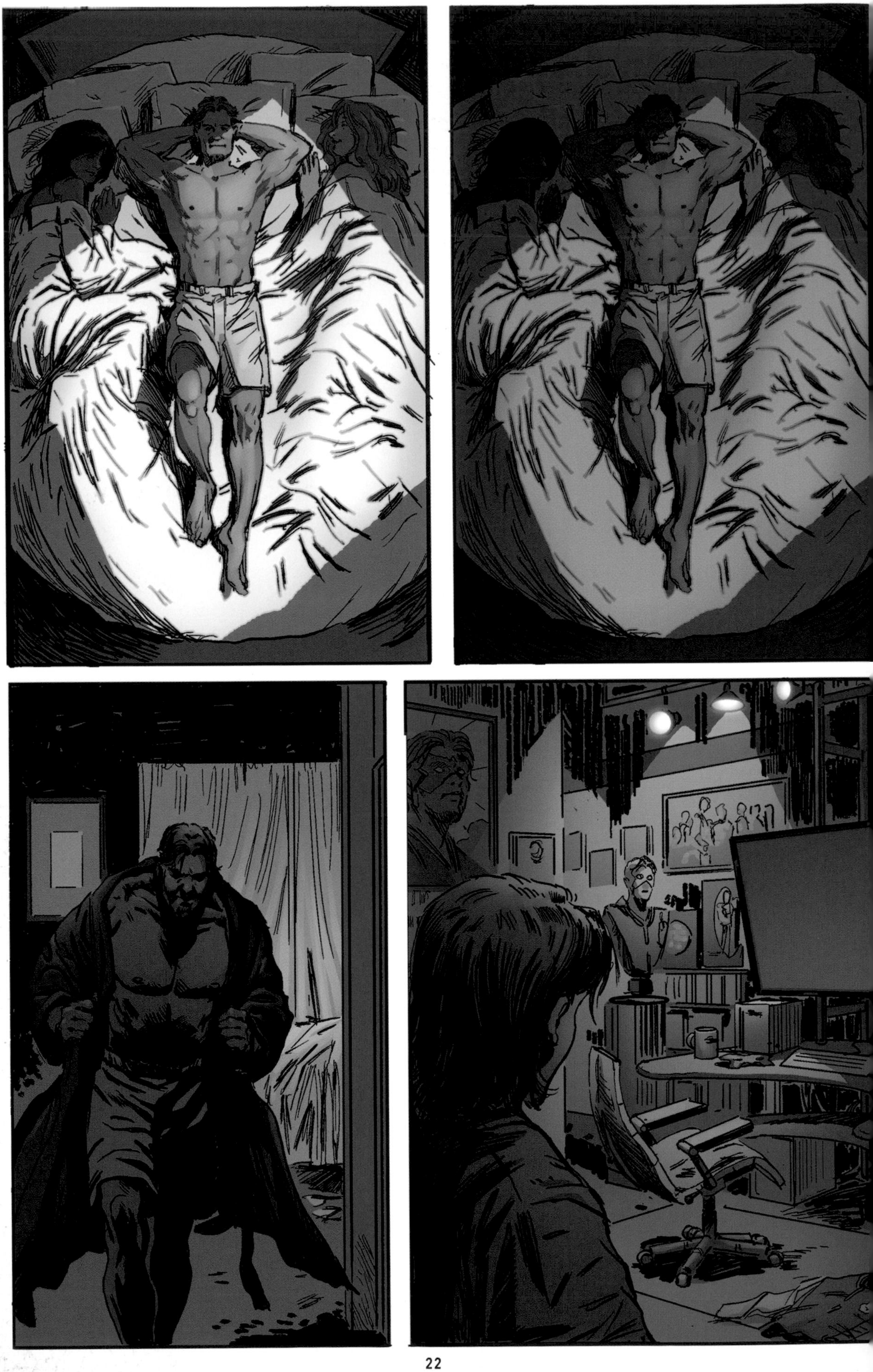

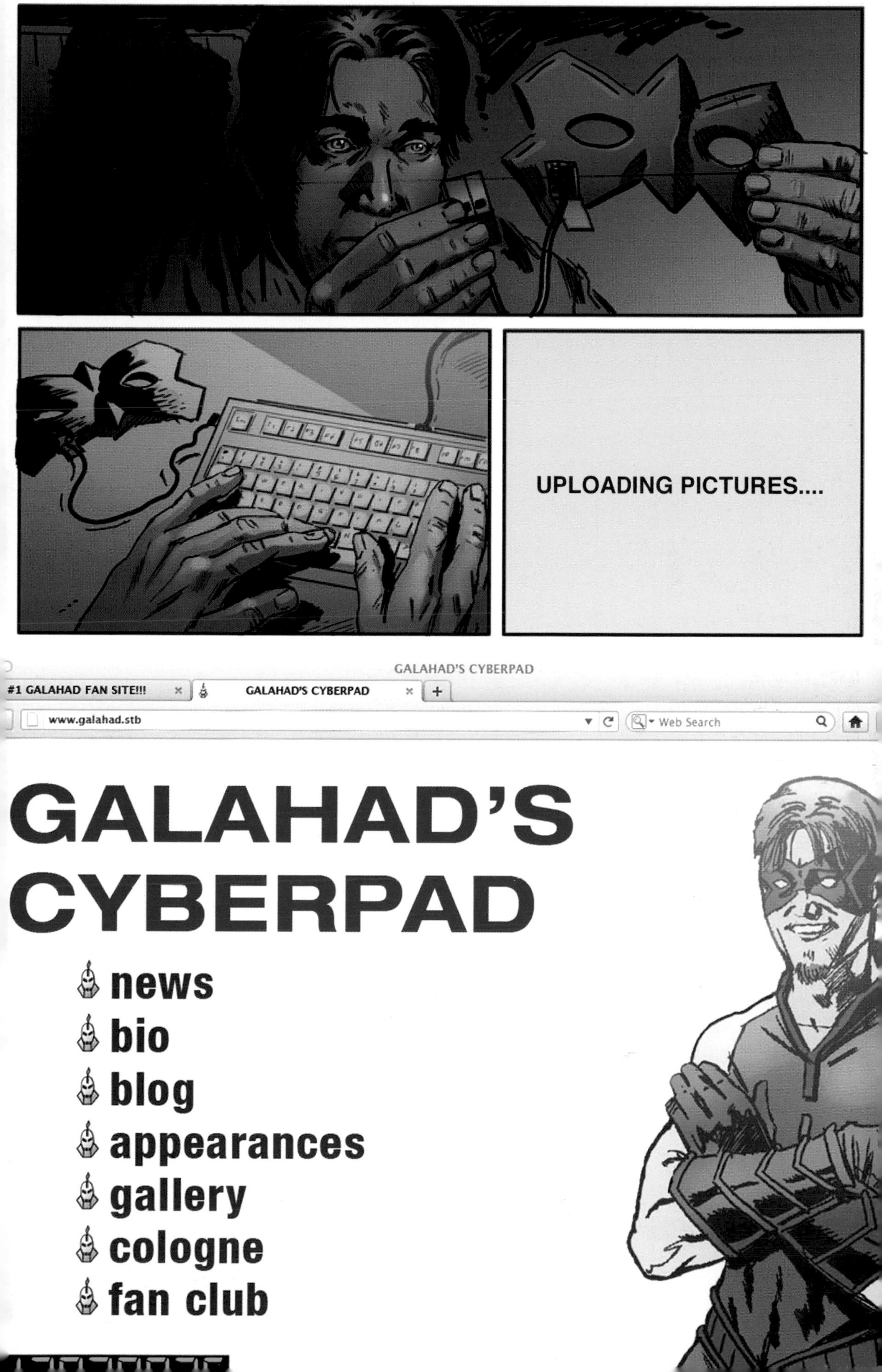
UPLOADING PICTURES....
GALAHAD'S CYBERPAD
#1 GALAHAD FAN SITE!!!
GALAHAD'S CYBERPAD
www.galahad.stb
Web Search
GALAHAD'S CYBERPAD
news
bio
blog
appearances
gallery
cologne
fan club

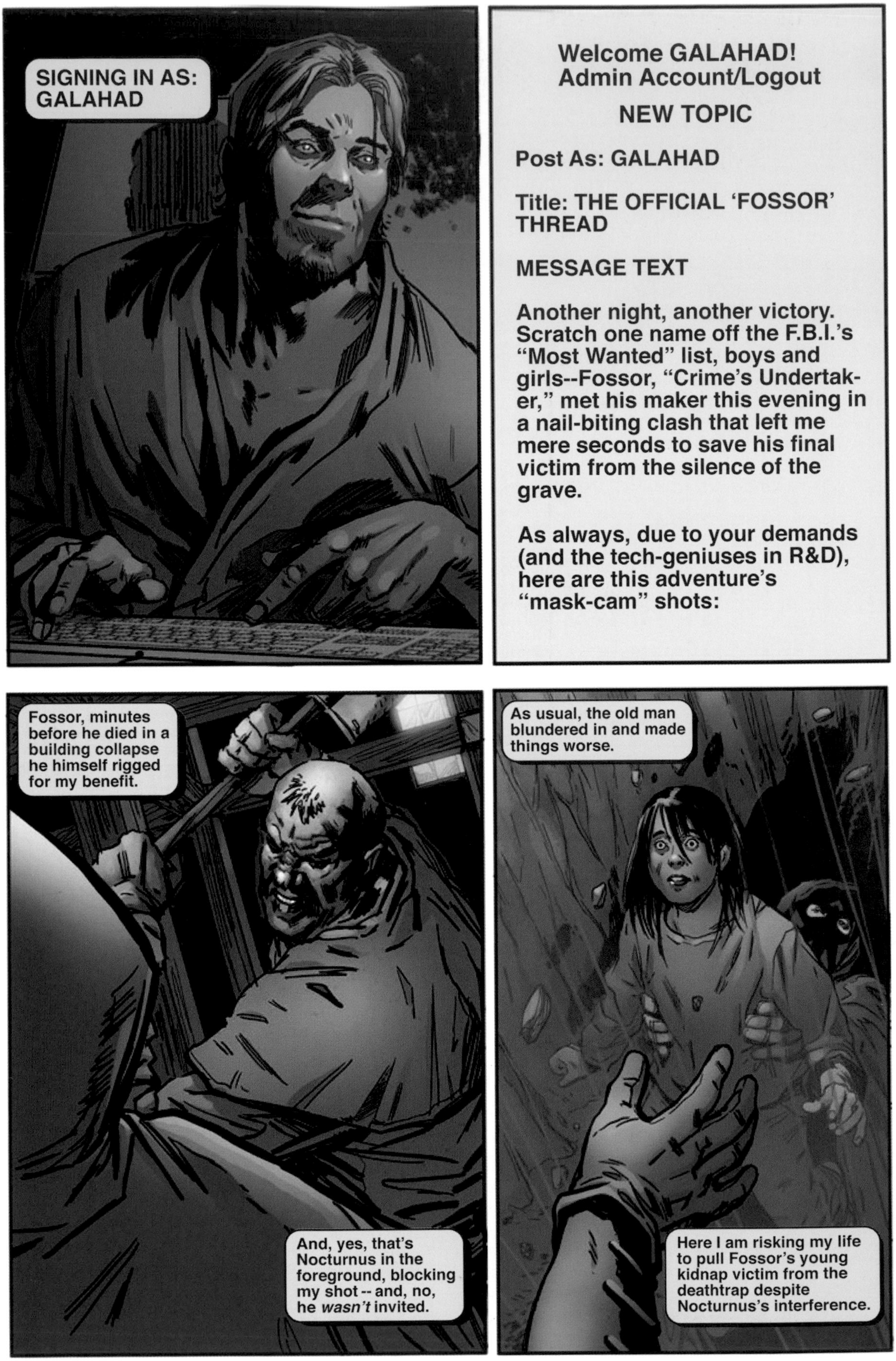
SIGNING IN AS: GALAHAD
Welcome GALAHAD!
Admin Account/Logout
NEW TOPIC
Post As: GALAHAD
Title: THE OFFICIAL 'FOSSOR' THREAD
MESSAGE TEXT
Another night, another victory. Scratch one name off the F.B.I.'s "Most Wanted" list, boys and girls--Fossor, "Crime's Undertaker," met his maker this evening in a nail-biting clash that left me mere seconds to save his final victim from the silence of the grave.
As always, due to your demands (and the tech-geniuses in R&D), here are this adventure's "mask-cam" shots:
Fossor, minutes before he died in a building collapse he himself rigged for my benefit.
And, yes, that's Nocturnus in the foreground, blocking my shot -- and, no, he *wasn't* invited.
As usual, the old man blundered in and made things worse.
Here I am risking my life to pull Fossor's young kidnap victim from the deathtrap despite Nocturnus's interference.

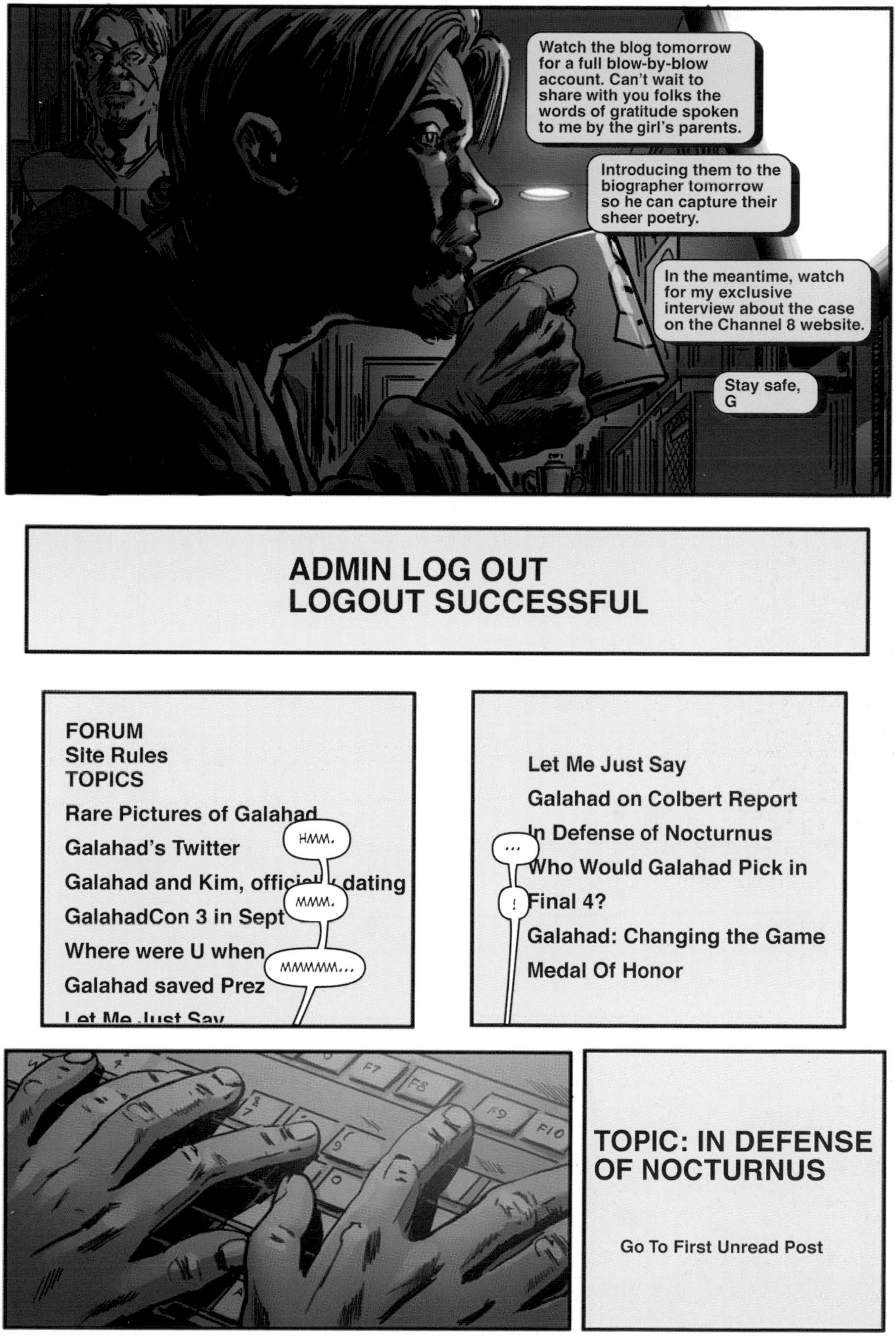
Watch the blog tomorrow for a full blow-by-blow account. Can't wait to share with you folks the words of gratitude spoken to me by the girl's parents.
Introducing them to the biographer tomorrow so he can capture their sheer poetry.
In the meantime, watch for my exclusive interview about the case on the Channel 8 website.
Stay safe, G
ADMIN LOG OUT
LOGOUT SUCCESSFUL
FORUM
Site Rules
TOPICS
Rare Pictures of Galahad
HMM.
Galahad's Twitter
Galahad and Kim, officially dating
MMM.
GalahadCon 3 in Sept
Where were U when
MMMMM...
Galahad saved Prez
Let Me Just Say
Galahad on Colbert Report
...
In Defense of Nocturnus
Who Would Galahad Pick in Final 4?
!
Galahad: Changing the Game
Medal Of Honor
TOPIC: IN DEFENSE OF NOCTURNUS
Go To First Unread Post

StBarryman posted 5-13-12

I, for one, miss the Nocturnus/Galahad TEAM. That's right, TEAM. What an ingrate. Imagine if you were Nocturnus and you had to put up with that loudmouth for all those years? You'd dump him, too! I can't stand all the badmouthing Galahad does about the man who taught him everything he knows-- his own DAD!
Who the hell does he think he is? St. Barrington doesn't need a friggin' celebrity, it needs a HERO.
And we HAVE one in NOCTURNUS

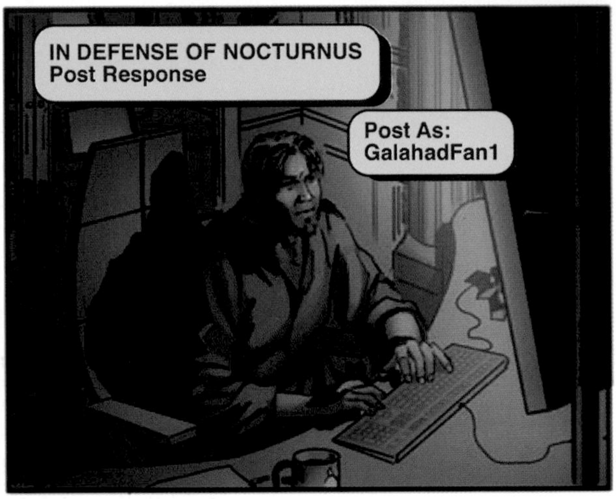
IN DEFENSE OF NOCTURNUS
Post Response
Post As:
GalahadFan1

StBarryman, a few points.
First, get it straight--
Galahad dumped NOCTURNUS as a partner, NOT the other way around.

Second, you don't have the SLIGHTEST IDEA what kind of a man you're defending. You're assuming he was some kind of MODEL FATHER.

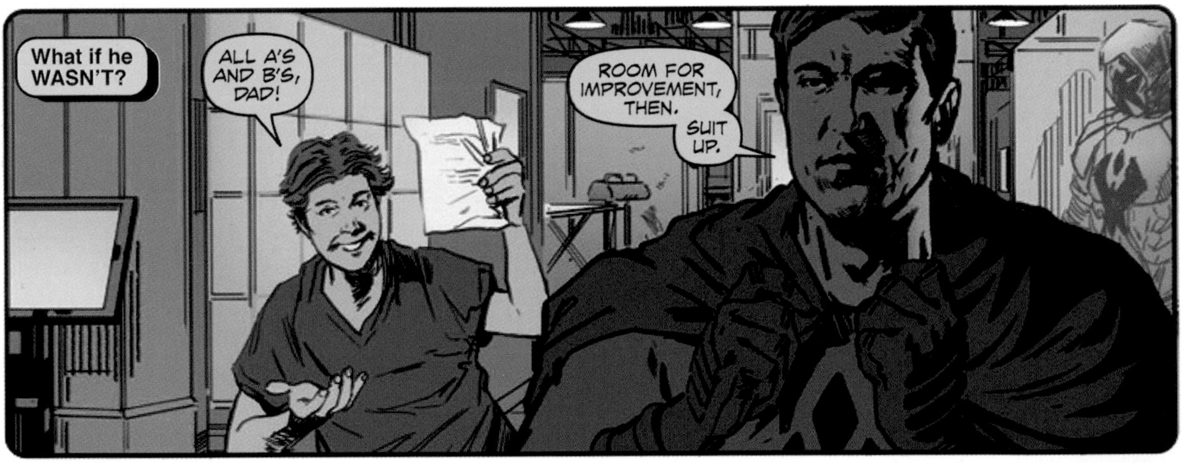
What if he WASN'T?
ALL A'S AND B'S, DAD!
ROOM FOR IMPROVEMENT, THEN.
SUIT UP.

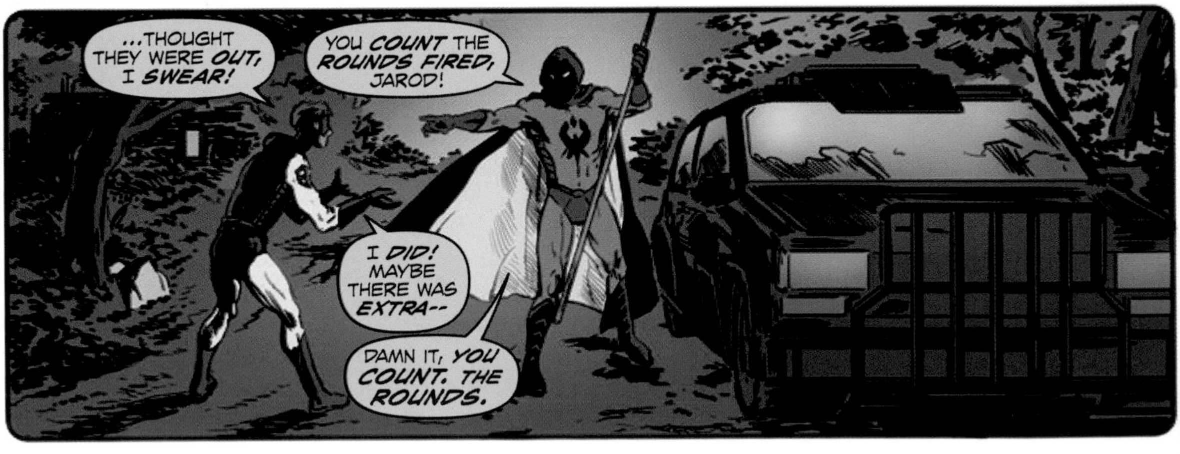
...THOUGHT THEY WERE OUT, I SWEAR!
YOU COUNT THE ROUNDS FIRED, JAROD!
I DID! MAYBE THERE WAS EXTRA--
DAMN IT, YOU COUNT. THE ROUNDS.

For all we know, Nocturnus was a demanding jerk that Galahad could never please.

What do you suppose it was like, anyway, to be a kid with all that responsibility on your shoulders? What kind of life was that for a boy, do you think? Did he miss being a normal kid?

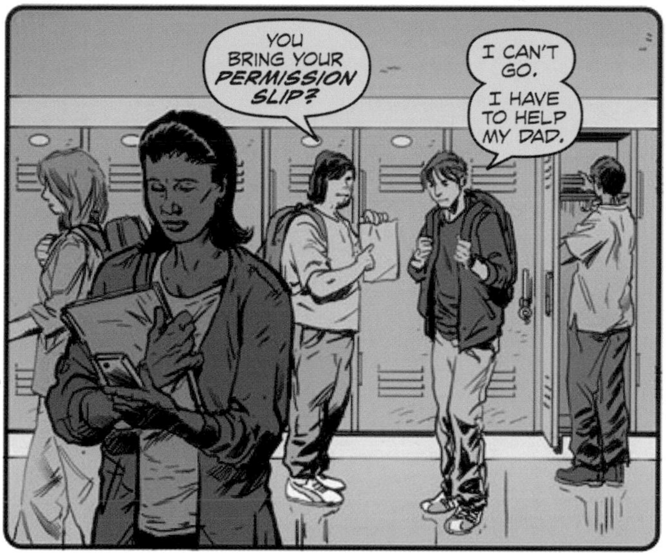
YOU BRING YOUR PERMISSION SLIP?
I CAN'T GO.
I HAVE TO HELP MY DAD.

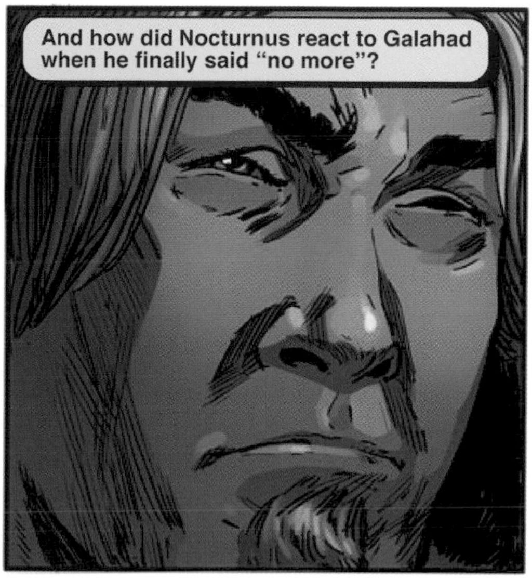
And how did Nocturnus react to Galahad when he finally said "no more"?

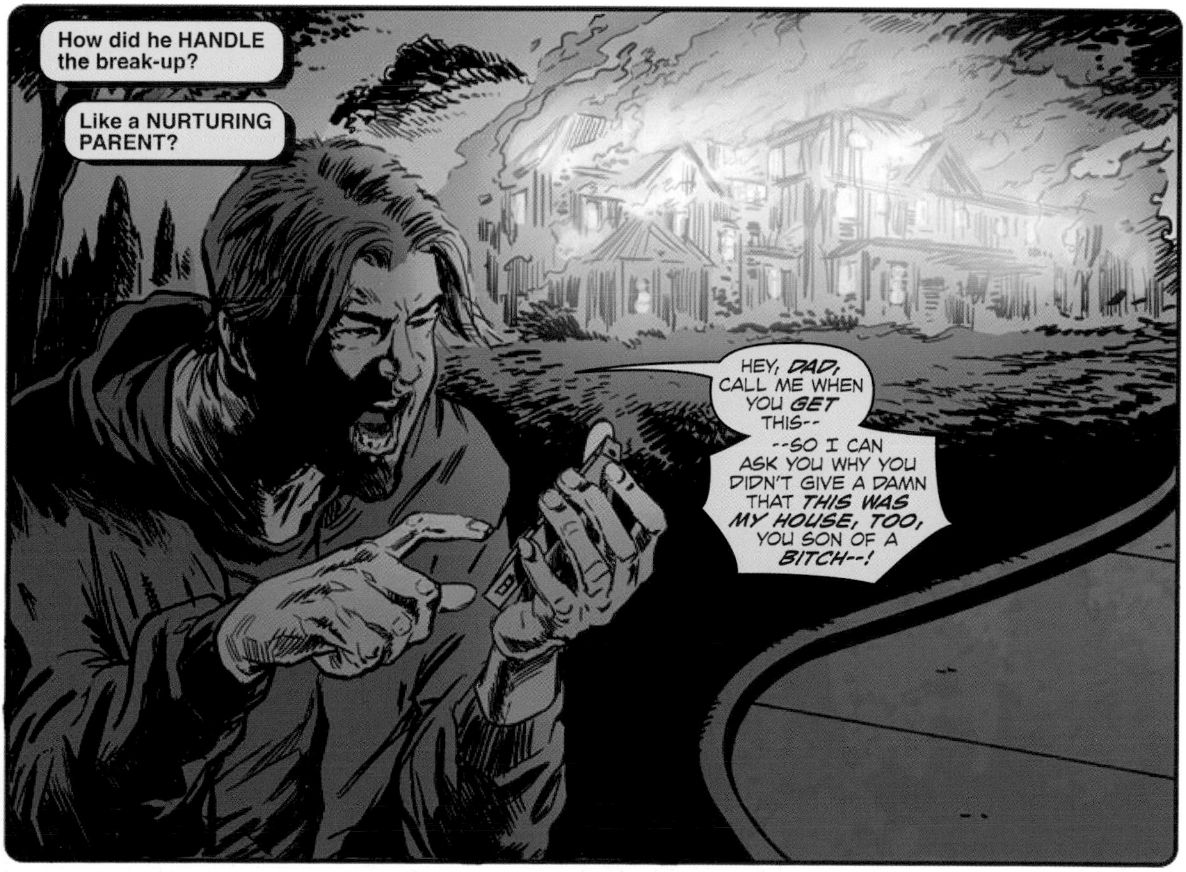
How did he HANDLE the break-up?
Like a NURTURING PARENT?
HEY, DAD, CALL ME WHEN YOU GET THIS--
--SO I CAN ASK YOU WHY YOU DIDN'T GIVE A DAMN THAT THIS WAS MY HOUSE, TOO, YOU SON OF A BITCH--!

...MY HOUSE, *TOO*...

WHAT WOULD YOU HAVE TO SAY ABOUT *THAT,* MR. MESSAGEBOARD DICK...?

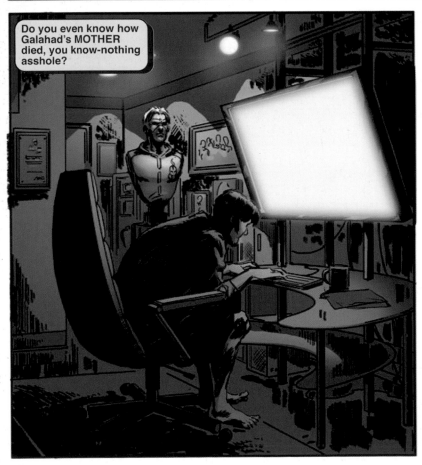

Do you even know how Galahad's MOTHER died, you know-nothing asshole?

Do you know how he could have SAVED her...?

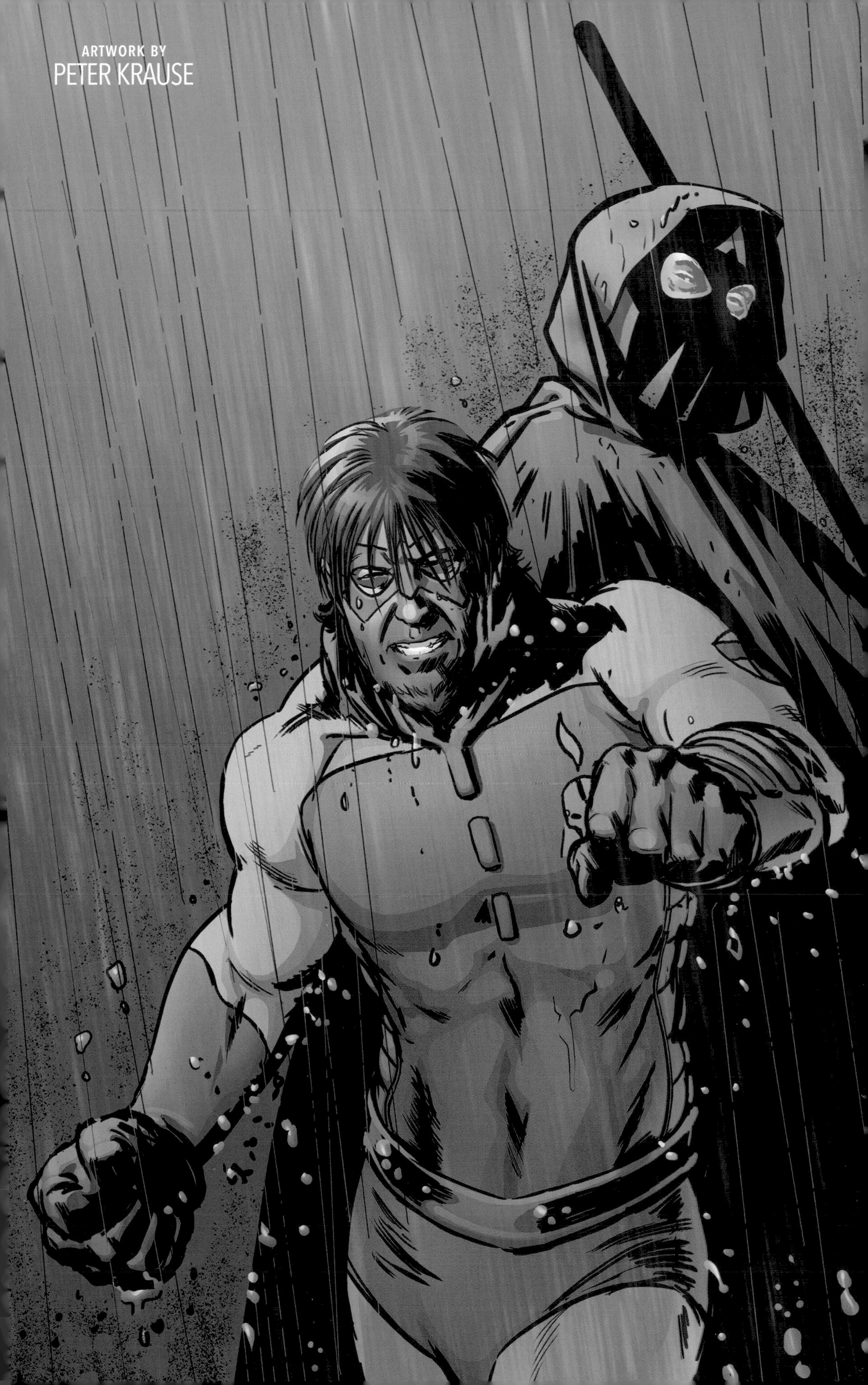
ARTWORK BY
PETER KRAUSE

CHAPTER TWO

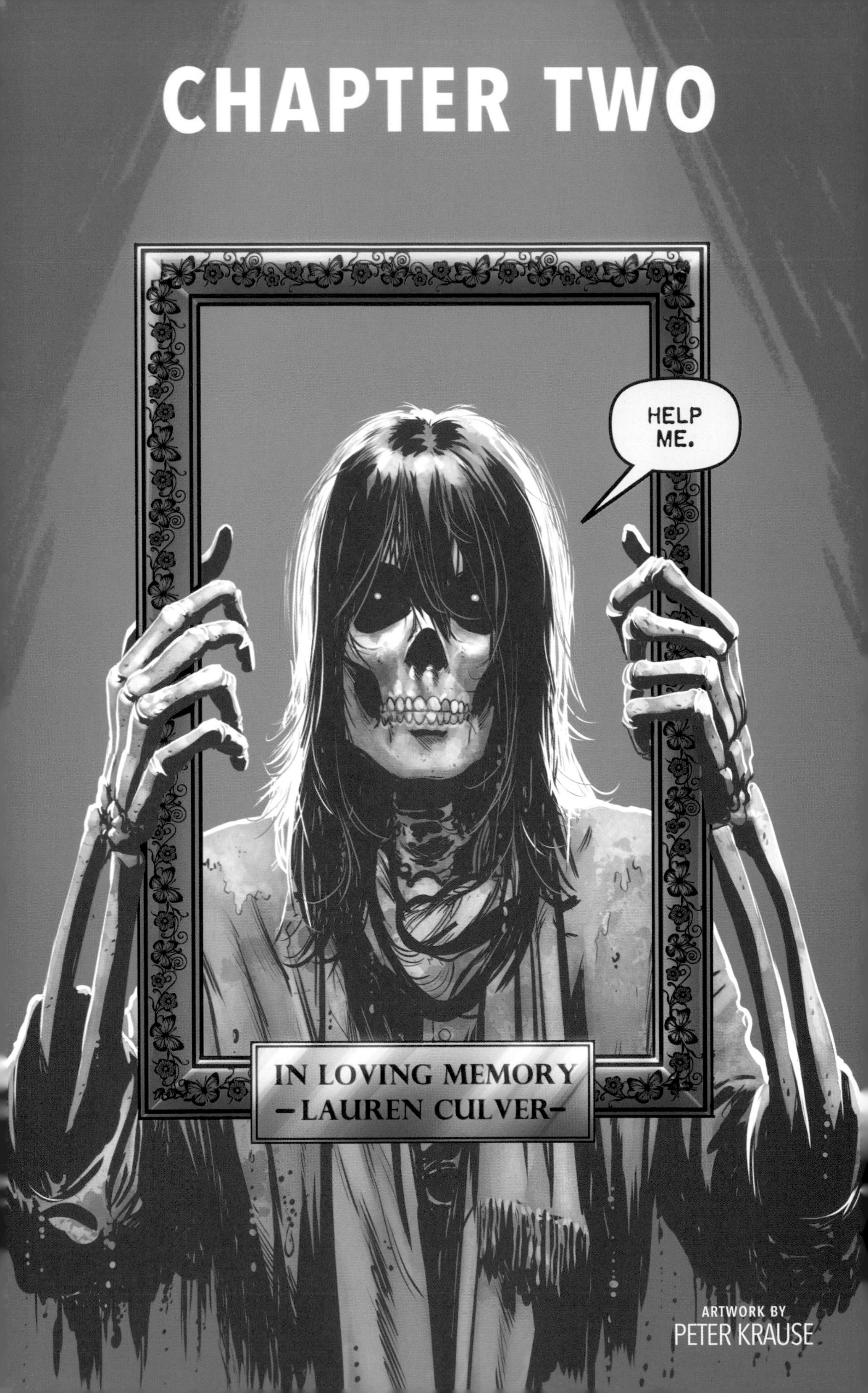
HELP ME.
IN LOVING MEMORY
-LAUREN CULVER-

ARTWORK BY
PETER KRAUSE

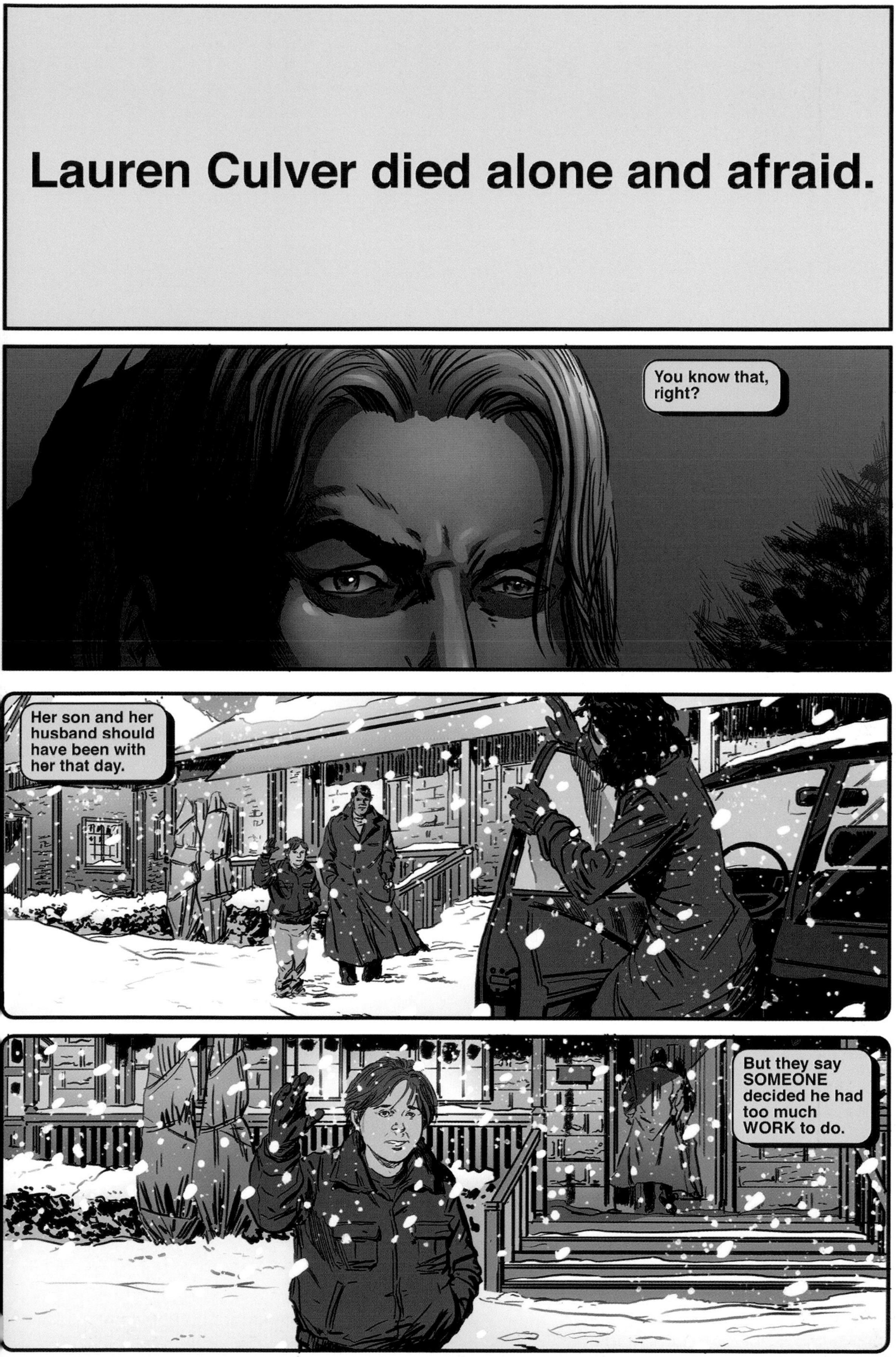
Lauren Culver died alone and afraid.
You know that, right?
Her son and her husband should have been with her that day.
But they say SOMEONE decided he had too much WORK to do.

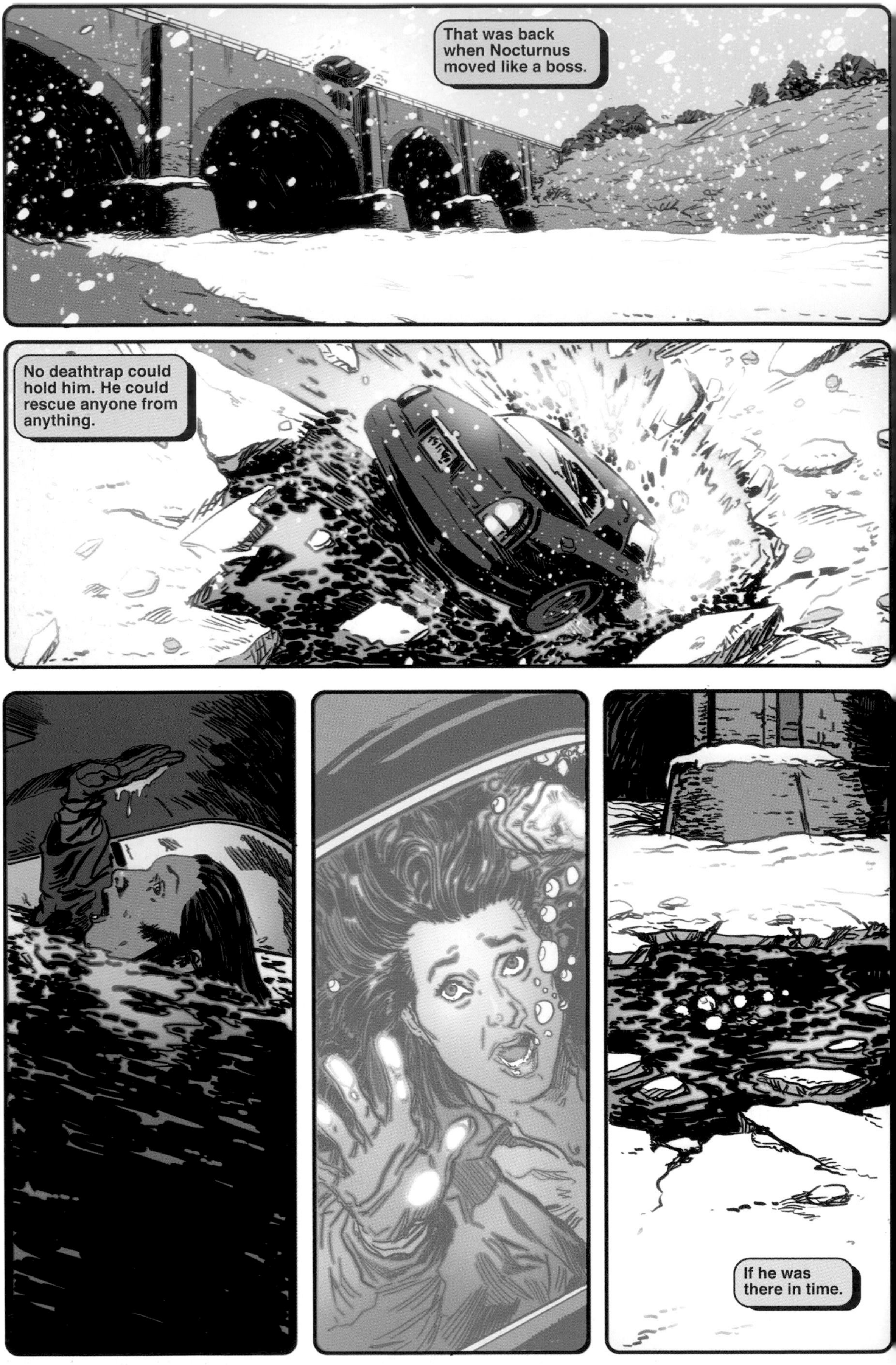
That was back when Nocturnus moved like a boss.
No deathtrap could hold him. He could rescue anyone from anything.
If he was there in time.

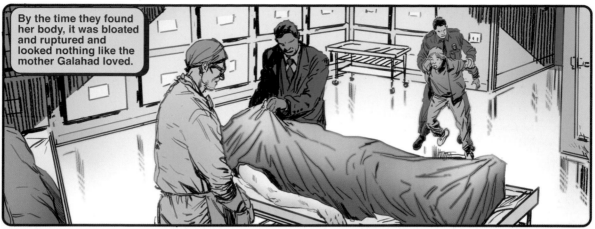

By the time they found her body, it was bloated and ruptured and looked nothing like the mother Galahad loved.

Galahad didn't blame his dad, not then. Not for years.

Not until he could finally afford to.

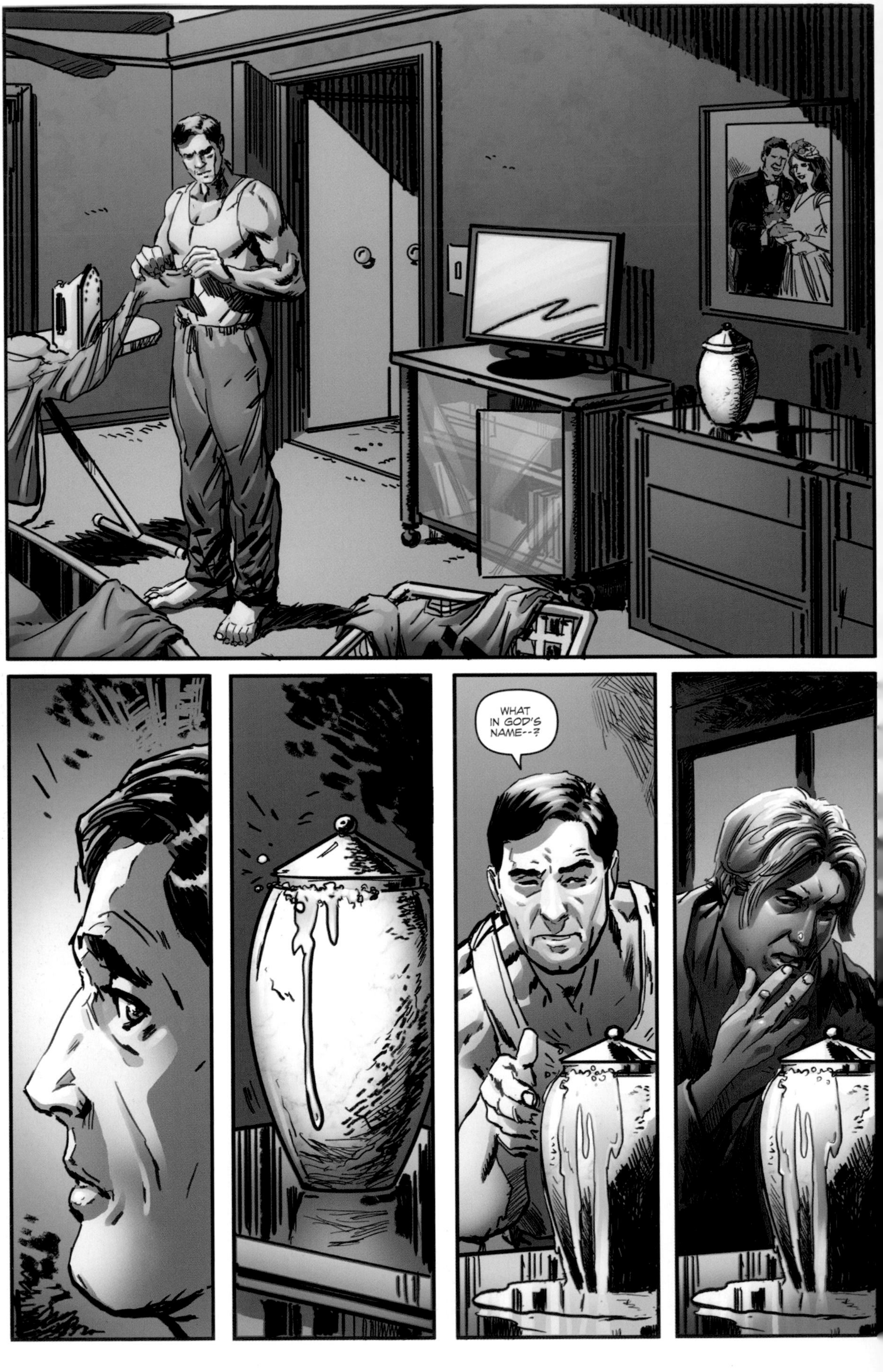
WHAT IN GOD'S NAME--?

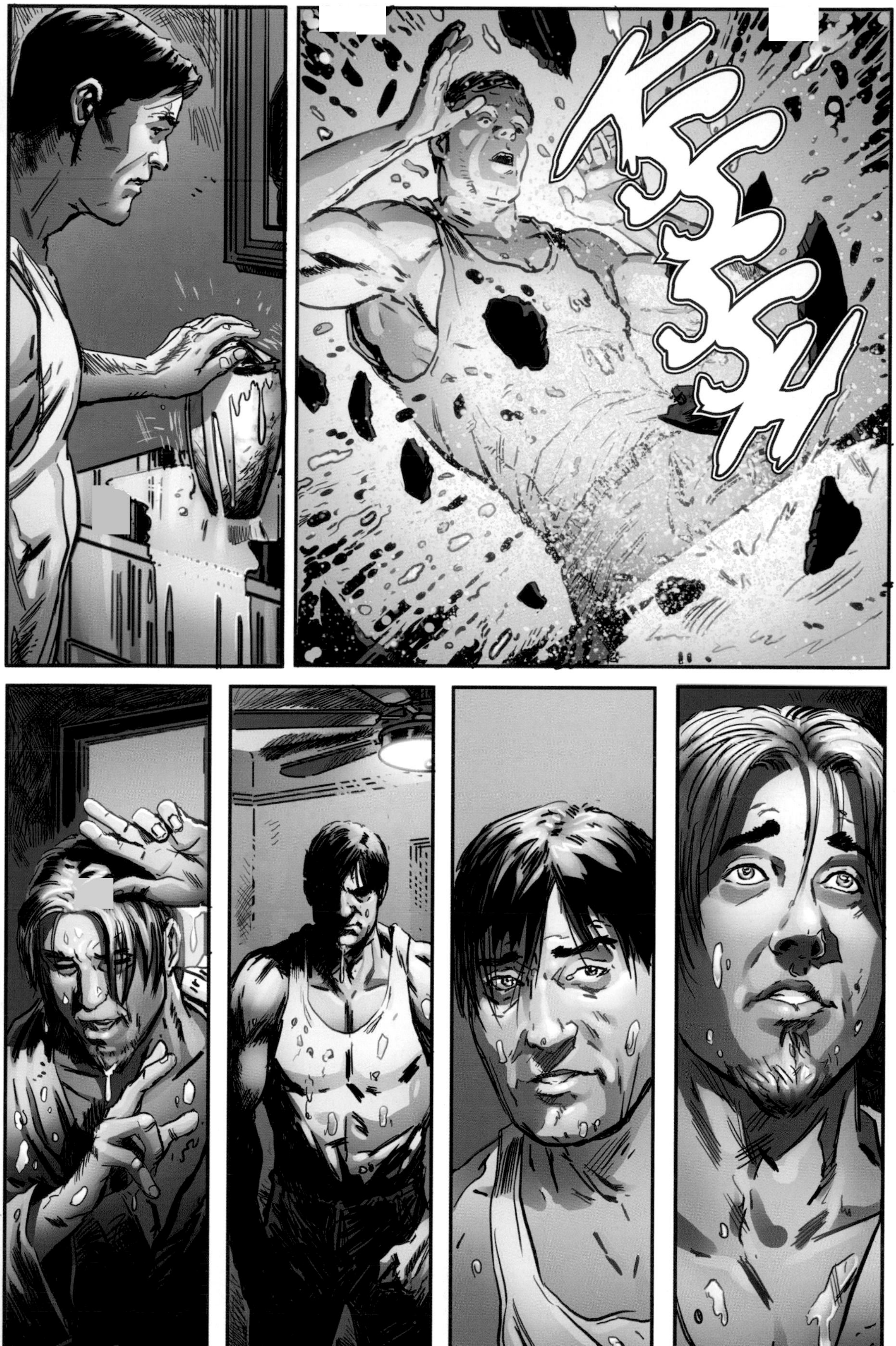
KRSSSH

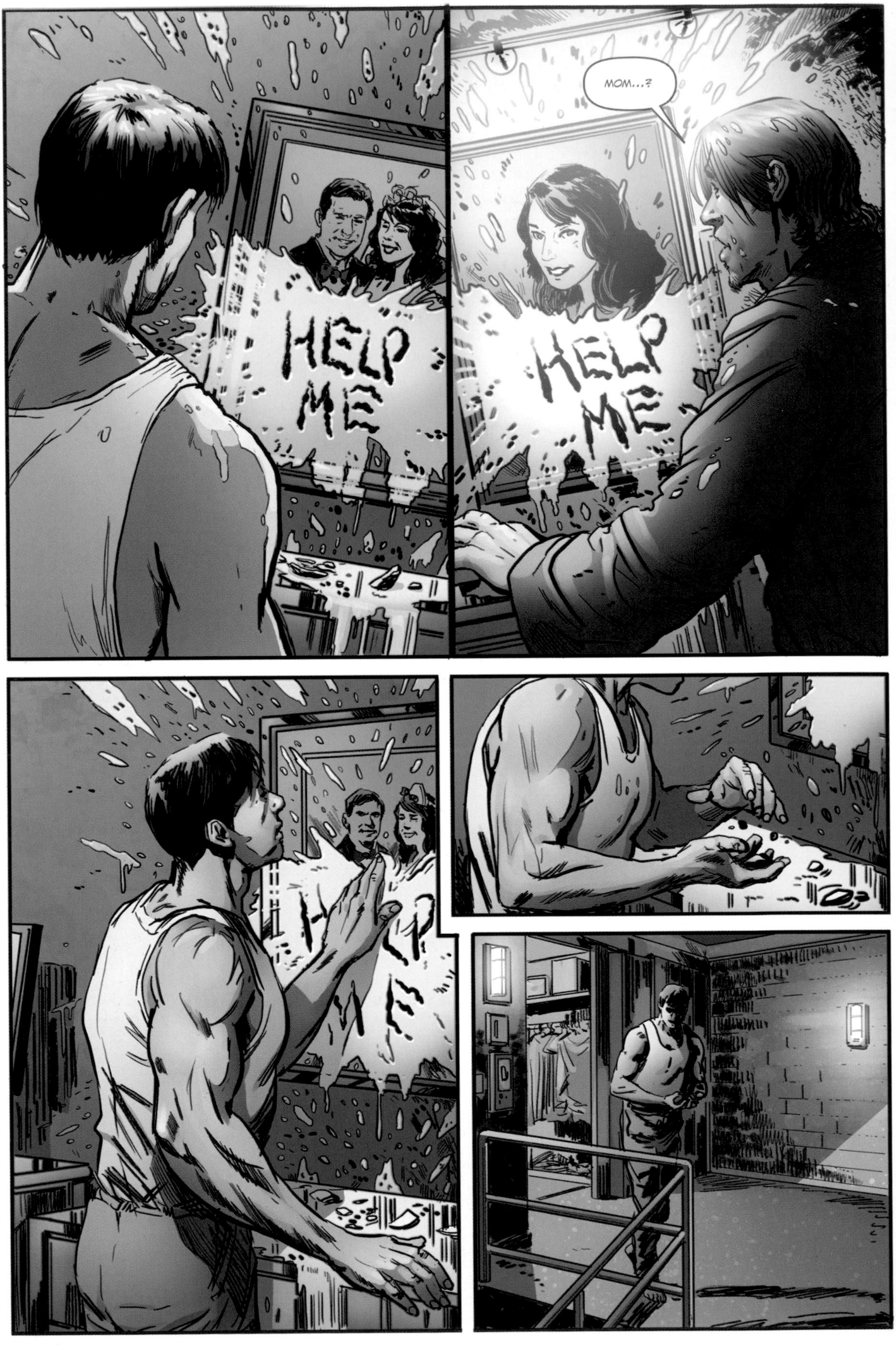
HELP ME
MOM...?
HELP ME

COME ON...
WORK...!

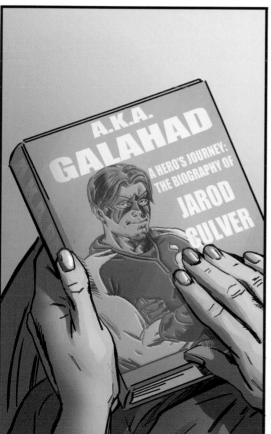

A.K.A.
GALAHAD

A HERO'S JOURNEY:
THE BIOGRAPHY OF

JAROD
CULVER

TAP
TAP

LT. RAINWOOD...?

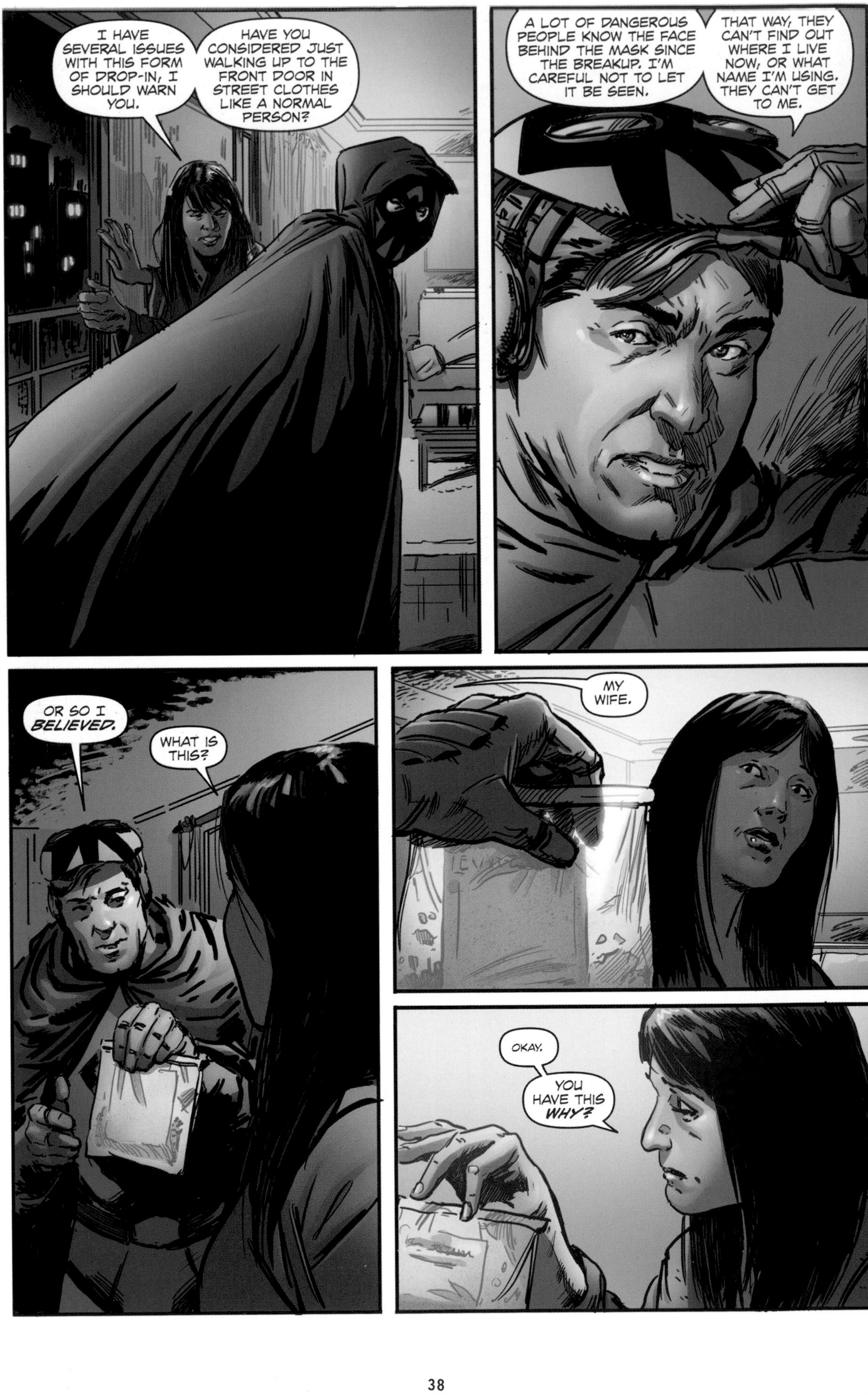
I HAVE SEVERAL ISSUES WITH THIS FORM OF DROP-IN, I SHOULD WARN YOU.
HAVE YOU CONSIDERED JUST WALKING UP TO THE FRONT DOOR IN STREET CLOTHES LIKE A NORMAL PERSON?
A LOT OF DANGEROUS PEOPLE KNOW THE FACE BEHIND THE MASK SINCE THE BREAKUP. I'M CAREFUL NOT TO LET IT BE SEEN.
THAT WAY, THEY CAN'T FIND OUT WHERE I LIVE NOW, OR WHAT NAME I'M USING. THEY CAN'T GET TO ME.
OR SO I *BELIEVED.*
WHAT IS THIS?
MY WIFE.
OKAY.
YOU HAVE THIS *WHY?*

EARLIER TODAY, HER URN *EXPLODED* IN A SHOWER OF WATER AND ASH THAT LEFT THE WORDS *"HELP ME"* ON A WALL IN MY--

--ON A WALL.

I RAN A CHEMICAL ANALYSIS ON THE CREMAINS. THEY ARE HUMAN ASH.

I WAS HOPING YOU COULD HAVE SOME DNA TESTING DONE TO VERIFY HER IDENTITY.

YOU DON'T HAVE THE *TECH?*

NOT THESE DAYS. ONCE MY SON UNMASKED ON *NATIONAL TELEVISION*, I HAD TO "BURY" JOHN CULVER IN A *HURRY.*

EARLY ON IN THIS CAREER, I BUILT SEVERAL *ALTER EGOS* FOR MYSELF AND MY FAMILY IN CASE I WAS EVER UNMASKED.

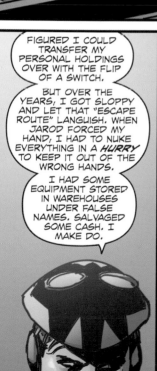

FIGURED I COULD TRANSFER MY PERSONAL HOLDINGS OVER WITH THE FLIP OF A SWITCH.

BUT OVER THE YEARS, I GOT SLOPPY AND LET THAT "ESCAPE ROUTE" LANGUISH. WHEN JAROD FORCED MY HAND, I HAD TO NUKE EVERYTHING IN A *HURRY* TO KEEP IT OUT OF THE WRONG HANDS.

I HAD SOME EQUIPMENT STORED IN WAREHOUSES UNDER FALSE NAMES. SALVAGED SOME CASH. I MAKE DO.

I THOUGHT I'D DROPPED OFF THE GRID--BUT IF SOMEONE'S TAMPERED WITH LAUREN'S REMAINS, THEY'RE *ONTO* ME.

YOU'RE SURE THERE *WAS* TAMPERING? THAT THIS ISN'T, I DON'T KNOW, SOME WEIRD MESSAGE FROM *HER?*

THAT'S ABSURD. WHY WOULD YOU EVEN GO THERE?

I DIDN'T.

HE DID.

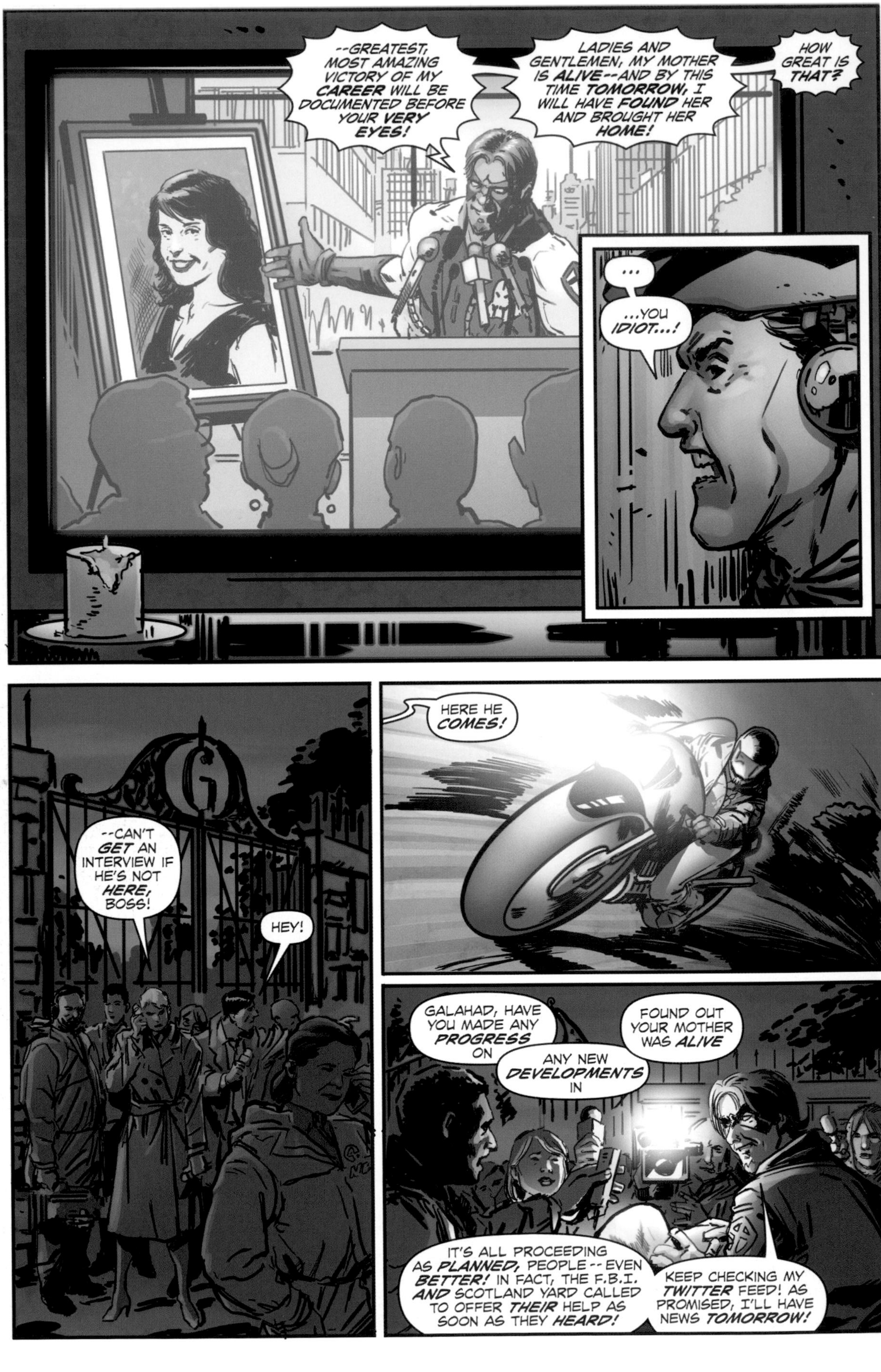
--GREATEST, MOST AMAZING VICTORY OF MY CAREER WILL BE DOCUMENTED BEFORE YOUR VERY EYES!
LADIES AND GENTLEMEN, MY MOTHER IS ALIVE--AND BY THIS TIME TOMORROW, I WILL HAVE FOUND HER AND BROUGHT HER HOME!
HOW GREAT IS THAT?
...
...YOU IDIOT...!
--CAN'T GET AN INTERVIEW IF HE'S NOT HERE, BOSS!
HEY!
HERE HE COMES!
GALAHAD, HAVE YOU MADE ANY PROGRESS ON
FOUND OUT YOUR MOTHER WAS ALIVE
ANY NEW DEVELOPMENTS IN
IT'S ALL PROCEEDING AS PLANNED, PEOPLE--EVEN BETTER! IN FACT, THE F.B.I. AND SCOTLAND YARD CALLED TO OFFER THEIR HELP AS SOON AS THEY HEARD!
KEEP CHECKING MY TWITTER FEED! AS PROMISED, I'LL HAVE NEWS TOMORROW!

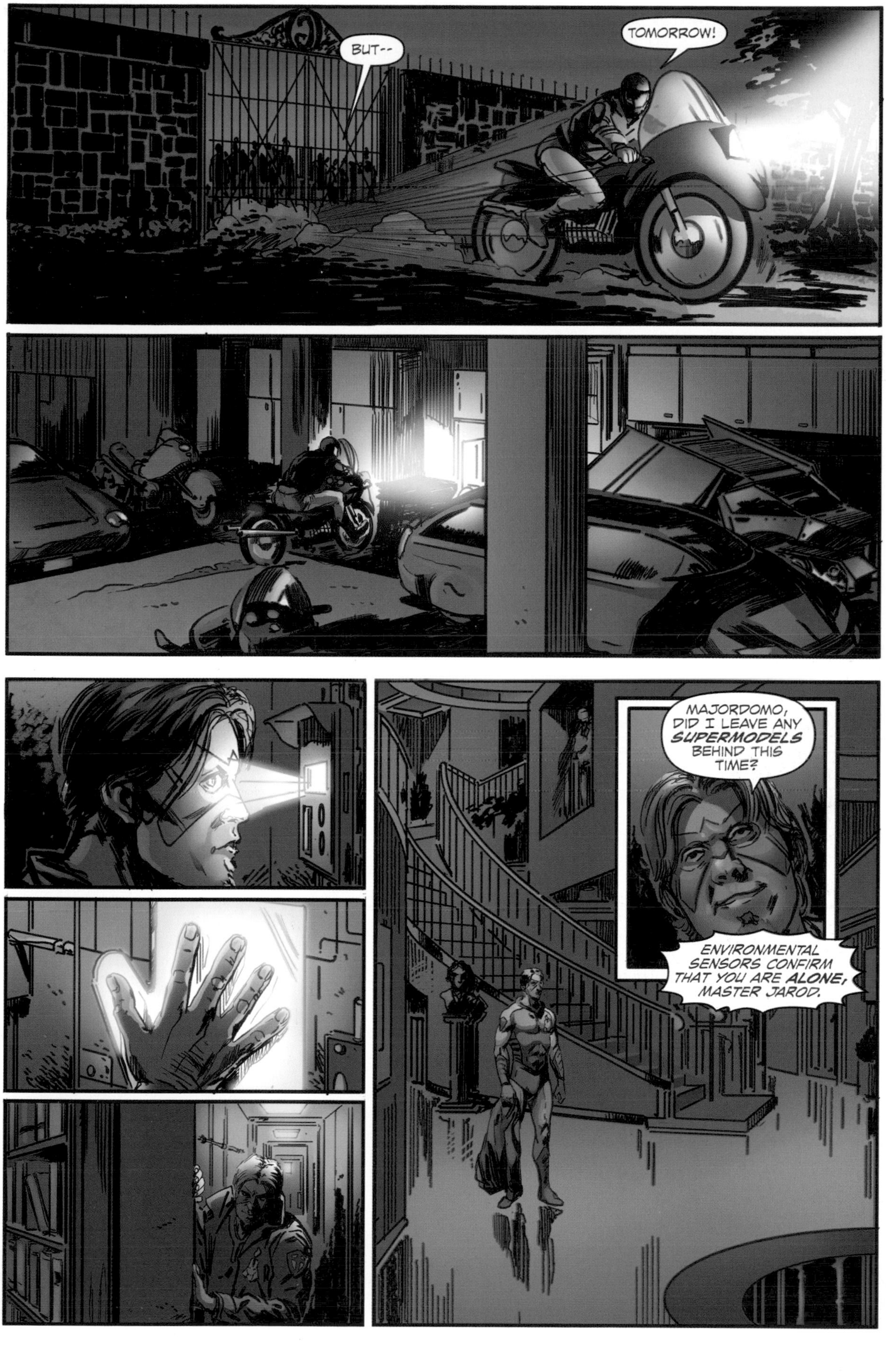
BUT--
TOMORROW!
MAJORDOMO, DID I LEAVE ANY SUPERMODELS BEHIND THIS TIME?
ENVIRONMENTAL SENSORS CONFIRM THAT YOU ARE ALONE, MASTER JAROD.

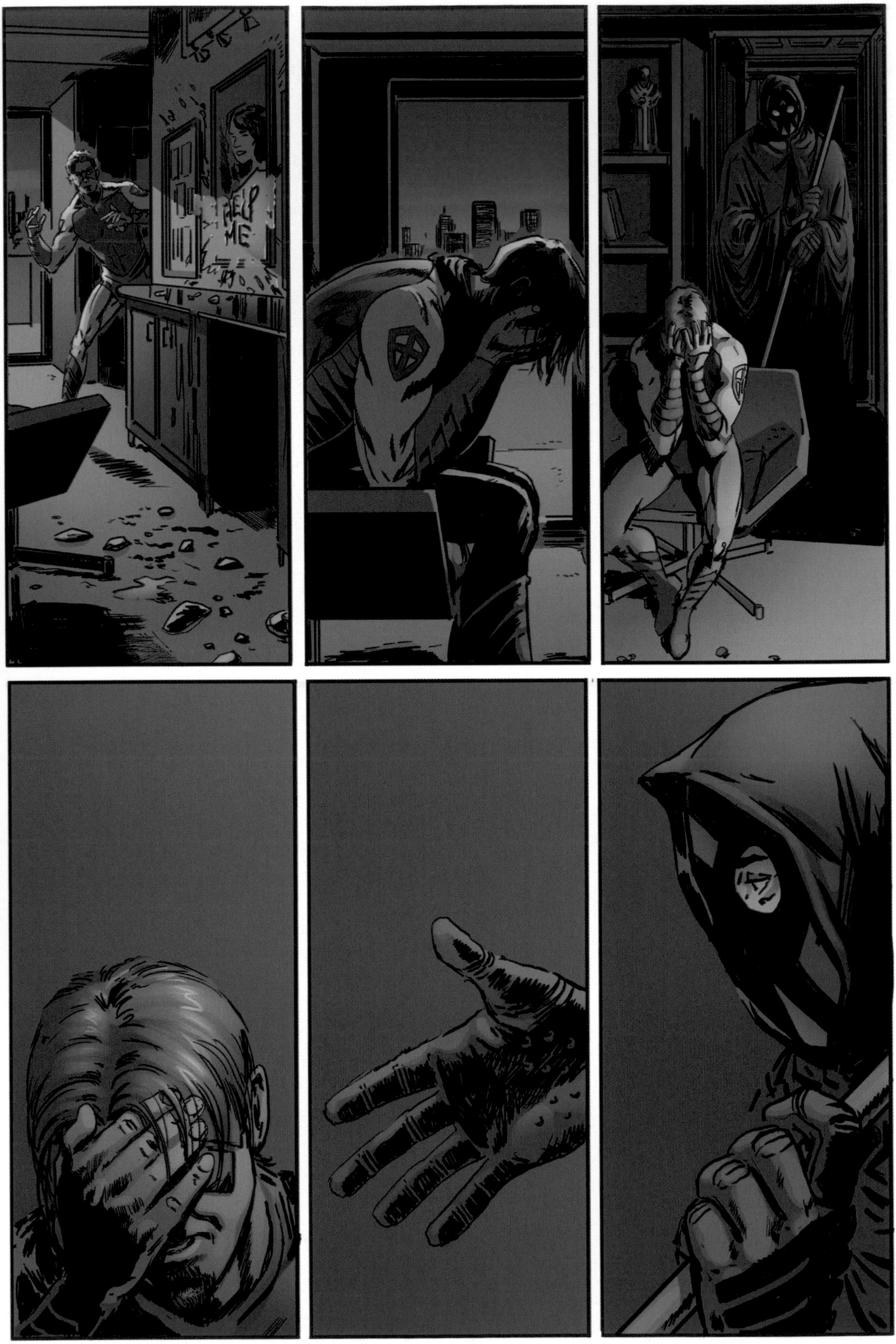
HELP
ME

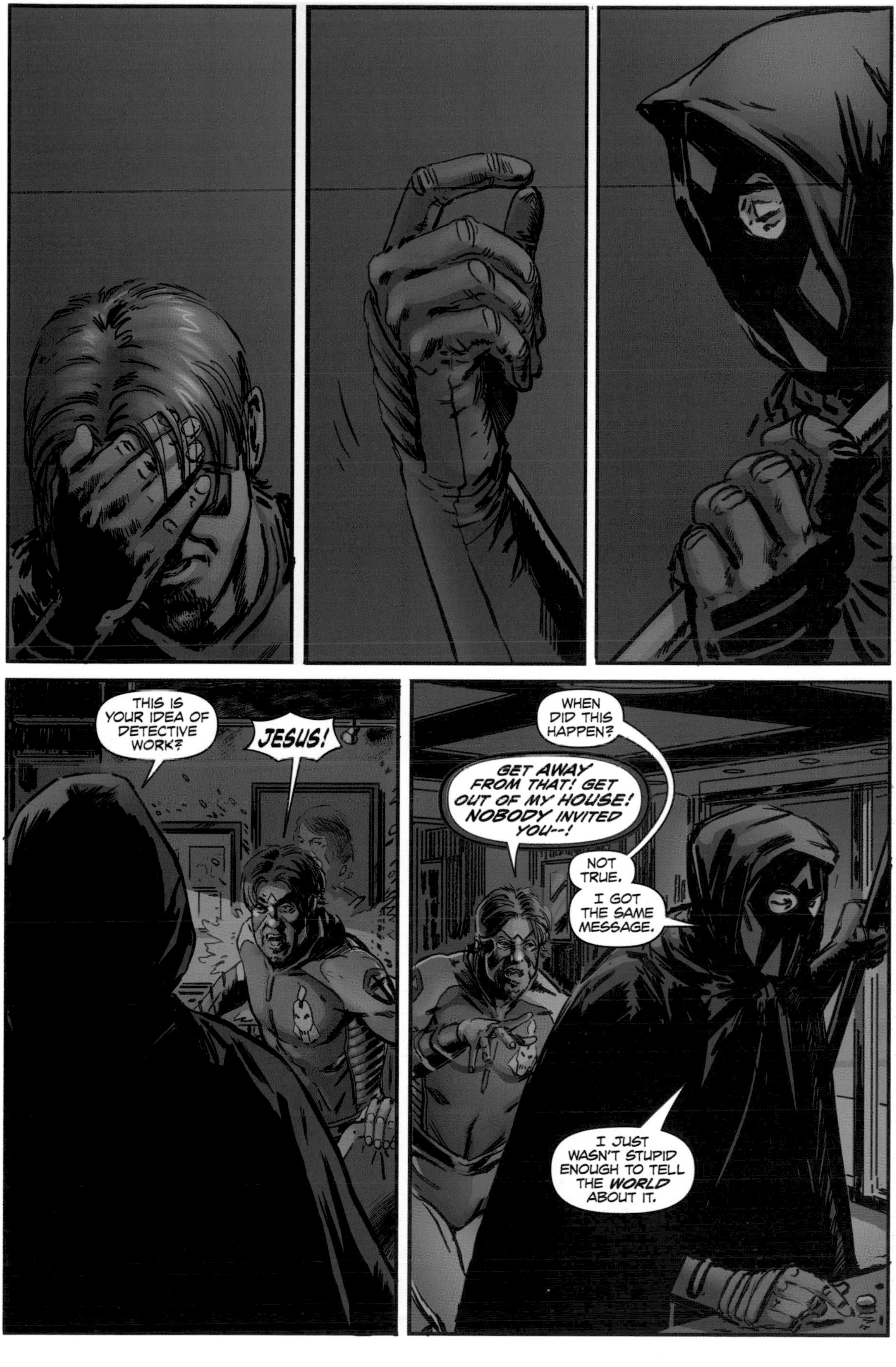
THIS IS YOUR IDEA OF DETECTIVE WORK?
JESUS!
WHEN DID THIS HAPPEN?
GET AWAY FROM THAT! GET OUT OF MY HOUSE! NOBODY INVITED YOU--!
NOT TRUE.
I GOT THE SAME MESSAGE.
I JUST WASN'T STUPID ENOUGH TO TELL THE WORLD ABOUT IT.

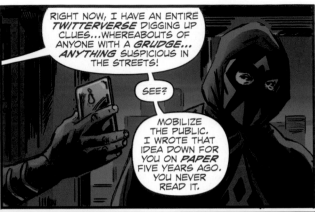

NOT STUPID. *SAVVY.*

USE THE MEDIA. INVITE PEOPLE *IN!*

YOU BUILD AND NURTURE A *FAN BASE,* THEY'LL BE YOUR *EYES* AND *EARS* IN THIS CITY!

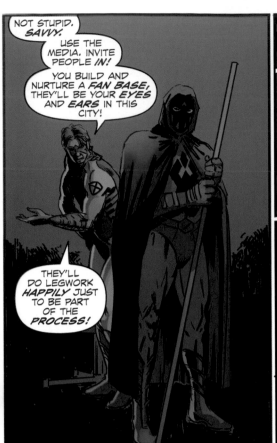

THEY'LL DO LEGWORK *HAPPILY* JUST TO BE PART OF THE *PROCESS!*

RIGHT NOW, I HAVE AN ENTIRE *TWITTERVERSE* DIGGING UP CLUES...WHEREABOUTS OF ANYONE WITH A *GRUDGE...* *ANYTHING* SUSPICIOUS IN THE STREETS!

SEE?

MOBILIZE THE PUBLIC. I WROTE THAT IDEA DOWN FOR YOU ON *PAPER* FIVE YEARS AGO. YOU NEVER READ IT.

THIS ISN'T *ABOUT* YOU.

IT NEVER *WAS.*

SO THIS ADORING PUBLIC YOU'RE PUTTING TO WORK...

...YOU DON'T MIND THEIR BLOOD ON YOUR HANDS?

WHAT ARE YOU TALKING ABOUT?

THAT THERE'S A *MASS MURDERER* WALKING AROUND THE *HARBORFRONT...*

SPOTTED MALVOLIA NEAR AQUARIUM

...AND HE DOESN'T LIKE BEING *FOLLOWED...!*

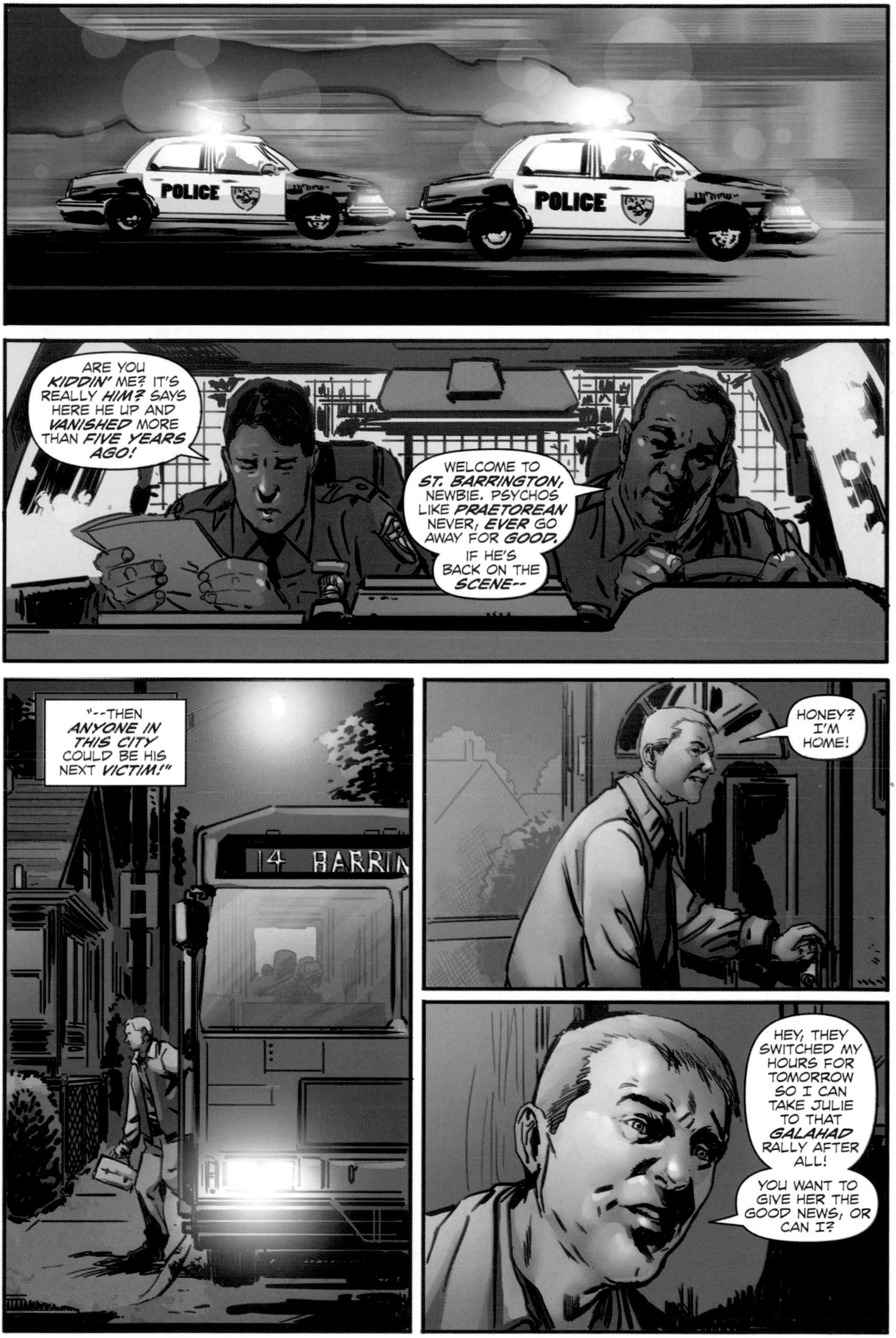
POLICE
POLICE
ARE YOU KIDDIN' ME? IT'S REALLY HIM? SAYS HERE HE UP AND VANISHED MORE THAN FIVE YEARS AGO!
WELCOME TO ST. BARRINGTON, NEWBIE. PSYCHOS LIKE PRAETOREAN NEVER, EVER GO AWAY FOR GOOD.
IF HE'S BACK ON THE SCENE--
"--THEN ANYONE IN THIS CITY COULD BE HIS NEXT VICTIM!"
14 BARRIN
HONEY? I'M HOME!
HEY, THEY SWITCHED MY HOURS FOR TOMORROW SO I CAN TAKE JULIE TO THAT GALAHAD RALLY AFTER ALL!
YOU WANT TO GIVE HER THE GOOD NEWS, OR CAN I?

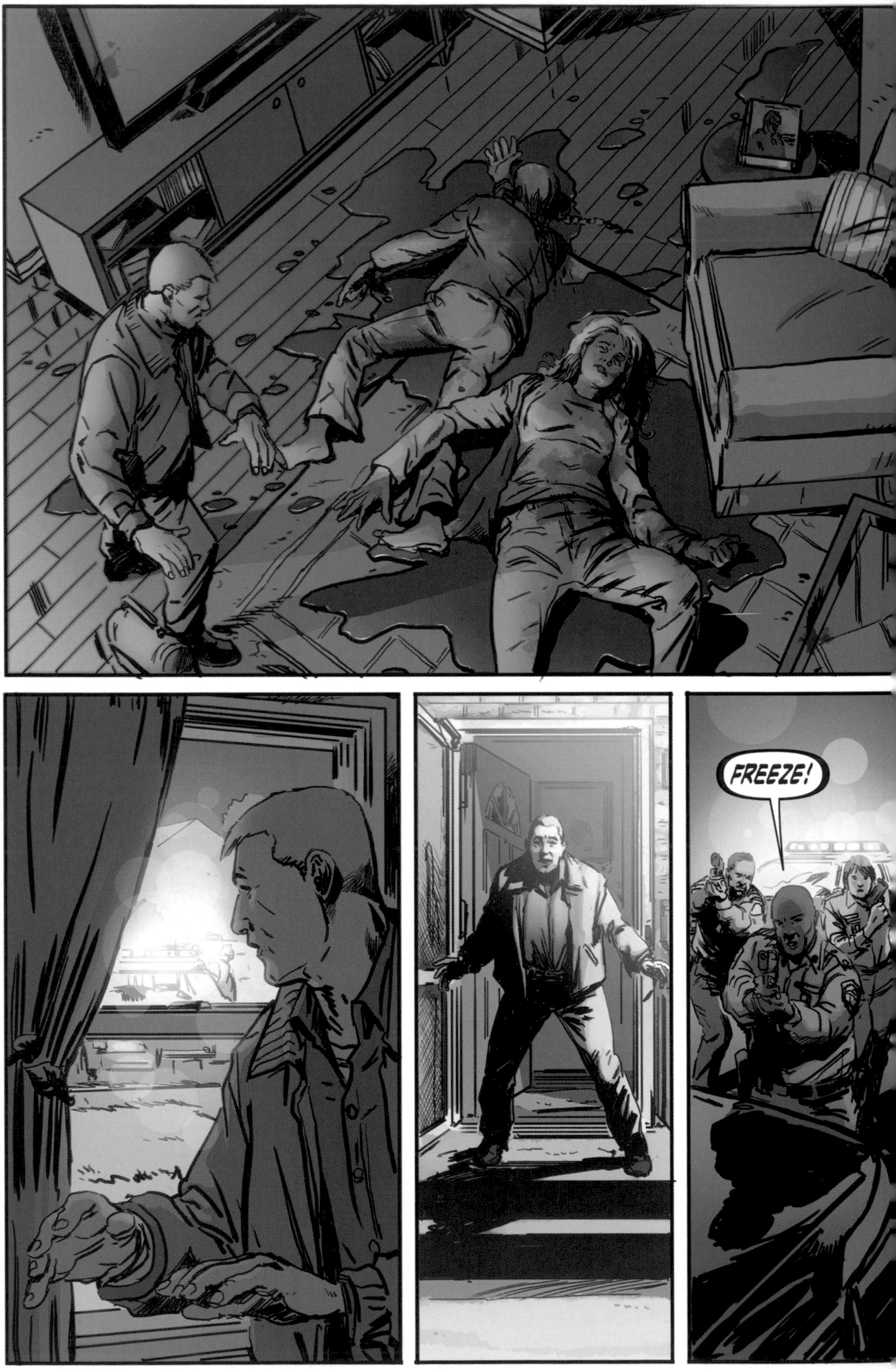
FREEZE!

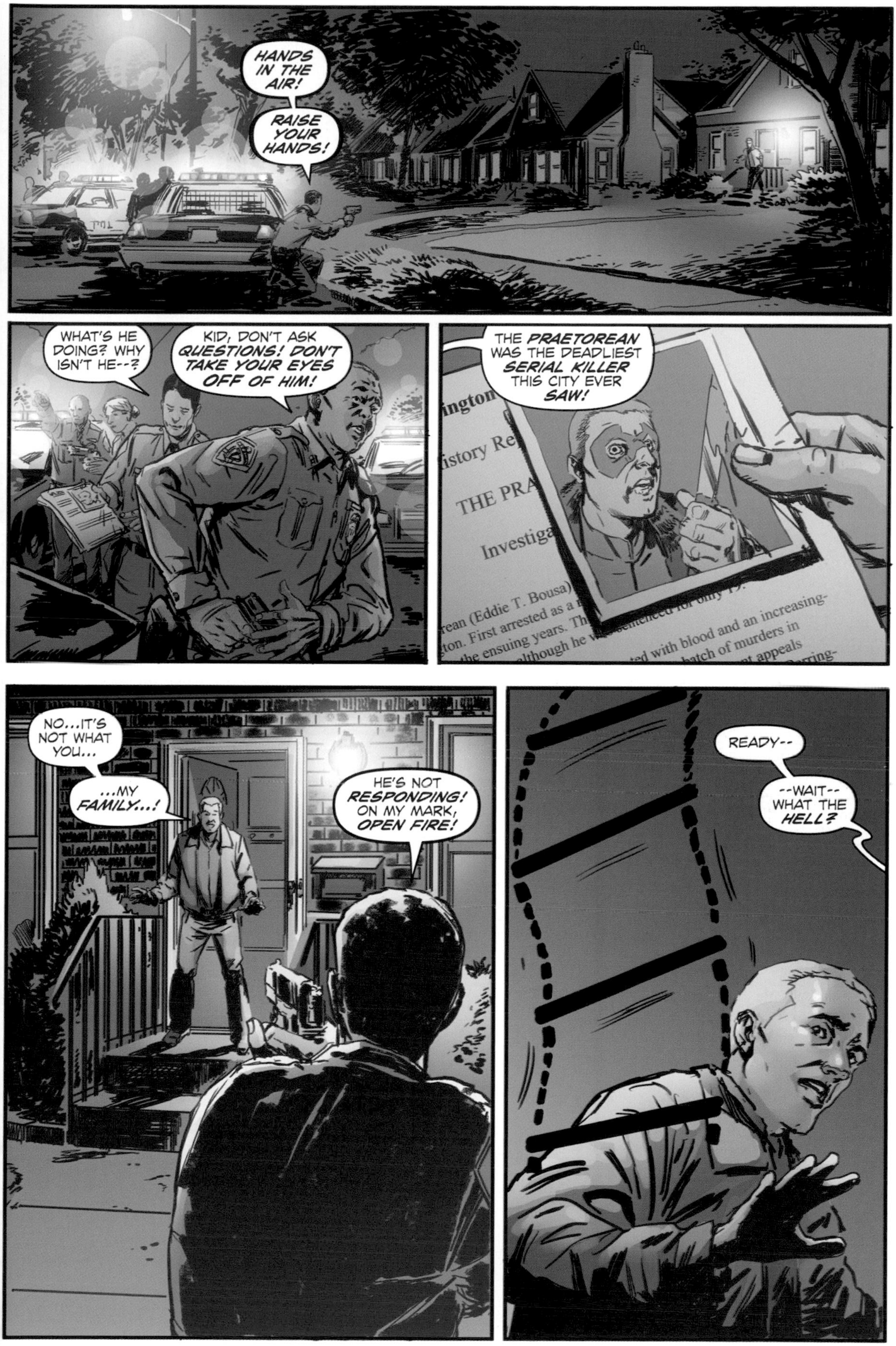
HANDS IN THE AIR!
RAISE YOUR HANDS!
WHAT'S HE DOING? WHY ISN'T HE--?
KID, DON'T ASK QUESTIONS! DON'T TAKE YOUR EYES OFF OF HIM!
THE PRAETOREAN WAS THE DEADLIEST SERIAL KILLER THIS CITY EVER SAW!
NO...IT'S NOT WHAT YOU...
...MY FAMILY...!
HE'S NOT RESPONDING! ON MY MARK, OPEN FIRE!
READY--
--WAIT-- WHAT THE HELL?

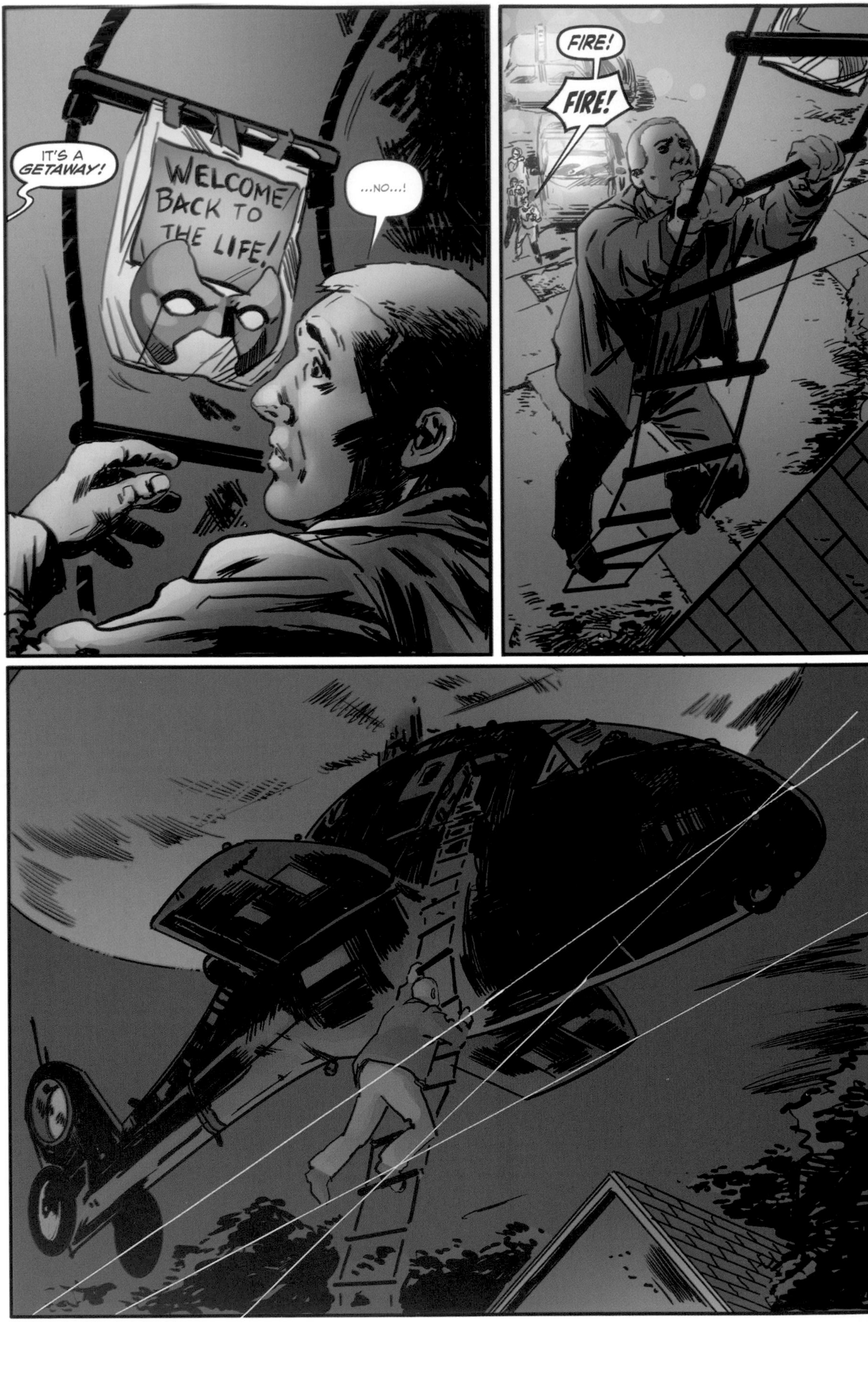
IT'S A GETAWAY!
WELCOME BACK TO THE LIFE!
...NO...!
FIRE!
FIRE!

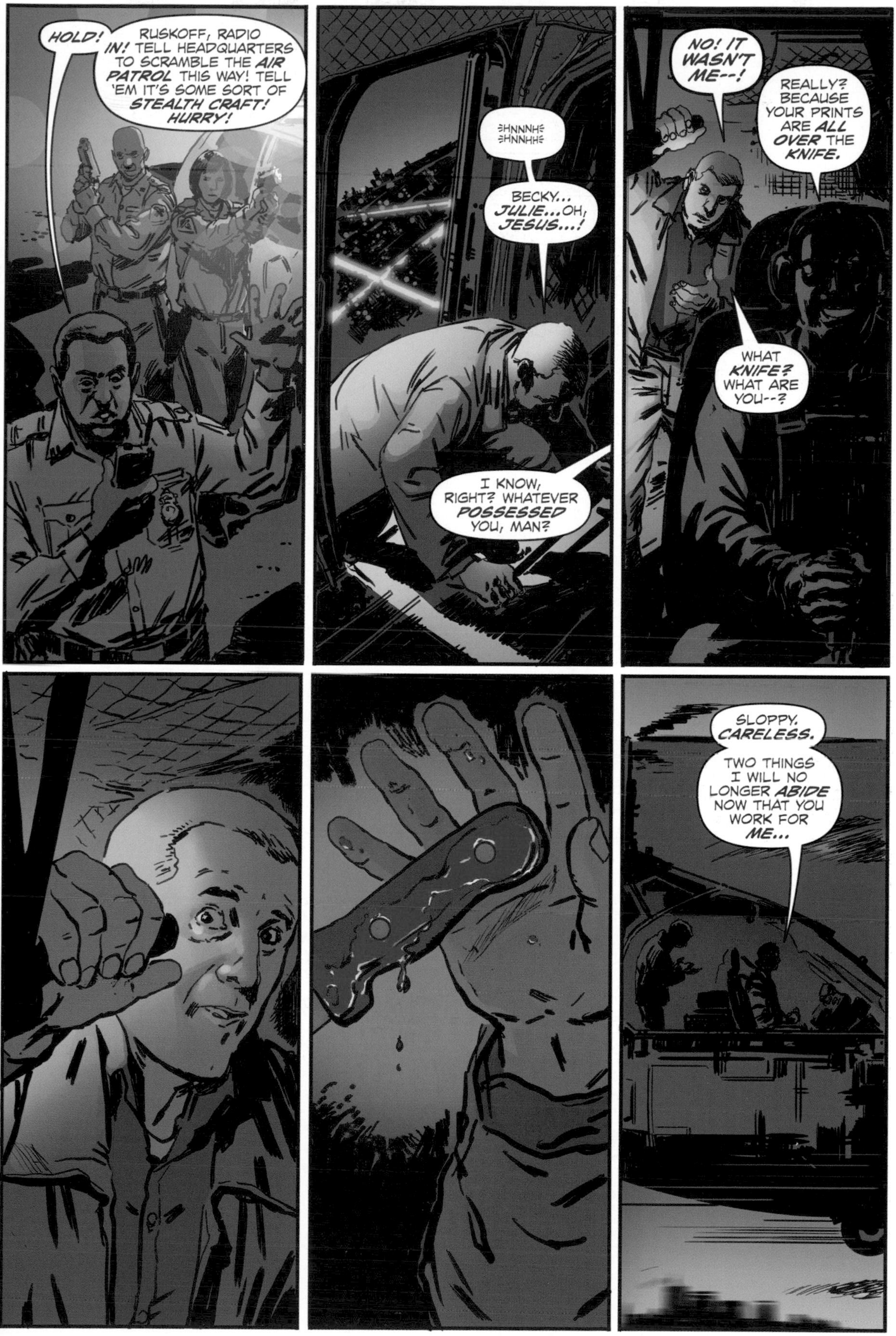
HOLD!
RUSKOFF, RADIO IN! TELL HEADQUARTERS TO SCRAMBLE THE AIR PATROL THIS WAY! TELL 'EM IT'S SOME SORT OF STEALTH CRAFT! HURRY!
HNNNH HNNNH
BECKY... JULIE...OH, JESUS...!
I KNOW, RIGHT? WHATEVER POSSESSED YOU, MAN?
NO! IT WASN'T ME--!
REALLY? BECAUSE YOUR PRINTS ARE ALL OVER THE KNIFE.
WHAT KNIFE? WHAT ARE YOU--?
SLOPPY. CARELESS.
TWO THINGS I WILL NO LONGER ABIDE NOW THAT YOU WORK FOR ME...

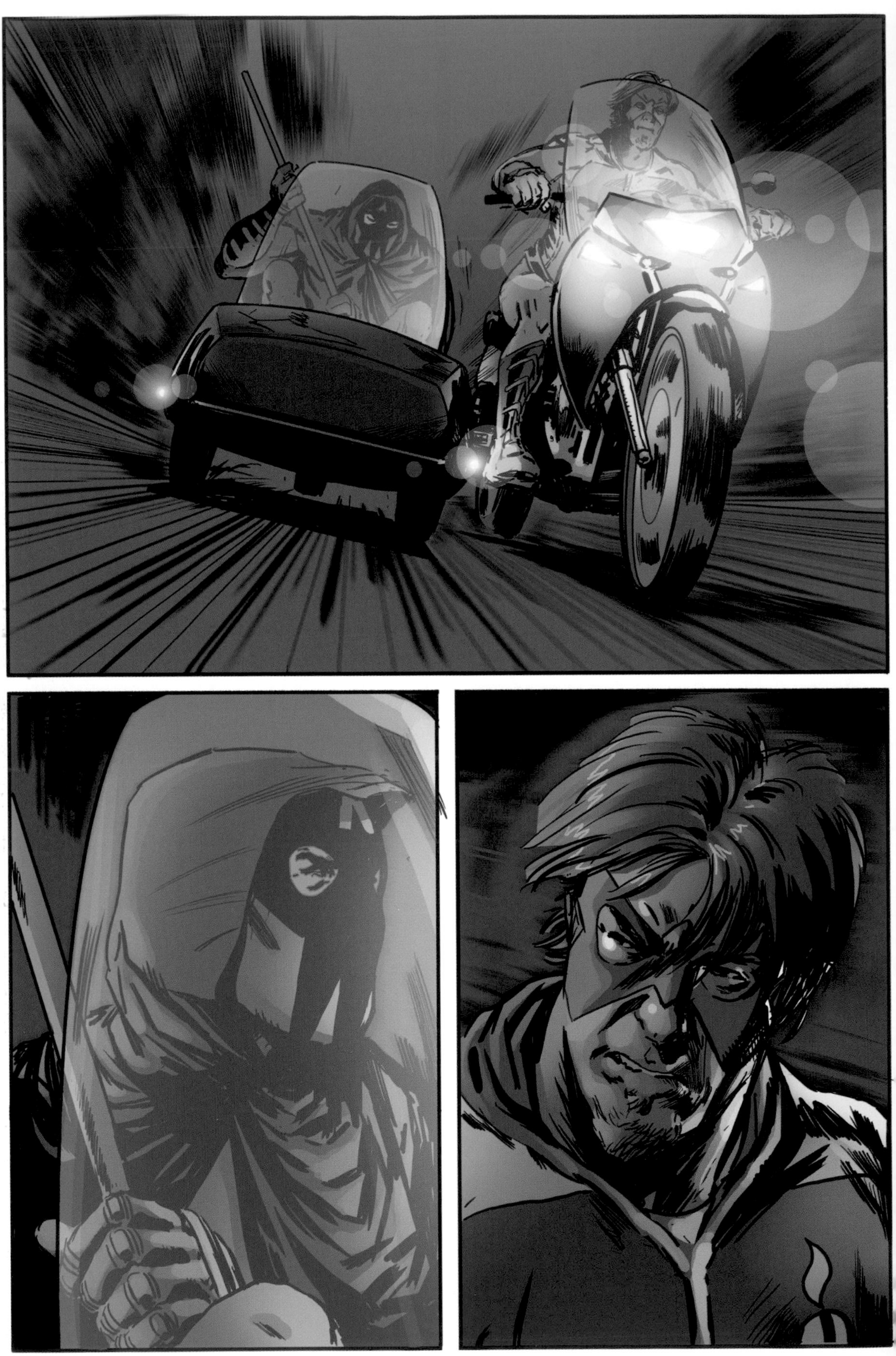

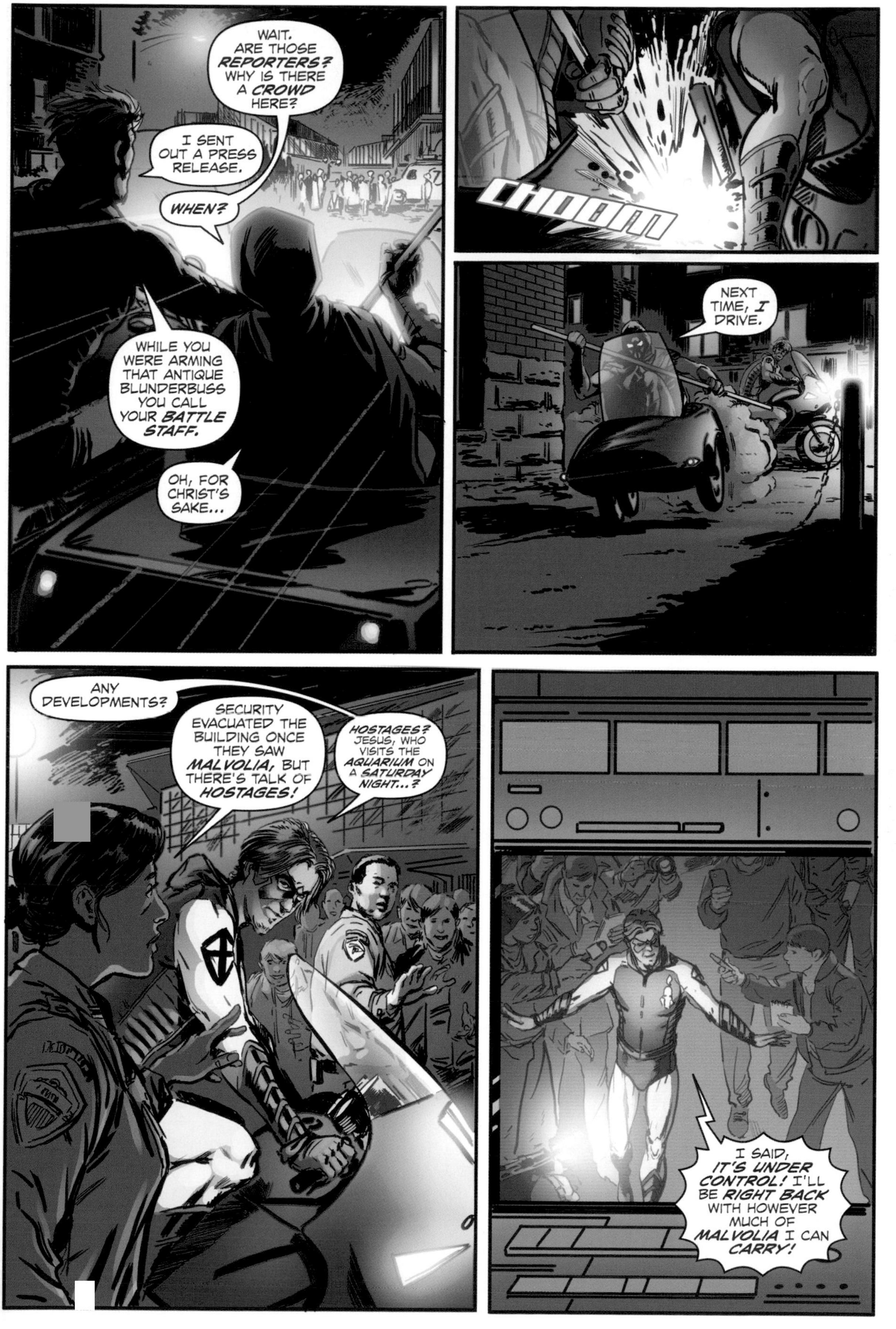
WAIT. ARE THOSE REPORTERS? WHY IS THERE A CROWD HERE?
I SENT OUT A PRESS RELEASE.
WHEN?
WHILE YOU WERE ARMING THAT ANTIQUE BLUNDERBUSS YOU CALL YOUR BATTLE STAFF.
OH, FOR CHRIST'S SAKE...
CHOOM
NEXT TIME, I DRIVE.
ANY DEVELOPMENTS?
SECURITY EVACUATED THE BUILDING ONCE THEY SAW MALVOLIA, BUT THERE'S TALK OF HOSTAGES!
HOSTAGES? JESUS, WHO VISITS THE AQUARIUM ON A SATURDAY NIGHT...?
I SAID, IT'S UNDER CONTROL! I'LL BE RIGHT BACK WITH HOWEVER MUCH OF MALVOLIA I CAN CARRY!

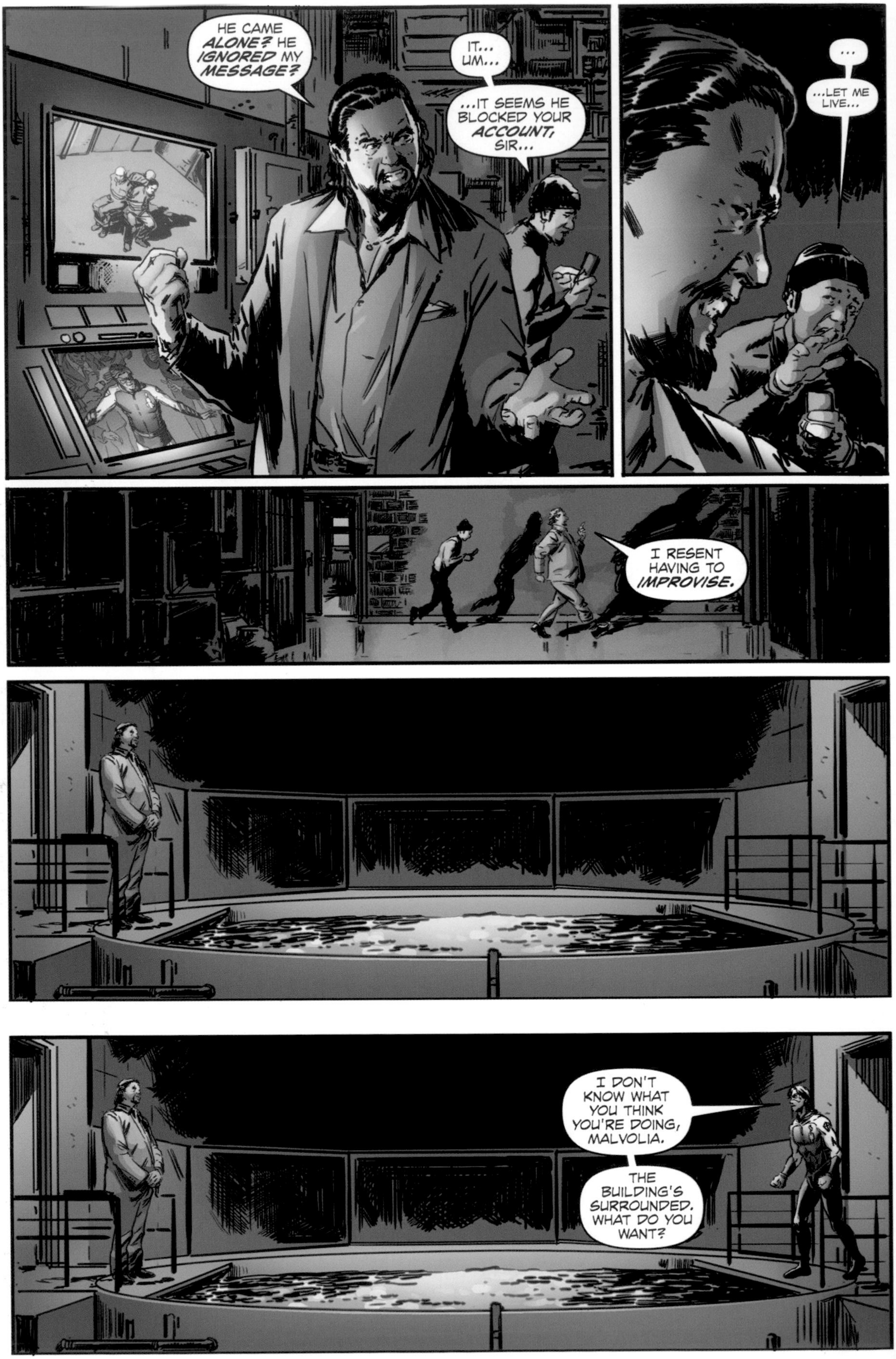
HE CAME *ALONE?* HE *IGNORED* MY *MESSAGE?*
IT... UM...
...IT SEEMS HE BLOCKED YOUR *ACCOUNT*, SIR...
...
...LET ME LIVE...
I RESENT HAVING TO *IMPROVISE.*
I DON'T KNOW WHAT YOU THINK YOU'RE DOING, MALVOLIA.
THE BUILDING'S SURROUNDED. WHAT DO YOU WANT?

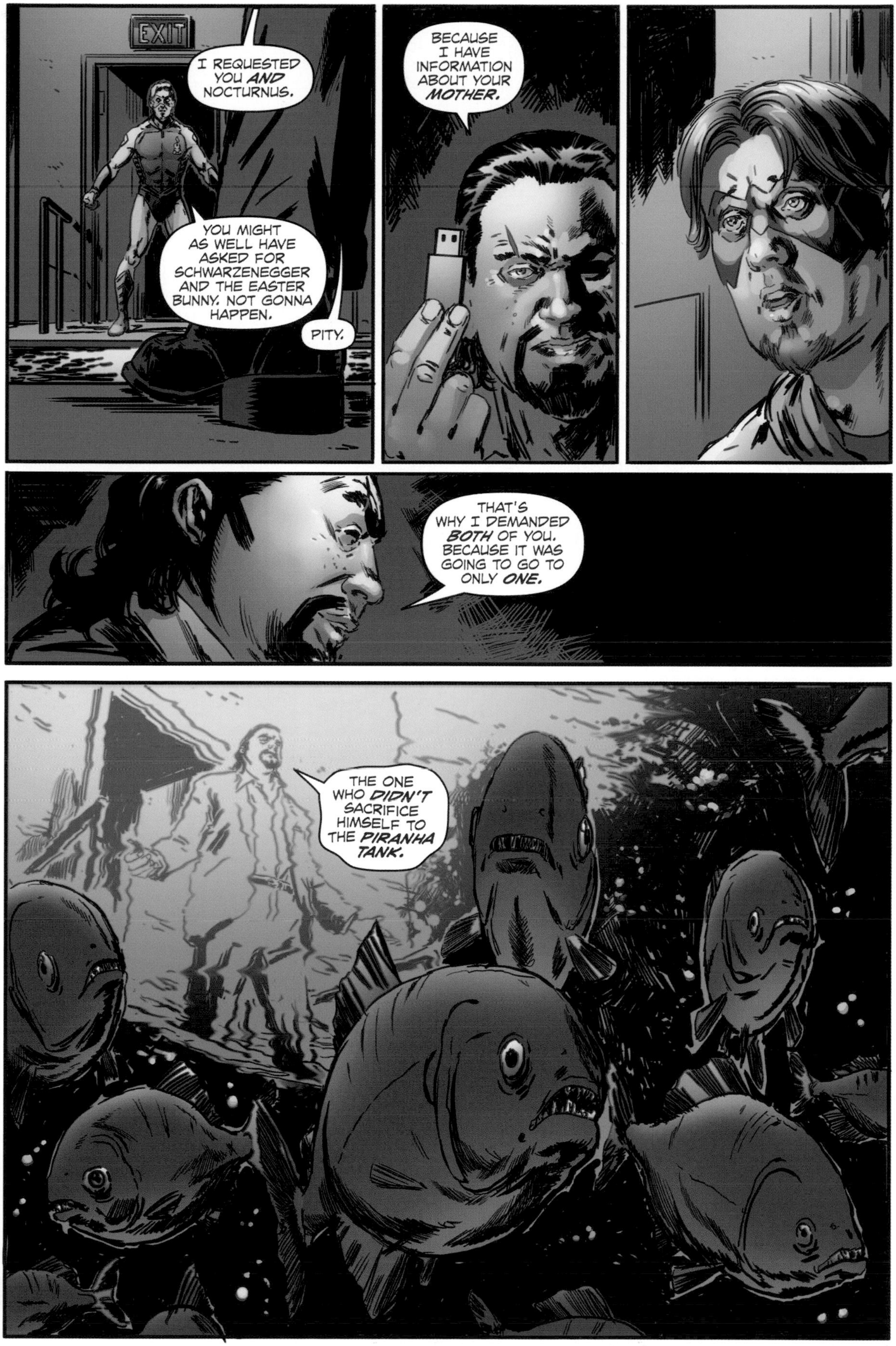
I REQUESTED YOU AND NOCTURNUS.
YOU MIGHT AS WELL HAVE ASKED FOR SCHWARZENEGGER AND THE EASTER BUNNY. NOT GONNA HAPPEN.
PITY.
EXIT
BECAUSE I HAVE INFORMATION ABOUT YOUR MOTHER.
THAT'S WHY I DEMANDED BOTH OF YOU. BECAUSE IT WAS GOING TO GO TO ONLY ONE.
THE ONE WHO DIDN'T SACRIFICE HIMSELF TO THE PIRANHA TANK.

YOU'RE INSANE. YOU EXPECTED ONE OF *US* TO JUST *JUMP IN?*

NOW...

...WHAT'S THAT ABOUT MY *WIFE...?*

54

ARTWORK BY
BRENT SCHOONOVER

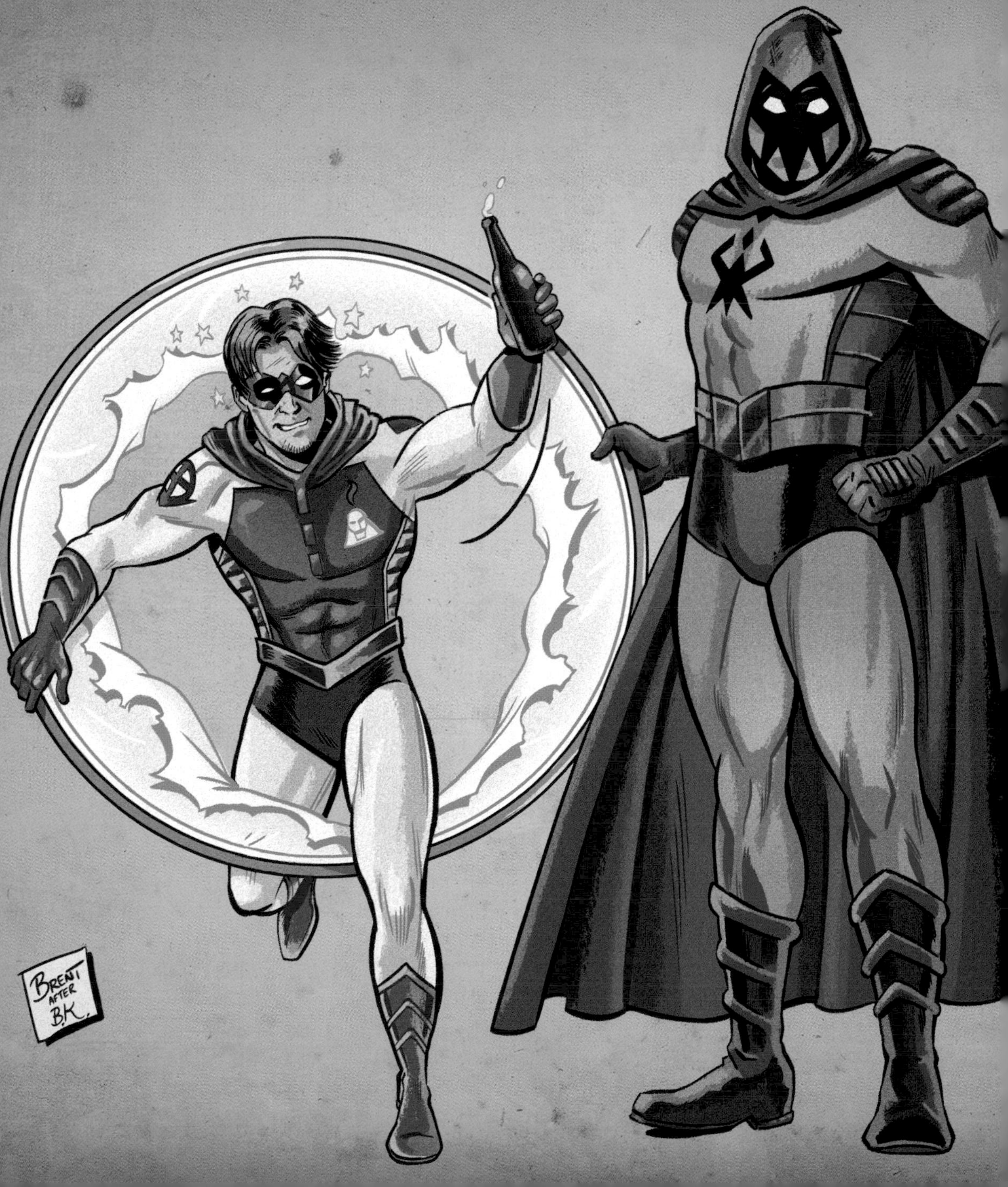
BRENT AFTER B.K.

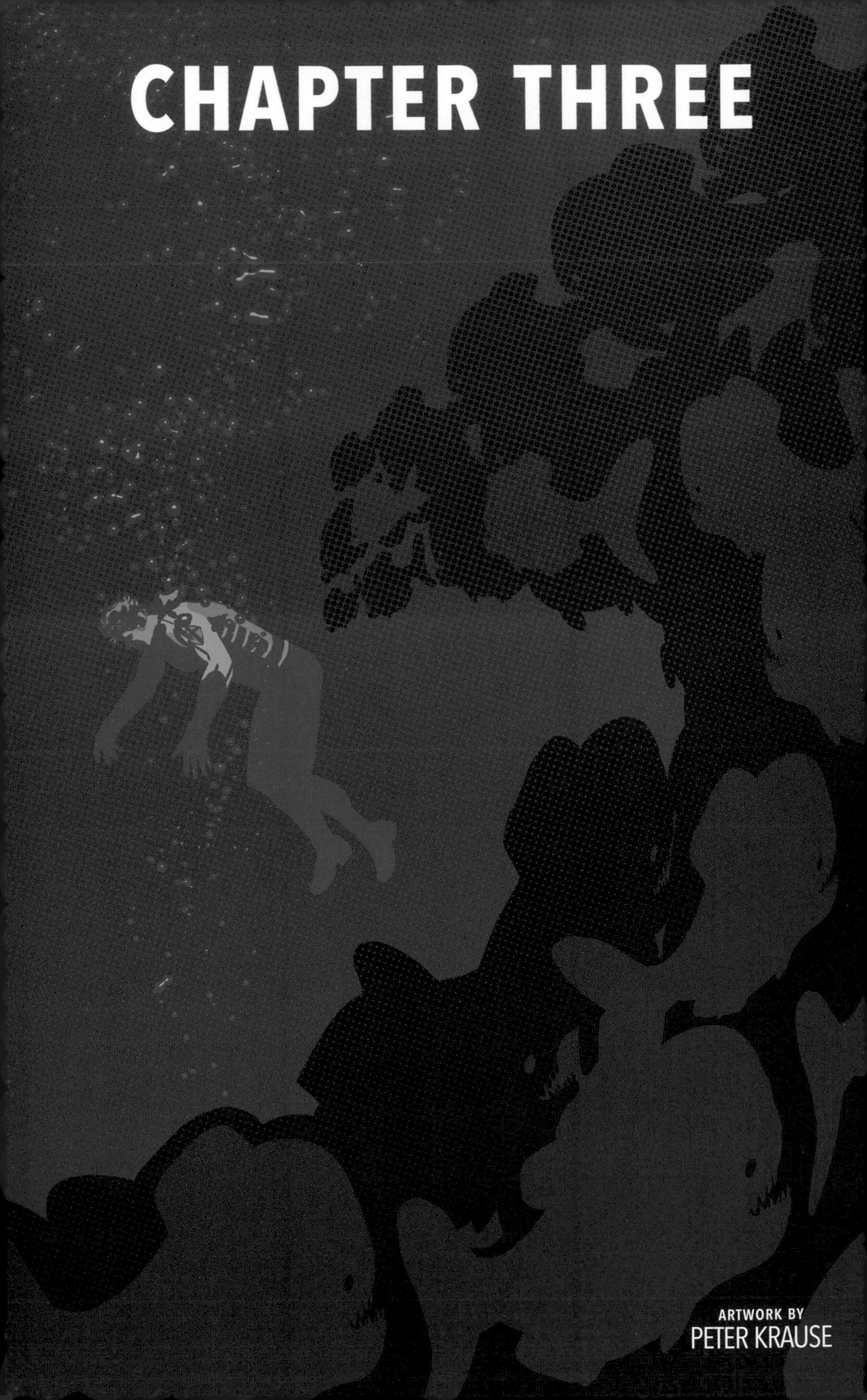
CHAPTER THREE
ARTWORK BY
PETER KRAUSE

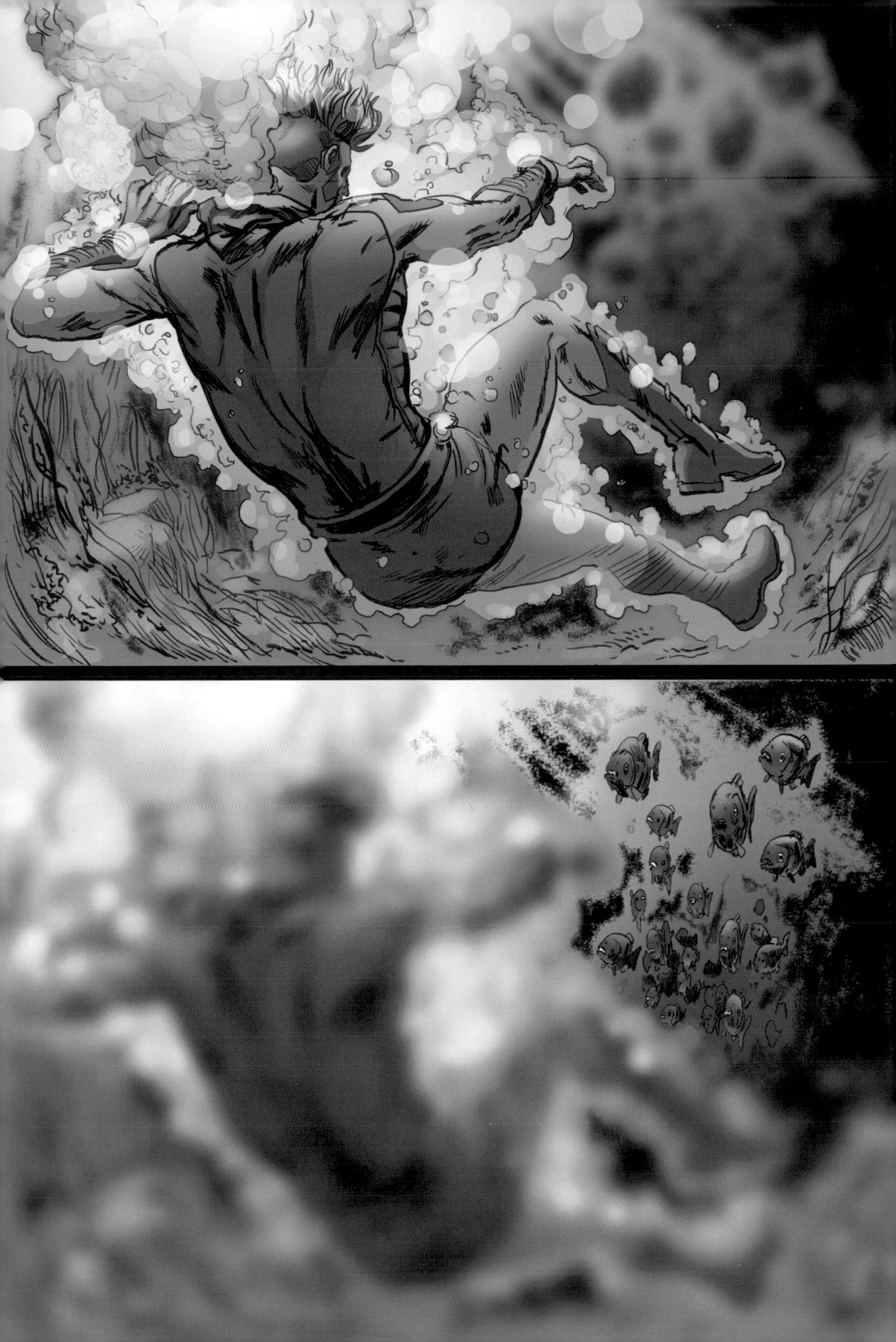

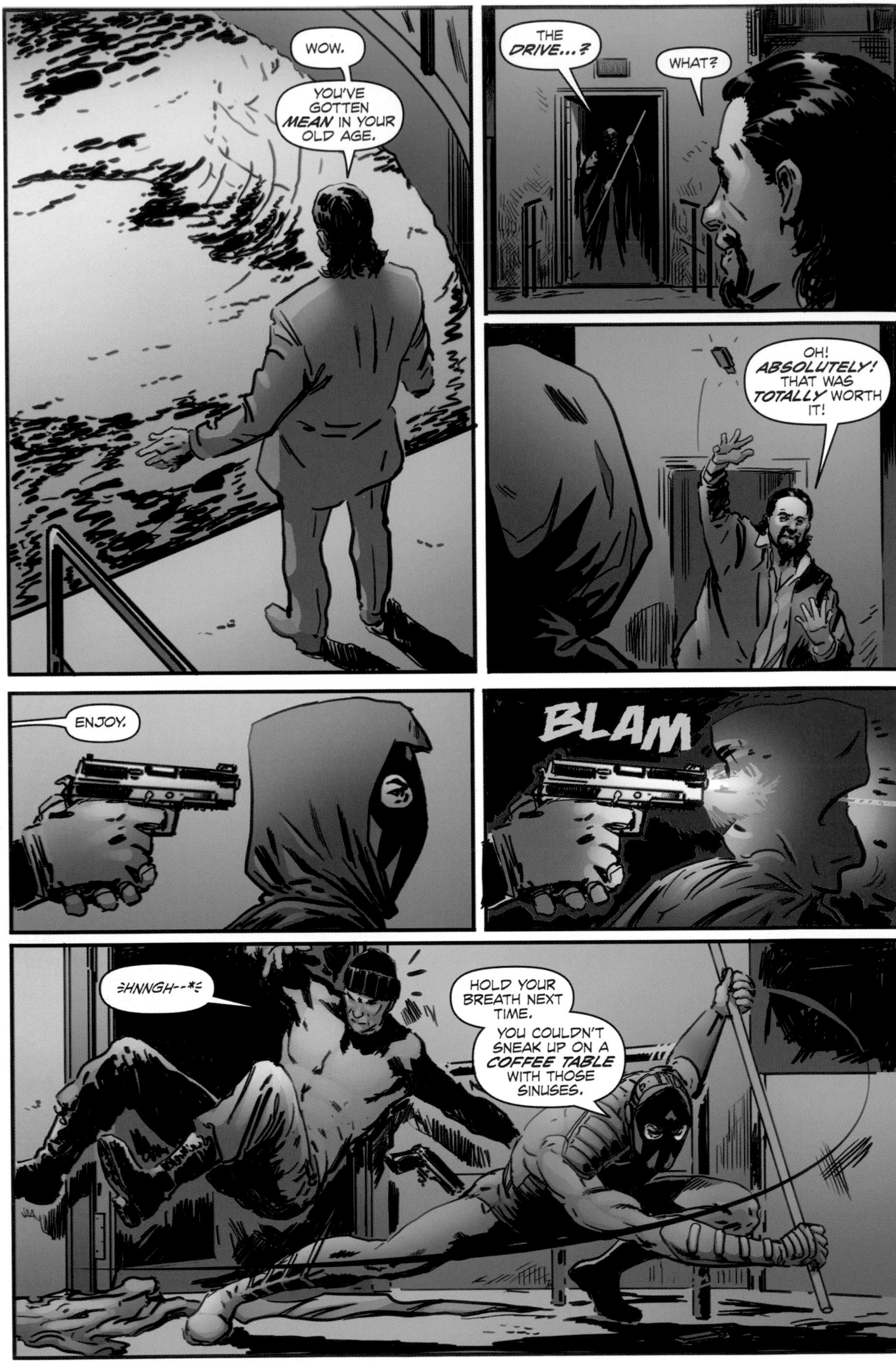
WOW.
YOU'VE GOTTEN MEAN IN YOUR OLD AGE.
THE DRIVE...?
WHAT?
OH! ABSOLUTELY! THAT WAS TOTALLY WORTH IT!
ENJOY.
BLAM
HNNGH--
HOLD YOUR BREATH NEXT TIME.
YOU COULDN'T SNEAK UP ON A COFFEE TABLE WITH THOSE SINUSES.

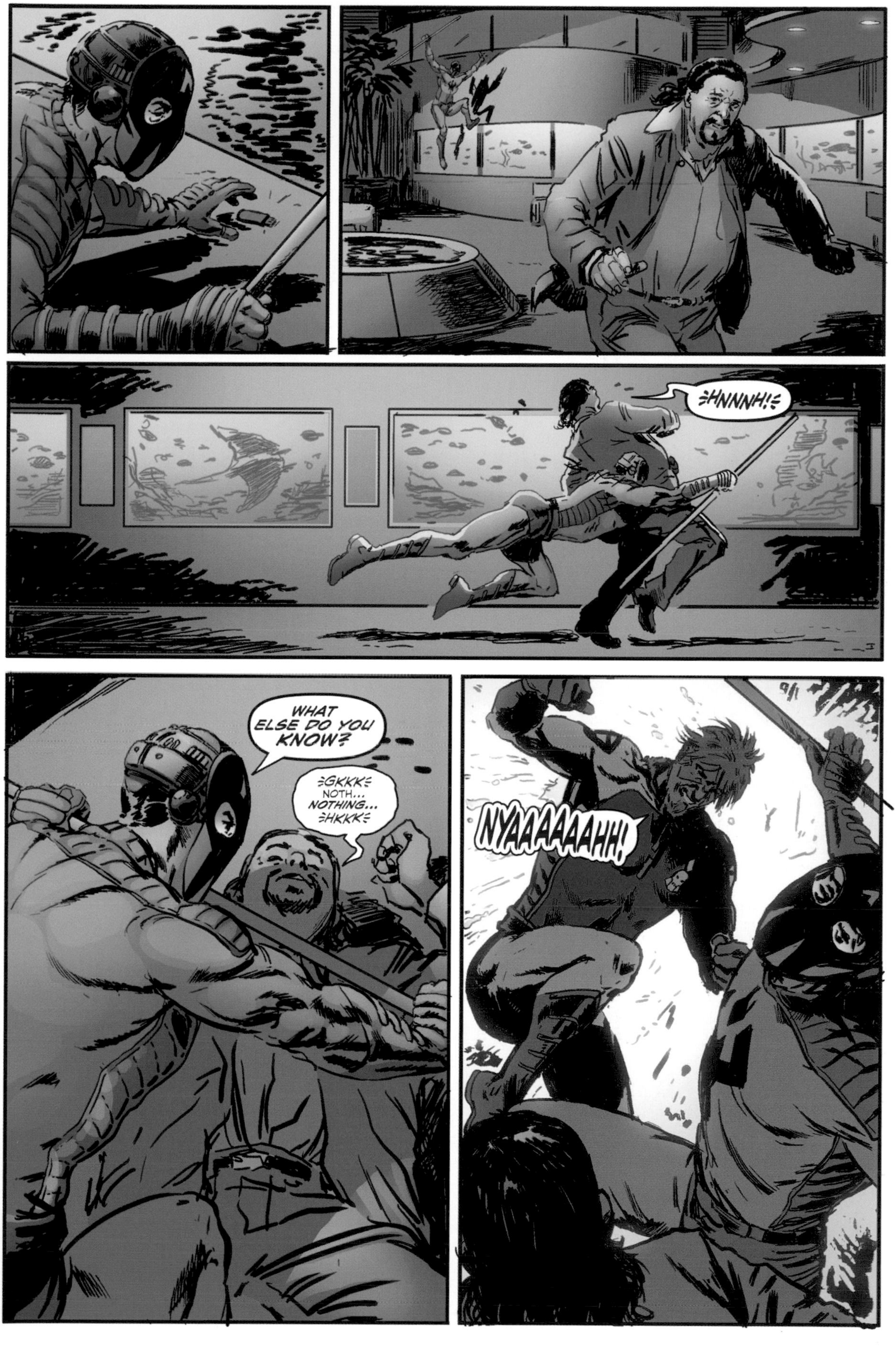

HNNNH!
WHAT ELSE DO YOU KNOW?
GKKK NOTH... NOTHING... HKKK
NYAAAAAAHH!

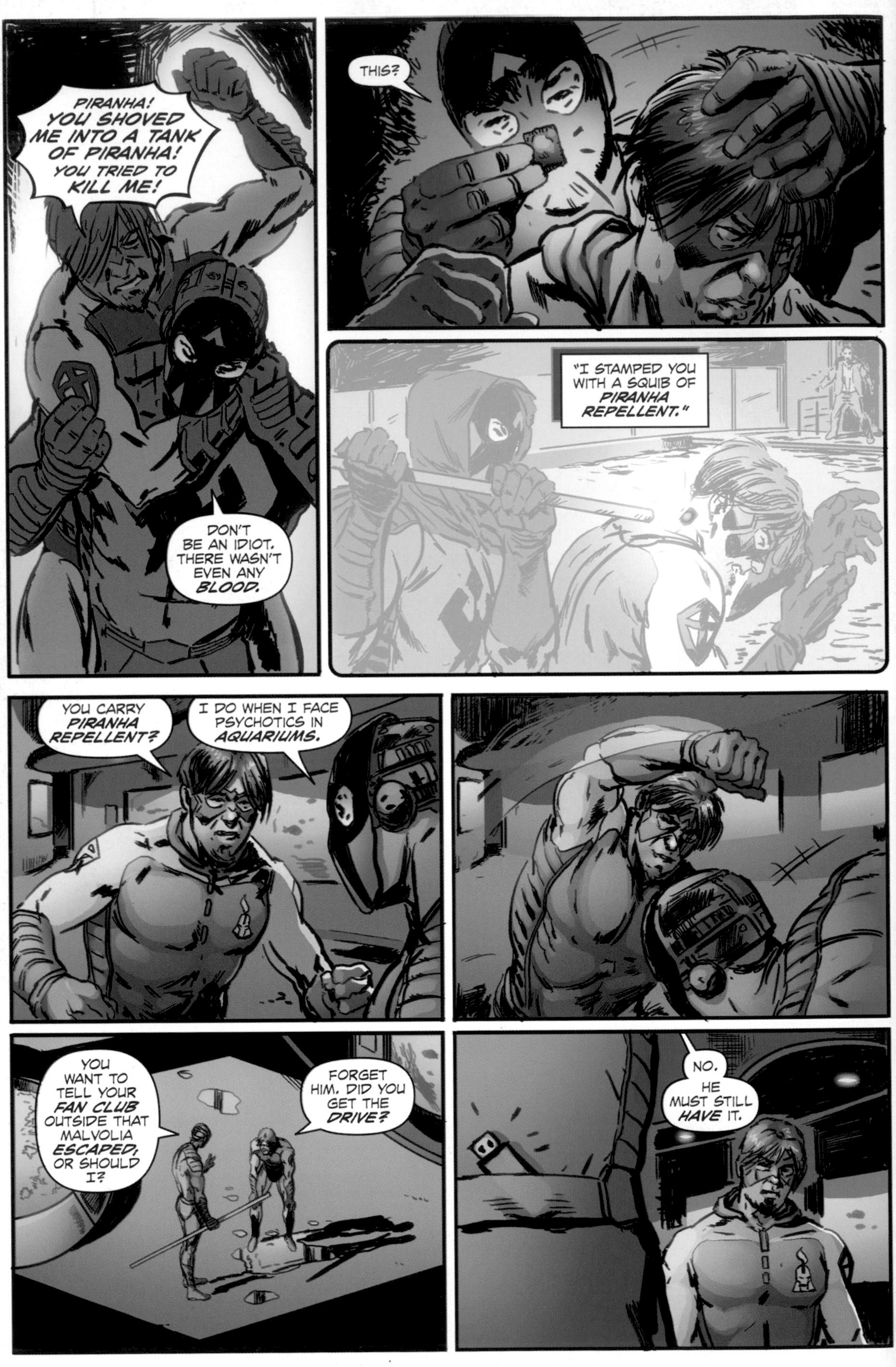
PIRANHA! YOU SHOVED ME INTO A TANK OF PIRANHA! YOU TRIED TO KILL ME!
DON'T BE AN IDIOT. THERE WASN'T EVEN ANY BLOOD.
THIS?
"I STAMPED YOU WITH A SQUIB OF PIRANHA REPELLENT."
YOU CARRY PIRANHA REPELLENT?
I DO WHEN I FACE PSYCHOTICS IN AQUARIUMS.
YOU WANT TO TELL YOUR FAN CLUB OUTSIDE THAT MALVOLIA ESCAPED, OR SHOULD I?
FORGET HIM. DID YOU GET THE DRIVE?
NO.
HE MUST STILL HAVE IT.

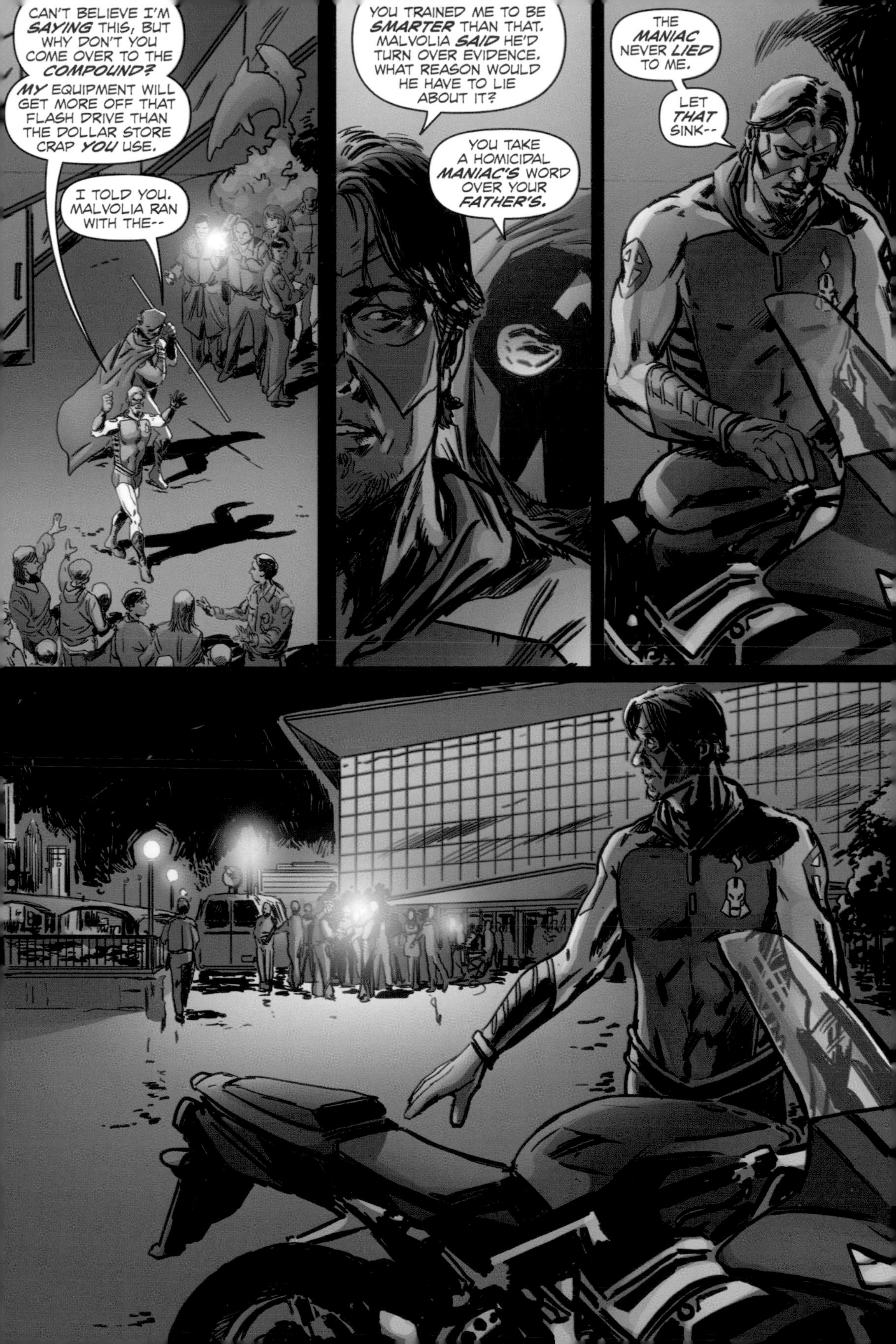
CAN'T BELIEVE I'M SAYING THIS, BUT WHY DON'T YOU COME OVER TO THE COMPOUND? MY EQUIPMENT WILL GET MORE OFF THAT FLASH DRIVE THAN THE DOLLAR STORE CRAP YOU USE.
I TOLD YOU. MALVOLIA RAN WITH THE--
YOU TRAINED ME TO BE SMARTER THAN THAT. MALVOLIA SAID HE'D TURN OVER EVIDENCE. WHAT REASON WOULD HE HAVE TO LIE ABOUT IT?
YOU TAKE A HOMICIDAL MANIAC'S WORD OVER YOUR FATHER'S.
THE MANIAC NEVER LIED TO ME.
LET THAT SINK--

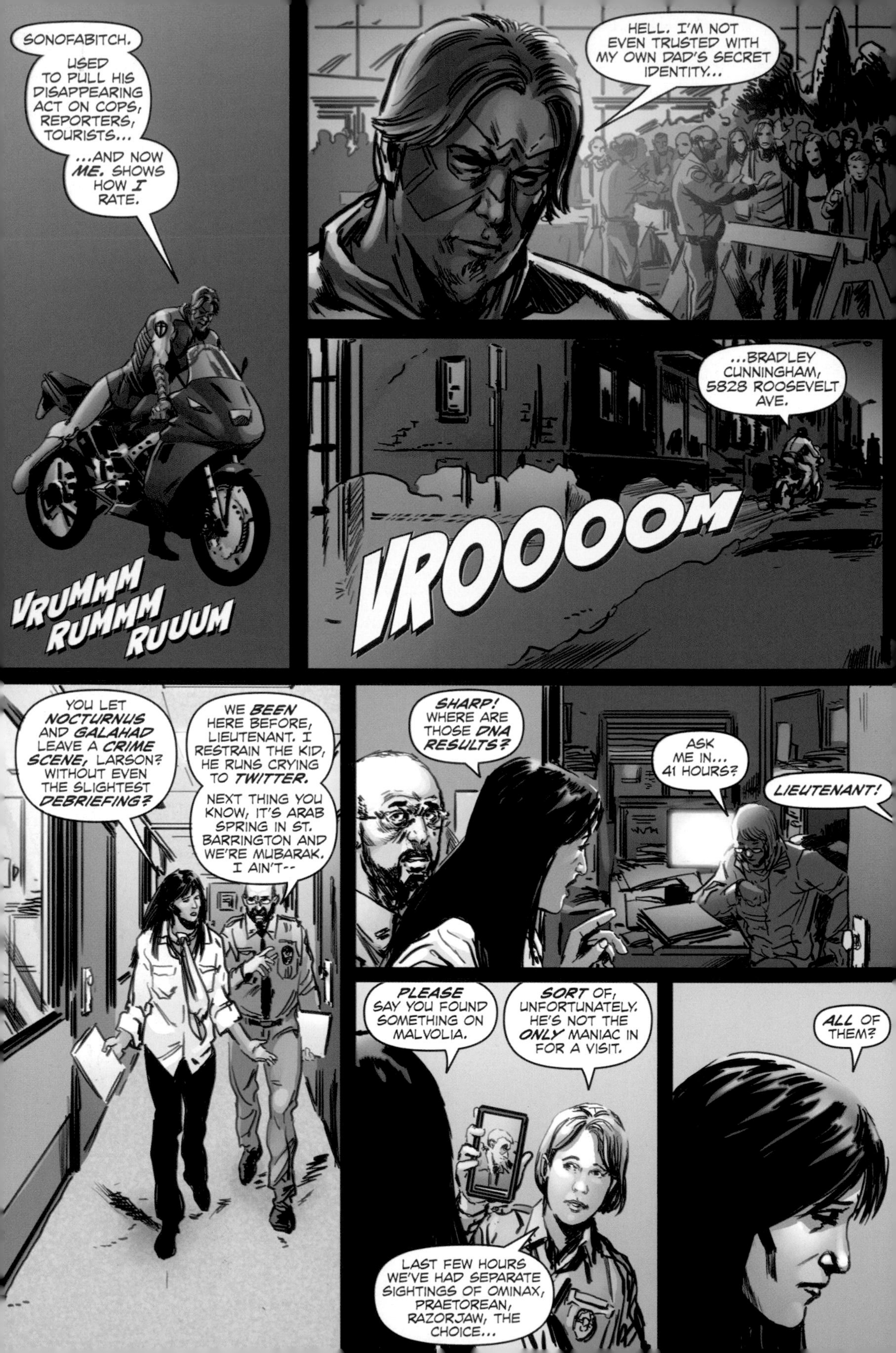
SONOFABITCH.
USED TO PULL HIS DISAPPEARING ACT ON COPS, REPORTERS, TOURISTS...
...AND NOW ME. SHOWS HOW I RATE.
VRUMMM RUMMM RUUUM
HELL. I'M NOT EVEN TRUSTED WITH MY OWN DAD'S SECRET IDENTITY...
...BRADLEY CUNNINGHAM, 5828 ROOSEVELT AVE.
VROOOOOM
YOU LET NOCTURNUS AND GALAHAD LEAVE A CRIME SCENE, LARSON? WITHOUT EVEN THE SLIGHTEST DEBRIEFING?
WE BEEN HERE BEFORE, LIEUTENANT. I RESTRAIN THE KID, HE RUNS CRYING TO TWITTER.
NEXT THING YOU KNOW, IT'S ARAB SPRING IN ST. BARRINGTON AND WE'RE MUBARAK. I AIN'T--
SHARP! WHERE ARE THOSE DNA RESULTS?
ASK ME IN... 41 HOURS?
LIEUTENANT!
PLEASE SAY YOU FOUND SOMETHING ON MALVOLIA.
SORT OF, UNFORTUNATELY. HE'S NOT THE ONLY MANIAC IN FOR A VISIT.
LAST FEW HOURS WE'VE HAD SEPARATE SIGHTINGS OF OMINAX, PRAETOREAN, RAZORJAW, THE CHOICE...
ALL OF THEM?

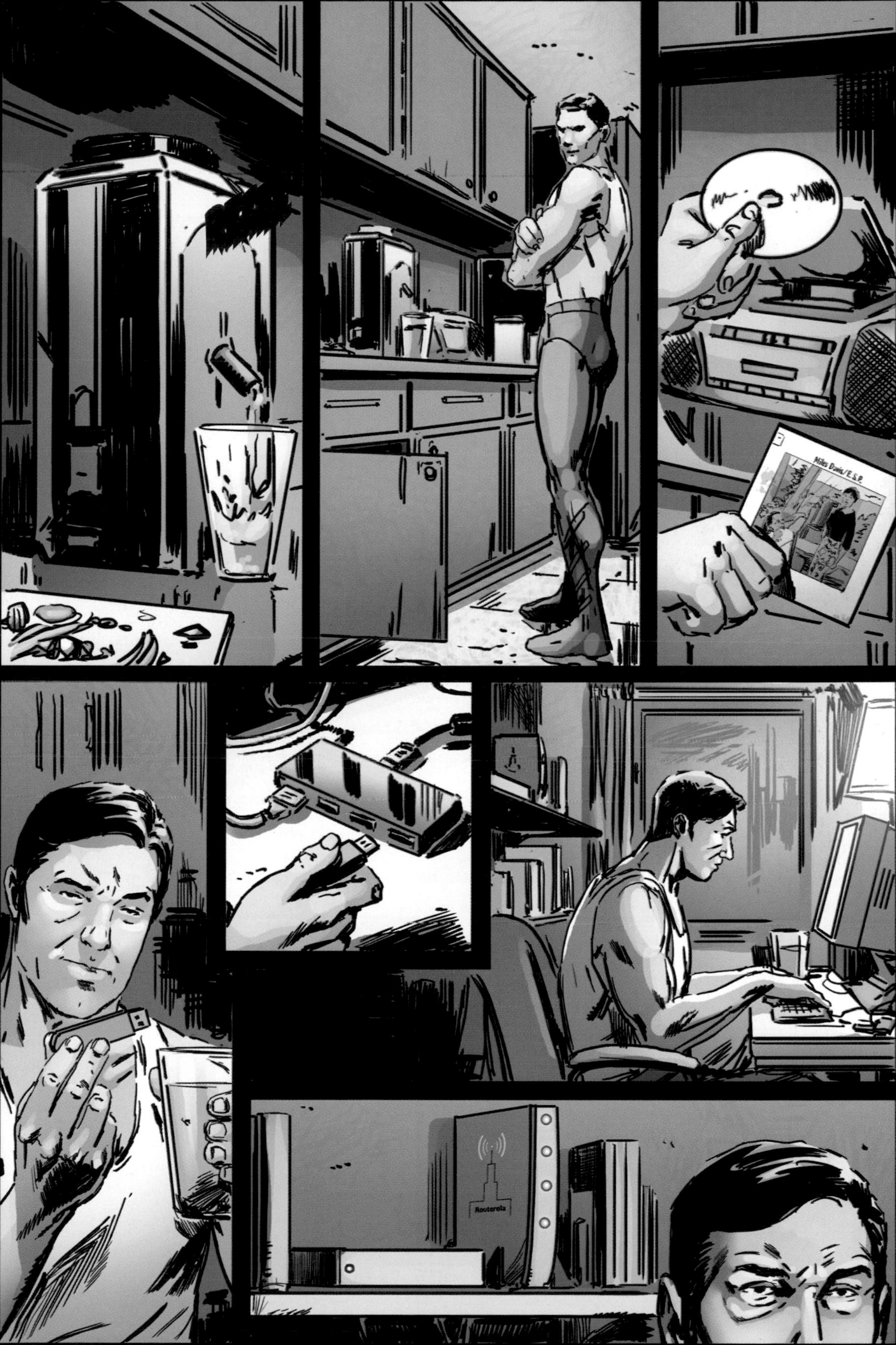
Miles Davis/E.S.P.
Routerola

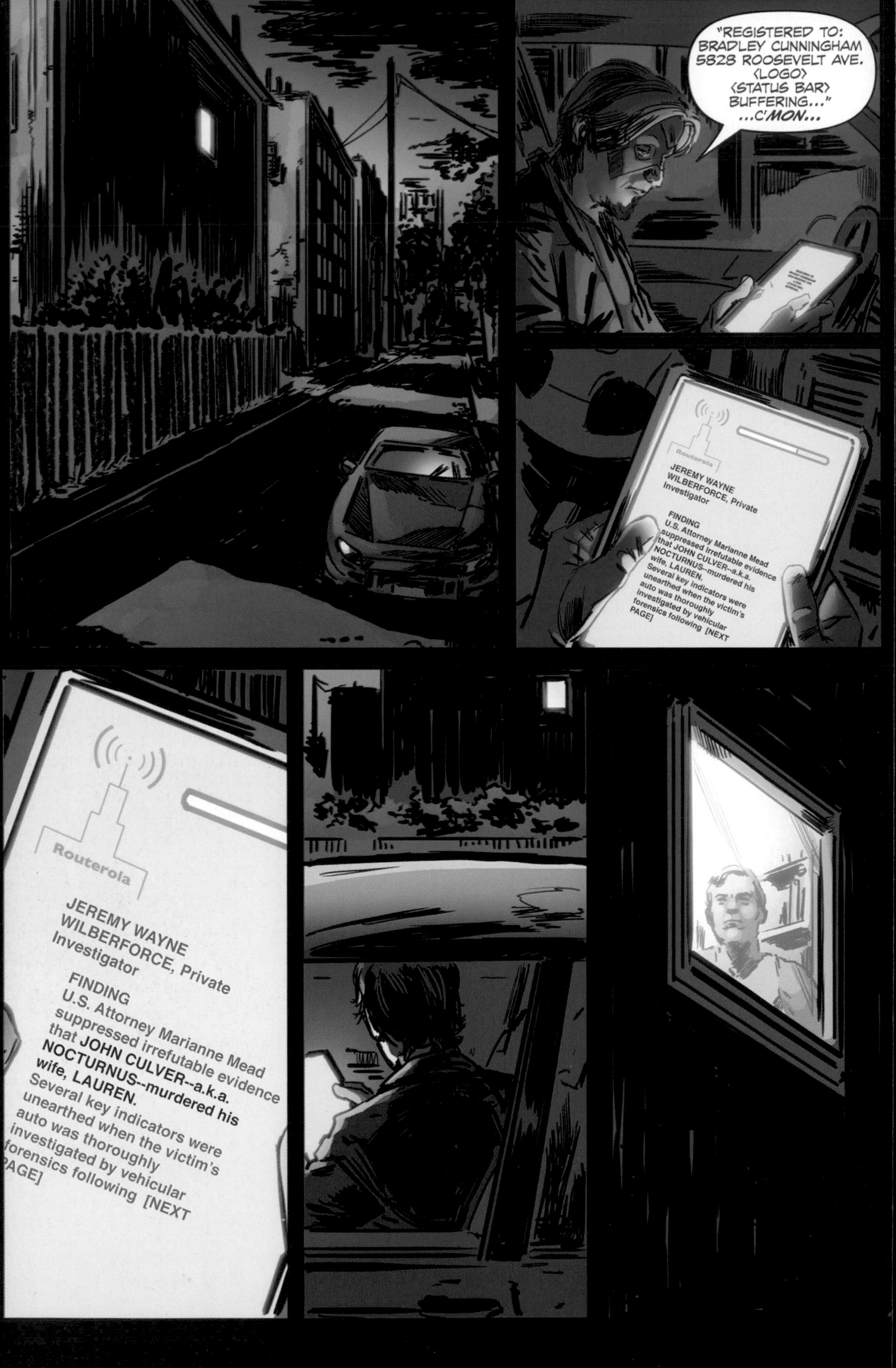
"REGISTERED TO: BRADLEY CUNNINGHAM 5828 ROOSEVELT AVE. <LOGO> <STATUS BAR> BUFFERING..." ...C'MON...
Routerola
JEREMY WAYNE WILBERFORCE, Private Investigator
FINDING
U.S. Attorney Marianne Mead suppressed irrefutable evidence that JOHN CULVER--a.k.a. NOCTURNUS--murdered his wife, LAUREN.
Several key indicators were unearthed when the victim's auto was thoroughly investigated by vehicular forensics following [NEXT PAGE]
Routerola
JEREMY WAYNE WILBERFORCE, Private Investigator
FINDING
U.S. Attorney Marianne Mead suppressed irrefutable evidence that JOHN CULVER--a.k.a. NOCTURNUS--murdered his wife, LAUREN.
Several key indicators were unearthed when the victim's auto was thoroughly investigated by vehicular forensics following [NEXT PAGE]

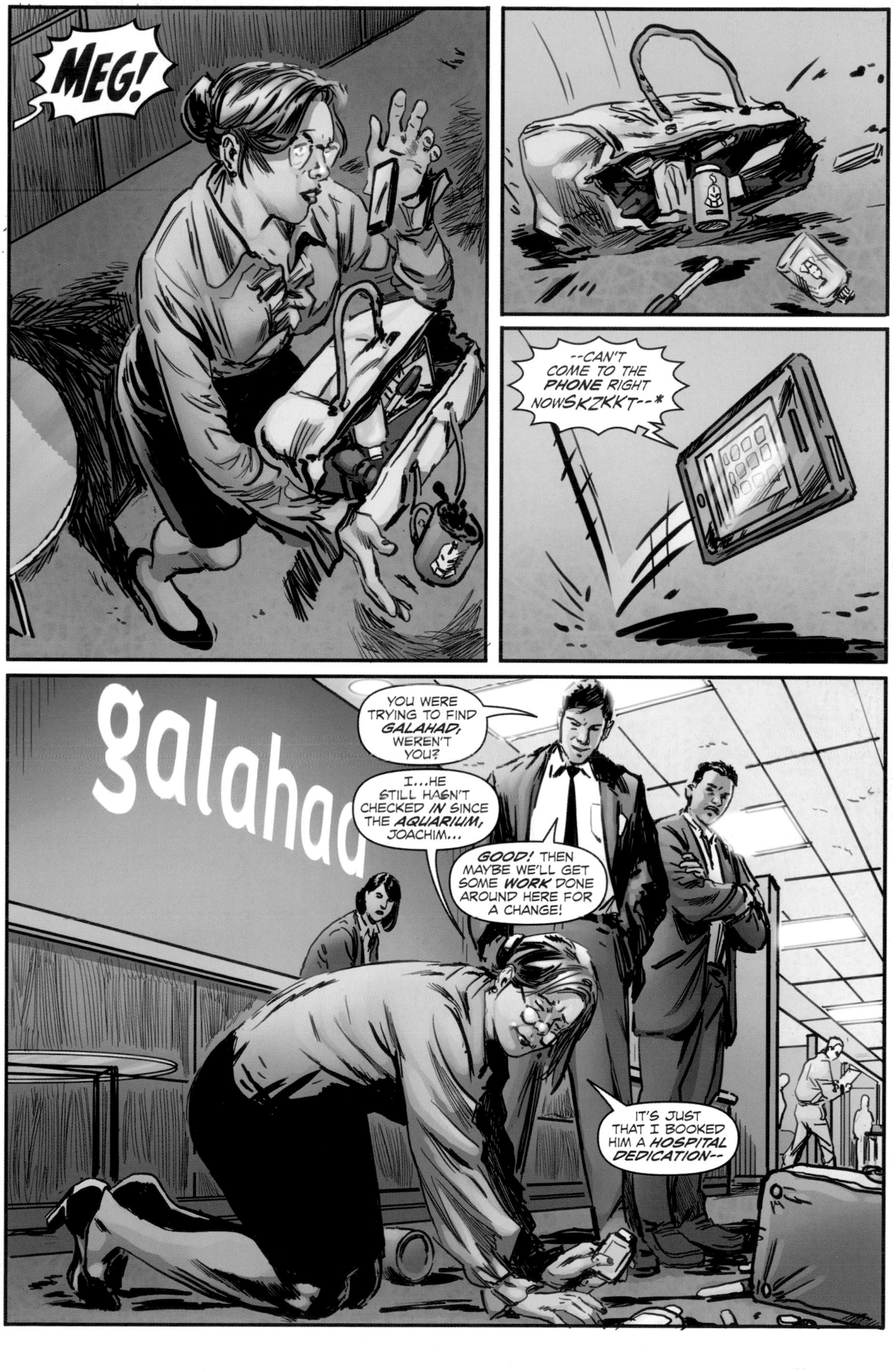
MEG!
--CAN'T COME TO THE PHONE RIGHT NOWSKZKKT--*
galahad
YOU WERE TRYING TO FIND GALAHAD, WEREN'T YOU?
I...HE STILL HASN'T CHECKED IN SINCE THE AQUARIUM, JOACHIM...
GOOD! THEN MAYBE WE'LL GET SOME WORK DONE AROUND HERE FOR A CHANGE!
IT'S JUST THAT I BOOKED HIM A HOSPITAL DEDICATION--

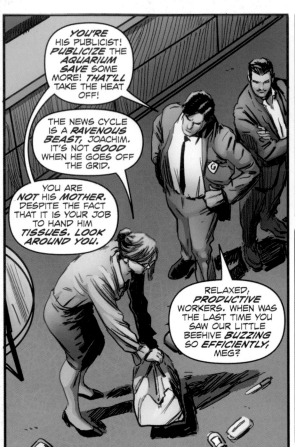

YOU'RE HIS PUBLICIST! *PUBLICIZE* THE *AQUARIUM SAVE* SOME MORE! *THAT'LL* TAKE THE HEAT OFF!

THE NEWS CYCLE IS A *RAVENOUS BEAST*, JOACHIM. IT'S NOT *GOOD* WHEN HE GOES OFF THE GRID.

YOU ARE *NOT* HIS *MOTHER.* DESPITE THE FACT THAT IT IS YOUR JOB TO HAND HIM *TISSUES. LOOK AROUND YOU.*

RELAXED, *PRODUCTIVE* WORKERS. WHEN WAS THE LAST TIME YOU SAW OUR LITTLE BEEHIVE *BUZZING* SO *EFFICIENTLY,* MEG?

WHEN GALAHAD WAS CAPTURED BY THE *BAHSHRA* FOR A WEEK.

AND WHAT HAPPENED AN *HOUR* AFTER HE *ESCAPED?*

HE CAME IN DEMANDING A *VICTORY PARADE* AND HIS FACE ON A *STAMP.*

WE HAD TO BOOK A *JAPANESE CAR COMMERCIAL* TO AFFORD *HUSH BONUSES* FOR THE *STAFF.*

I DON'T KNOW HOW YOU MAKE THAT ARROGANT PRICK LOOK GOOD. I WOULD NOT WANT YOUR JOB.

BUT IF YOU WAKE THE BEAR, *ALL* OF US WILL WANT YOUR *HEAD. WHEREVER* HE IS, MEG...

"...I'M SURE HE'S JUST *FINE.*"

--ALERT--
--ALERT--

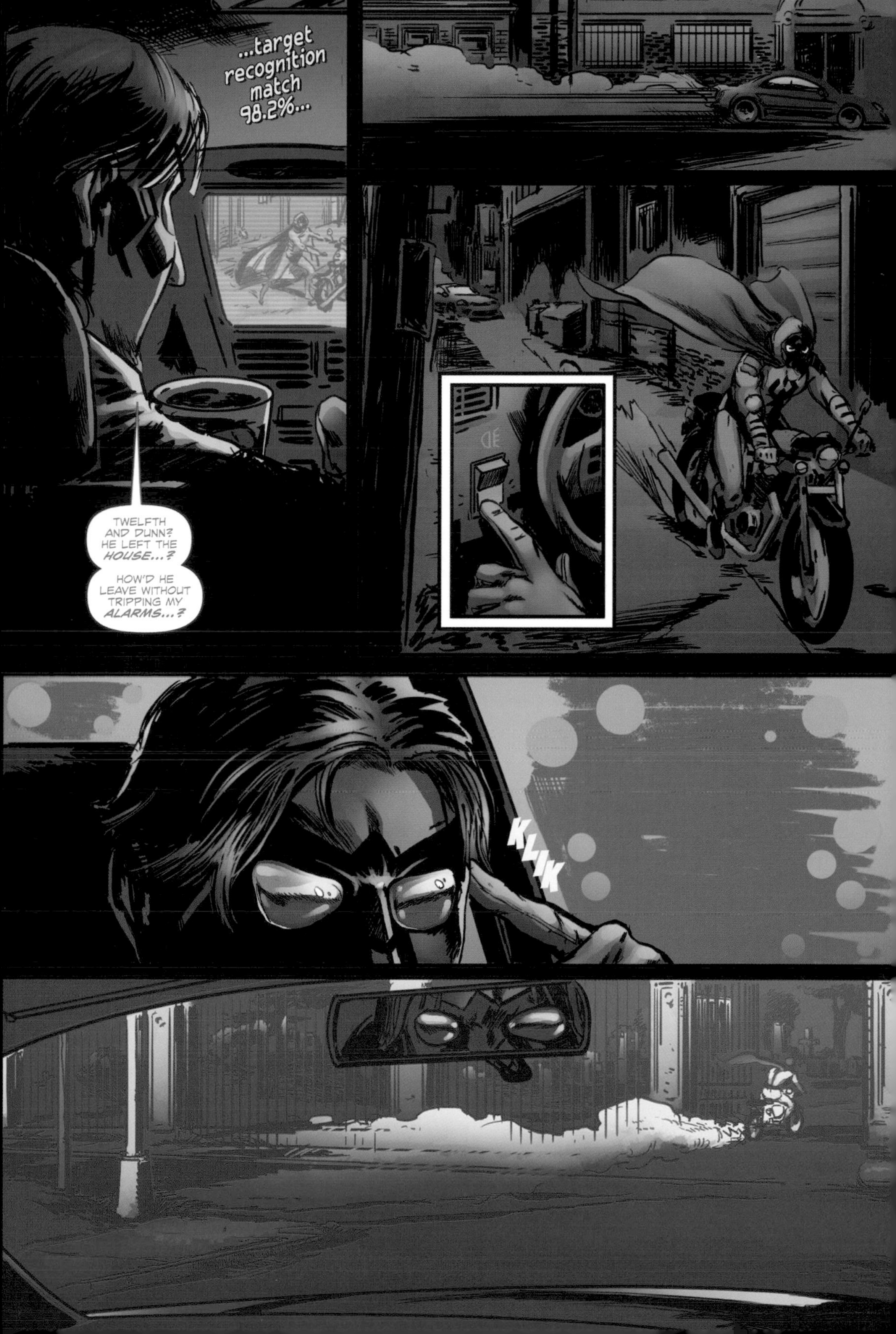
...target recognition match 98.2%...
TWELFTH AND DUNN? HE LEFT THE HOUSE...?
HOW'D HE LEAVE WITHOUT TRIPPING MY ALARMS...?
KLIK

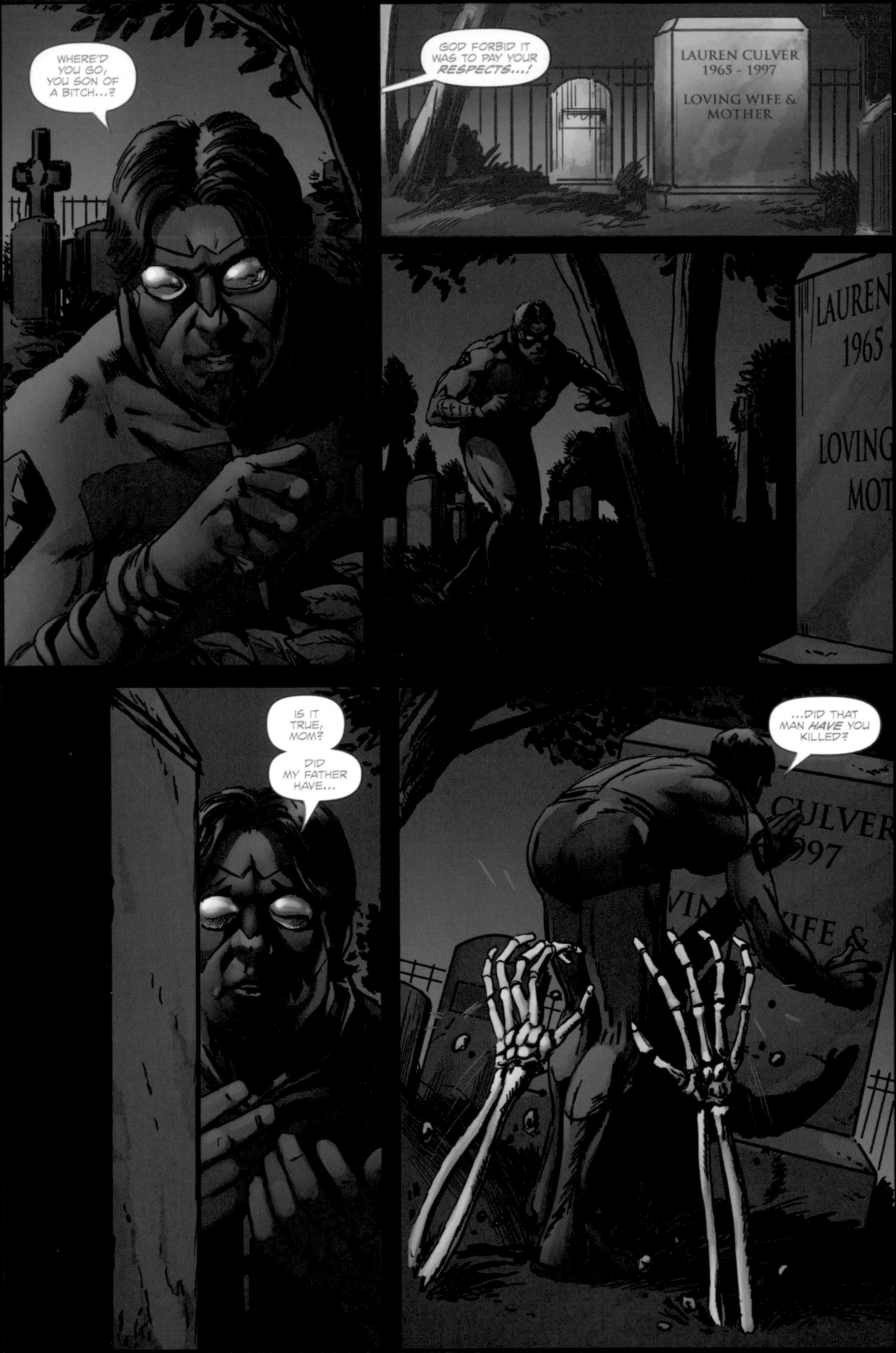
WHERE'D YOU GO, YOU SON OF A BITCH...?
GOD FORBID IT WAS TO PAY YOUR RESPECTS...!
LAUREN CULVER 1965 - 1997
LOVING WIFE & MOTHER
IS IT TRUE, MOM?
DID MY FATHER HAVE...
...DID THAT MAN HAVE YOU KILLED?

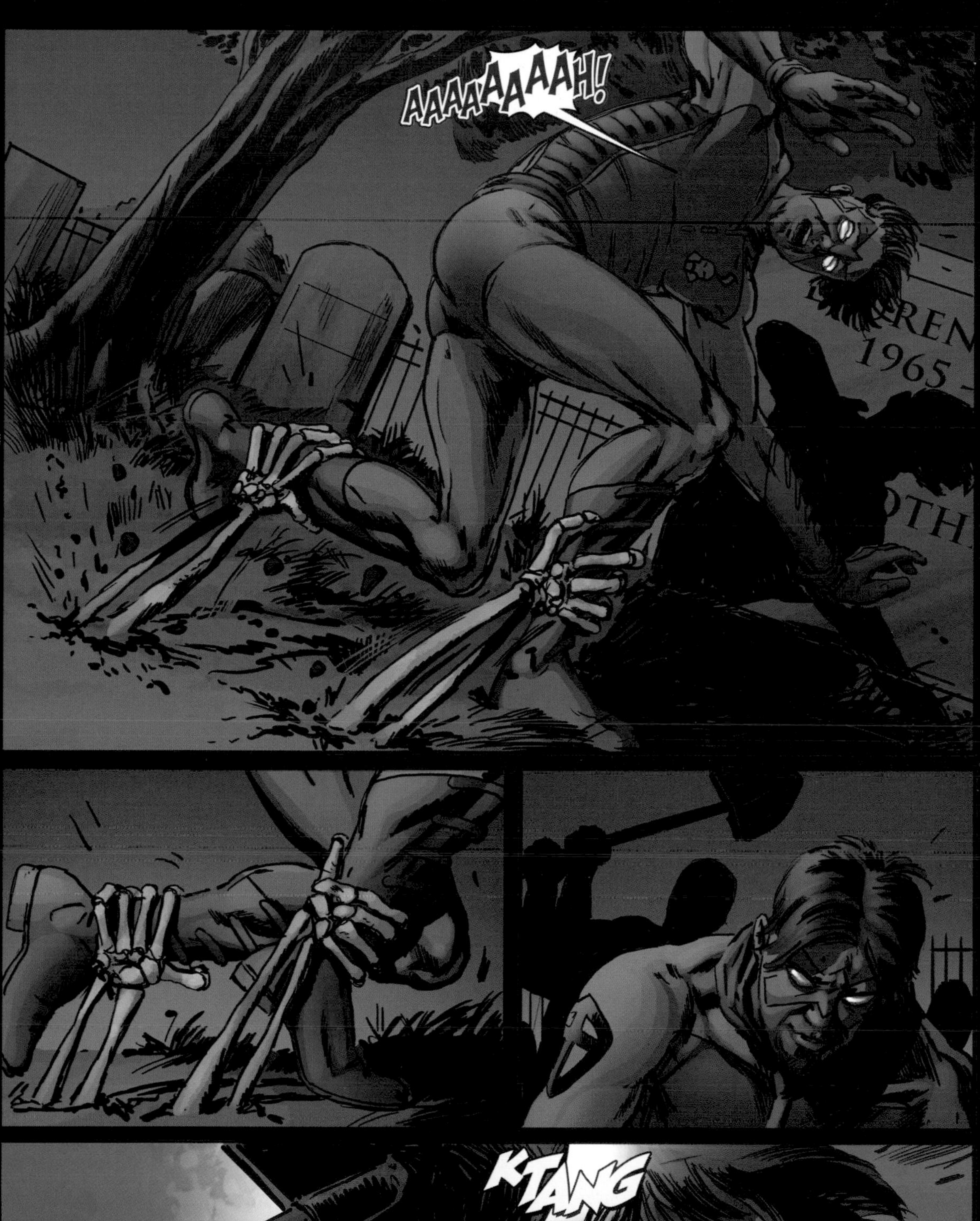
AAAAAAAAH!
1965 –
KTANG

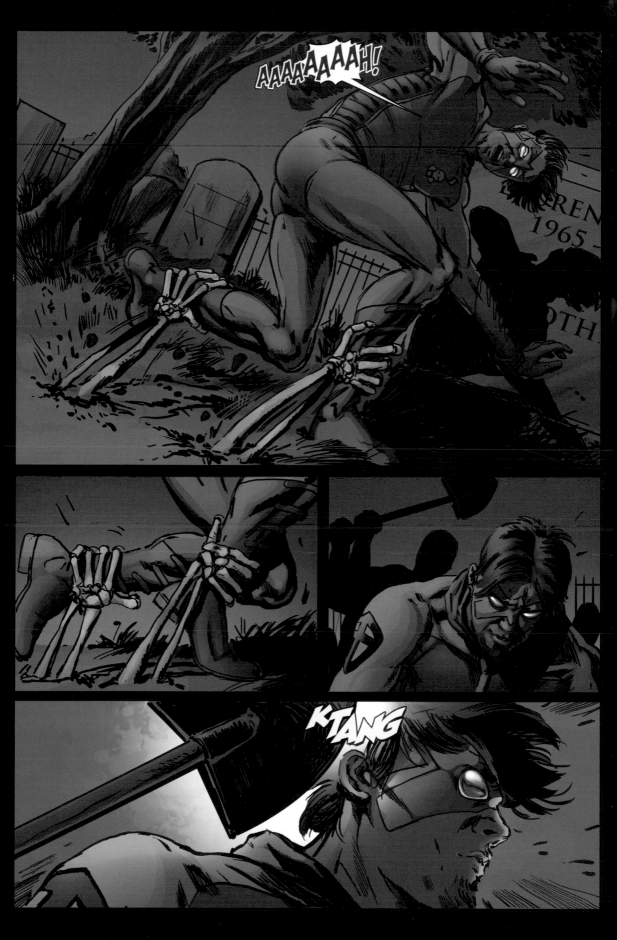

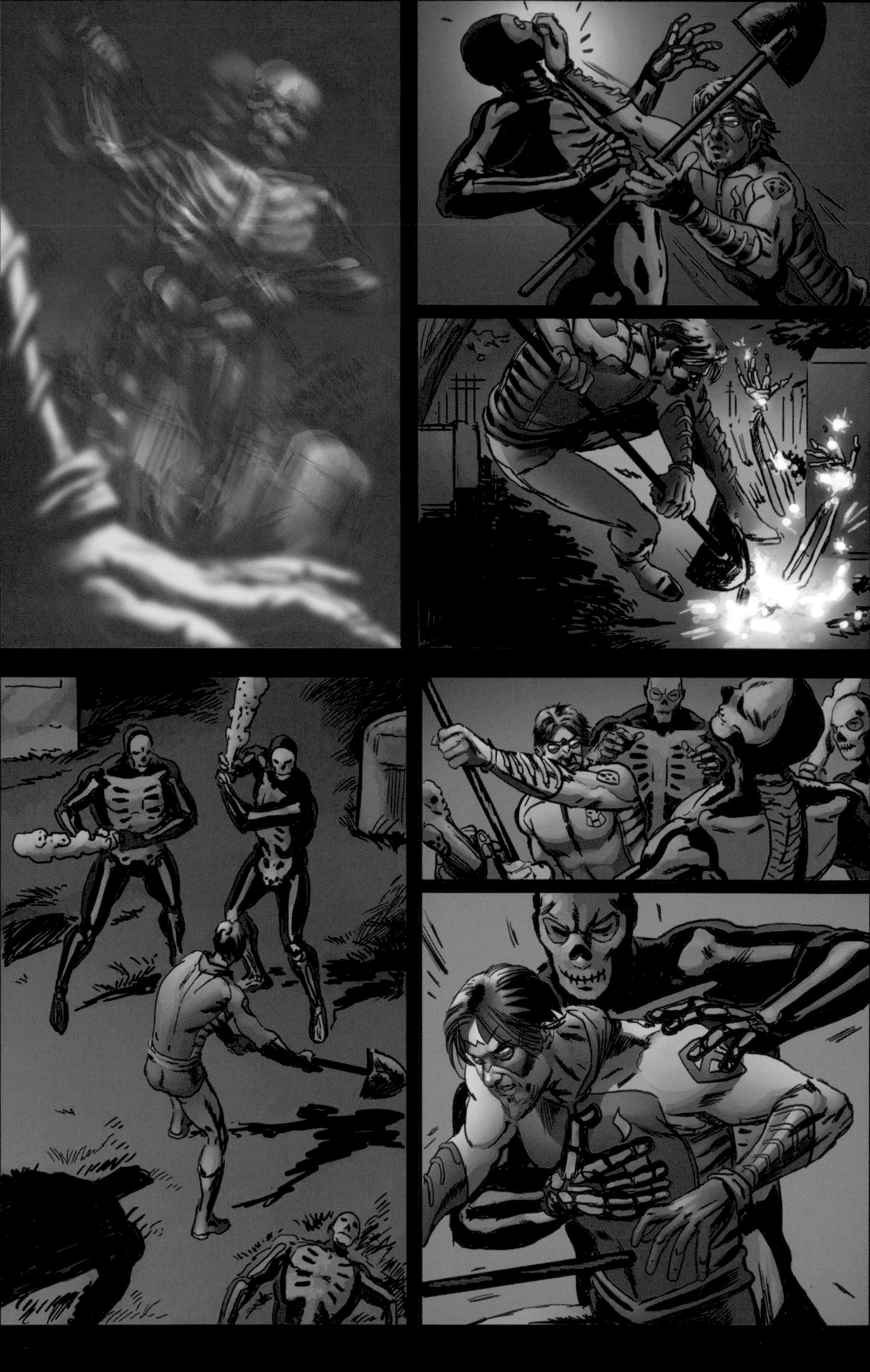

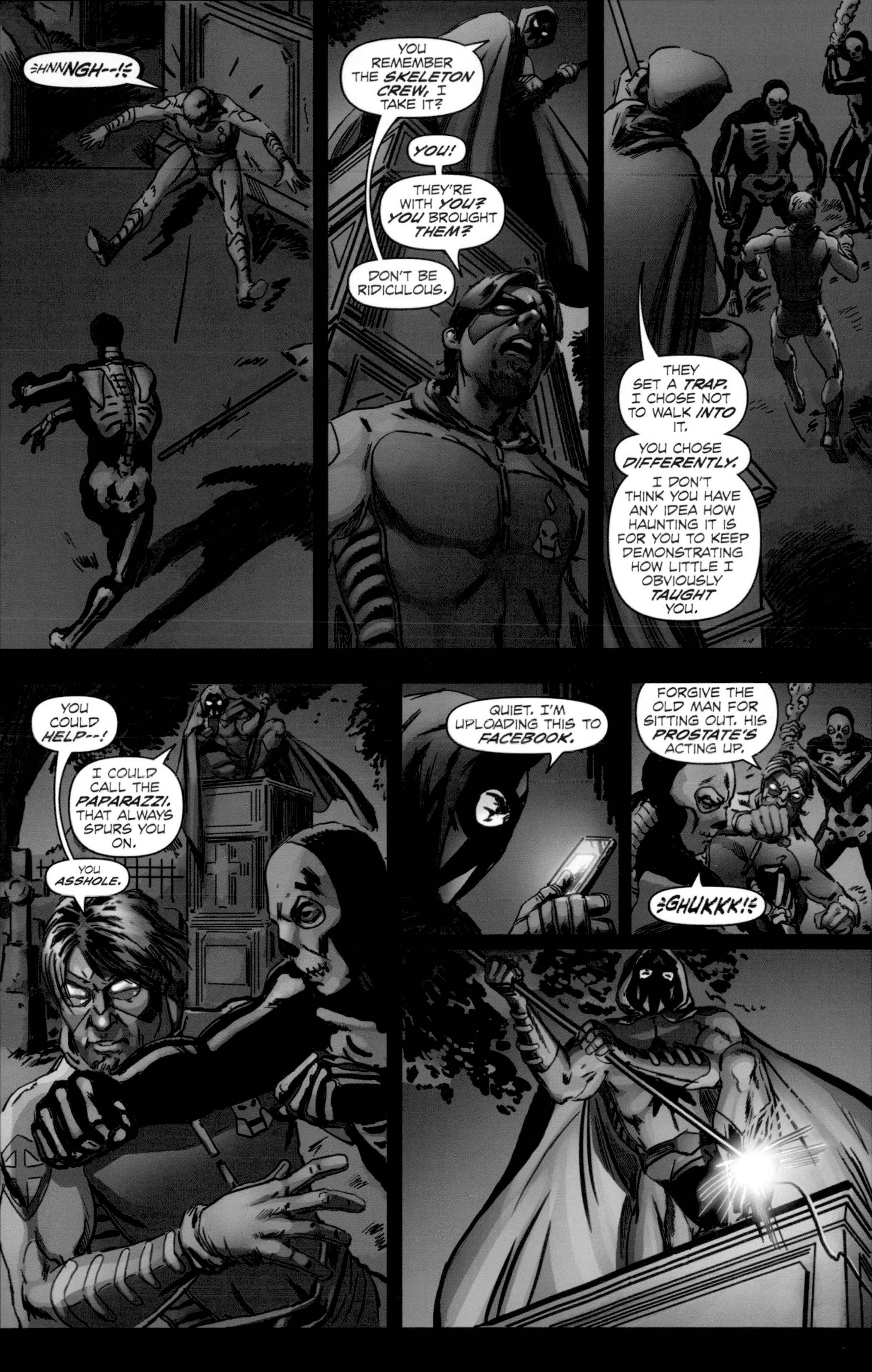

≈HNNNGH--!≈
YOU REMEMBER THE SKELETON CREW, I TAKE IT?
YOU!
THEY'RE WITH YOU? YOU BROUGHT THEM?
DON'T BE RIDICULOUS.
THEY SET A TRAP. I CHOSE NOT TO WALK INTO IT.
YOU CHOSE DIFFERENTLY.
I DON'T THINK YOU HAVE ANY IDEA HOW HAUNTING IT IS FOR YOU TO KEEP DEMONSTRATING HOW LITTLE I OBVIOUSLY TAUGHT YOU.
YOU COULD HELP--!
I COULD CALL THE PAPARAZZI. THAT ALWAYS SPURS YOU ON.
YOU ASSHOLE.
QUIET. I'M UPLOADING THIS TO FACEBOOK.
FORGIVE THE OLD MAN FOR SITTING OUT. HIS PROSTATE'S ACTING UP.
≈GHUKKK!≈

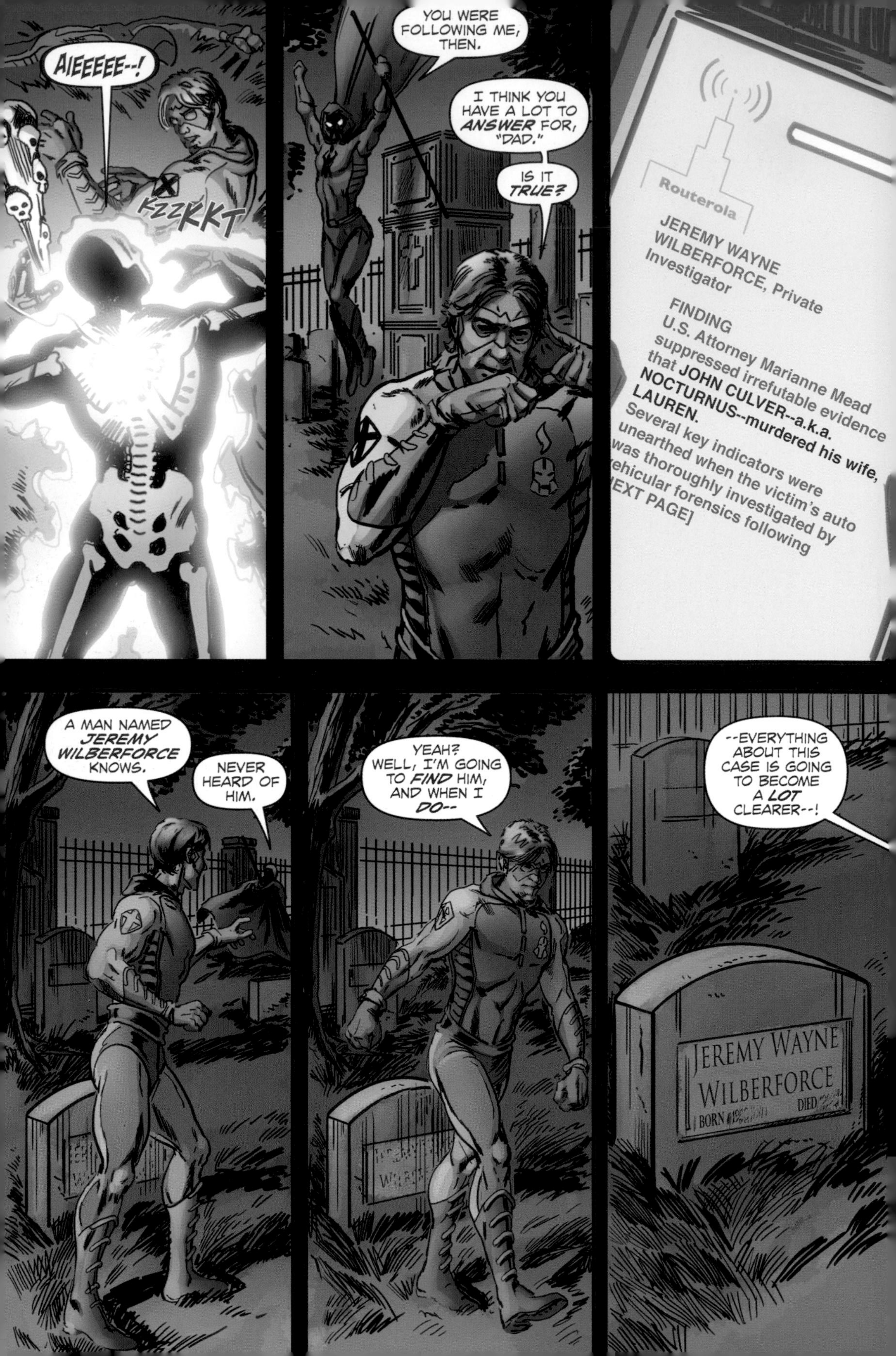

AIEEEEE--!
KZZKKT
YOU WERE FOLLOWING ME, THEN.
I THINK YOU HAVE A LOT TO *ANSWER* FOR, "DAD."
IS IT *TRUE?*
Routerola
JEREMY WAYNE WILBERFORCE, Private Investigator
FINDING
U.S. Attorney Marianne Mead suppressed irrefutable evidence that **JOHN CULVER--a.k.a. NOCTURNUS--murdered his wife, LAUREN.**
Several key indicators were unearthed when the victim's auto was thoroughly investigated by vehicular forensics following
[NEXT PAGE]
A MAN NAMED *JEREMY WILBERFORCE* KNOWS.
NEVER HEARD OF HIM.
YEAH? WELL, I'M GOING TO *FIND* HIM, AND WHEN I *DO--*
--EVERYTHING ABOUT THIS CASE IS GOING TO BECOME A *LOT* CLEARER--!
JEREMY WAYNE WILBERFORCE
BORN
DIED

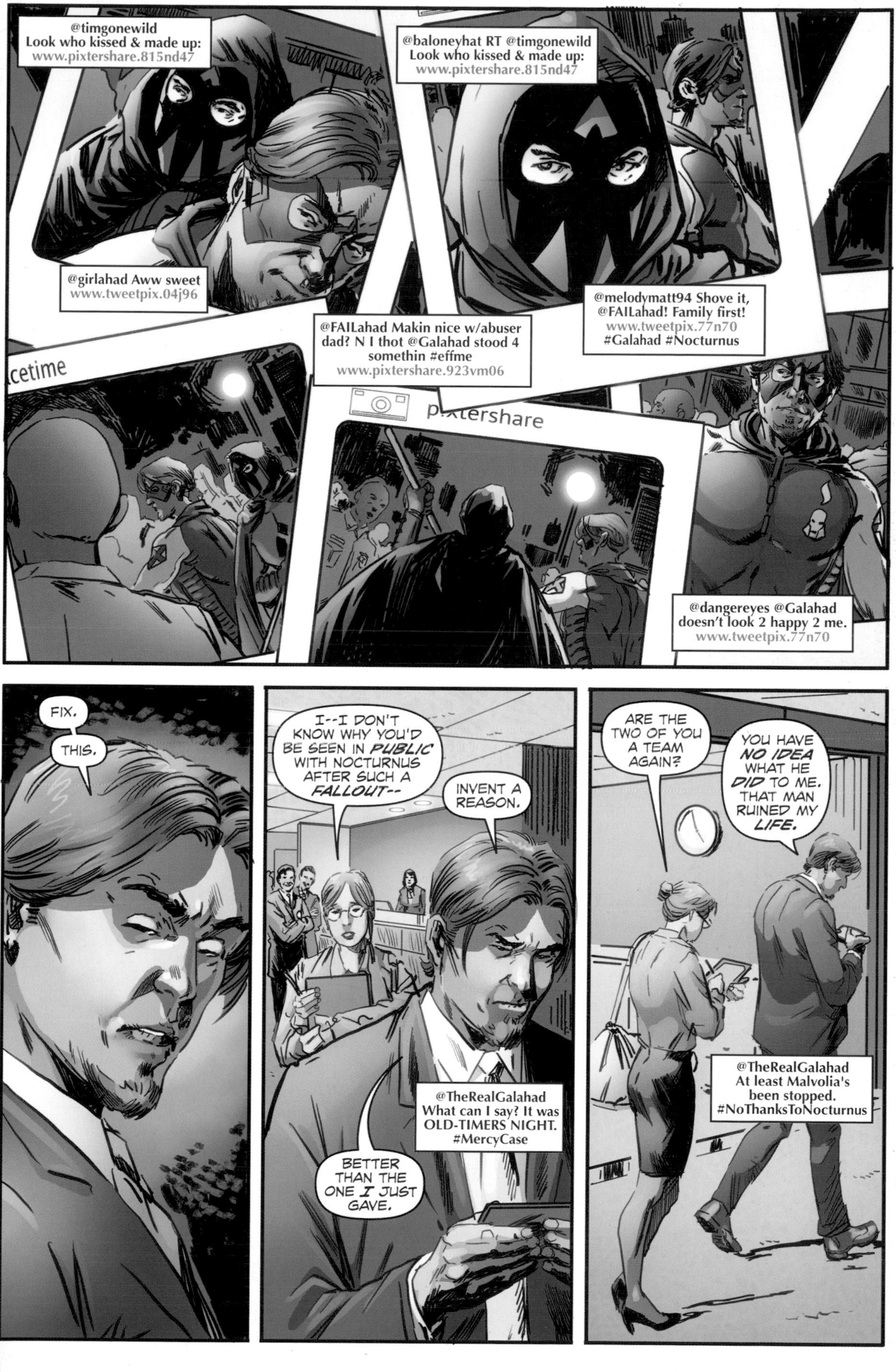
@timgonewild
Look who kissed & made up:
www.pixtershare.815nd47
@baloneyhat RT @timgonewild
Look who kissed & made up:
www.pixtershare.815nd47
@girlahad Aww sweet
www.tweetpix.04j96
@FAILahad Makin nice w/abuser dad? N I thot @Galahad stood 4 somethin #effme
www.pixtershare.923vm06
@melodymatt94 Shove it, @FAILahad! Family first!
www.tweetpix.77n70
#Galahad #Nocturnus
cetime
pixtershare
@dangereyes @Galahad doesn't look 2 happy 2 me.
www.tweetpix.77n70
FIX.
THIS.
I--I DON'T KNOW WHY YOU'D BE SEEN IN PUBLIC WITH NOCTURNUS AFTER SUCH A FALLOUT--
INVENT A REASON.
@TheRealGalahad
What can I say? It was OLD-TIMERS NIGHT.
#MercyCase
BETTER THAN THE ONE I JUST GAVE.
ARE THE TWO OF YOU A TEAM AGAIN?
YOU HAVE NO IDEA WHAT HE DID TO ME. THAT MAN RUINED MY LIFE.
@TheRealGalahad
At least Malvolia's been stopped.
#NoThanksToNocturnus

ANY NEWS ON YOUR MOTHER'S RETURN? THE FANBASE IS EXCITED TO SEE YOU *HAPPY--*

THAT I'M *BACK* WITH DADDY *AND* MY MOMMY'S ALIVE?

OH, I'M *TICKLED. SO* THRILLED ABOUT MY NEW *"GOOD BOY"* IMAGE, I NEED SOMEONE TO TAKE IT *OUT* ON.

WHO'S AT *LARGE?*

@anonydrone
"How DARE #Nocturnus make me richnfamous?"
#Galahad #hissy

@luvmyjob666
Veruca Salt thinks this kid's spoiled.
#Galahad

@rychboyzpet
Douchegeyser.
#guesswho

@careerh0micide
I smell bitchboy
#grandentrance

GETTING THAT INFORMATION FOR YOU...

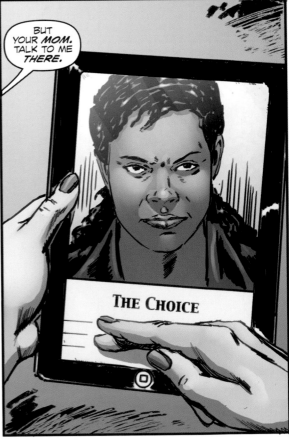

BUT YOUR *MOM.* TALK TO ME *THERE.*

THE CHOICE

IS SHE *SAFE*?

PRAETOREAN

HOW DID YOU FIND OUT SHE'S--

OMINAX

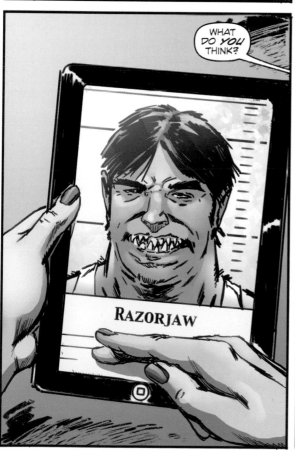

WHAT DO *YOU* THINK?

RAZORJAW

OH. MY. *GOD.*

YOU HAVE *NO IDEA* IF SHE'S REALLY ALIVE!

WOW, YOU'RE *GOOD.*

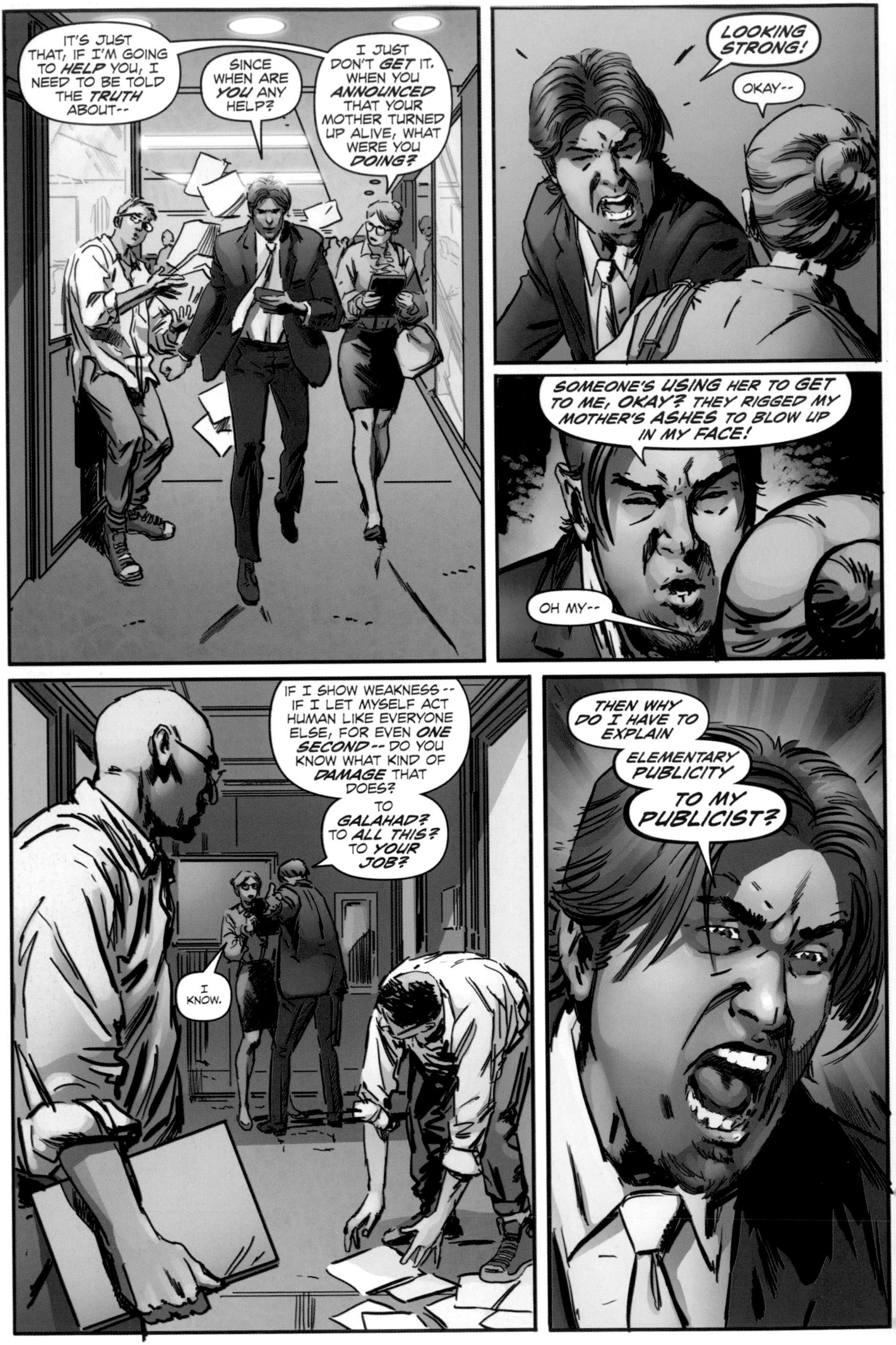
IT'S JUST THAT, IF I'M GOING TO *HELP* YOU, I NEED TO BE TOLD THE *TRUTH* ABOUT--
SINCE WHEN ARE *YOU* ANY HELP?
I JUST DON'T *GET* IT. WHEN YOU *ANNOUNCED* THAT YOUR MOTHER TURNED UP ALIVE, WHAT WERE YOU *DOING?*
LOOKING STRONG!
OKAY--
SOMEONE'S *USING* HER TO GET TO ME, *OKAY?* THEY RIGGED MY *MOTHER'S ASHES* TO BLOW UP IN MY FACE!
OH MY--
IF I SHOW WEAKNESS -- IF I LET MYSELF ACT HUMAN LIKE EVERYONE ELSE, FOR EVEN *ONE SECOND* -- DO YOU KNOW WHAT KIND OF *DAMAGE* THAT DOES?
TO *GALAHAD?* TO *ALL THIS?* TO *YOUR JOB?*
I KNOW.
THEN WHY DO I HAVE TO EXPLAIN
ELEMENTARY PUBLICITY
TO MY PUBLICIST?

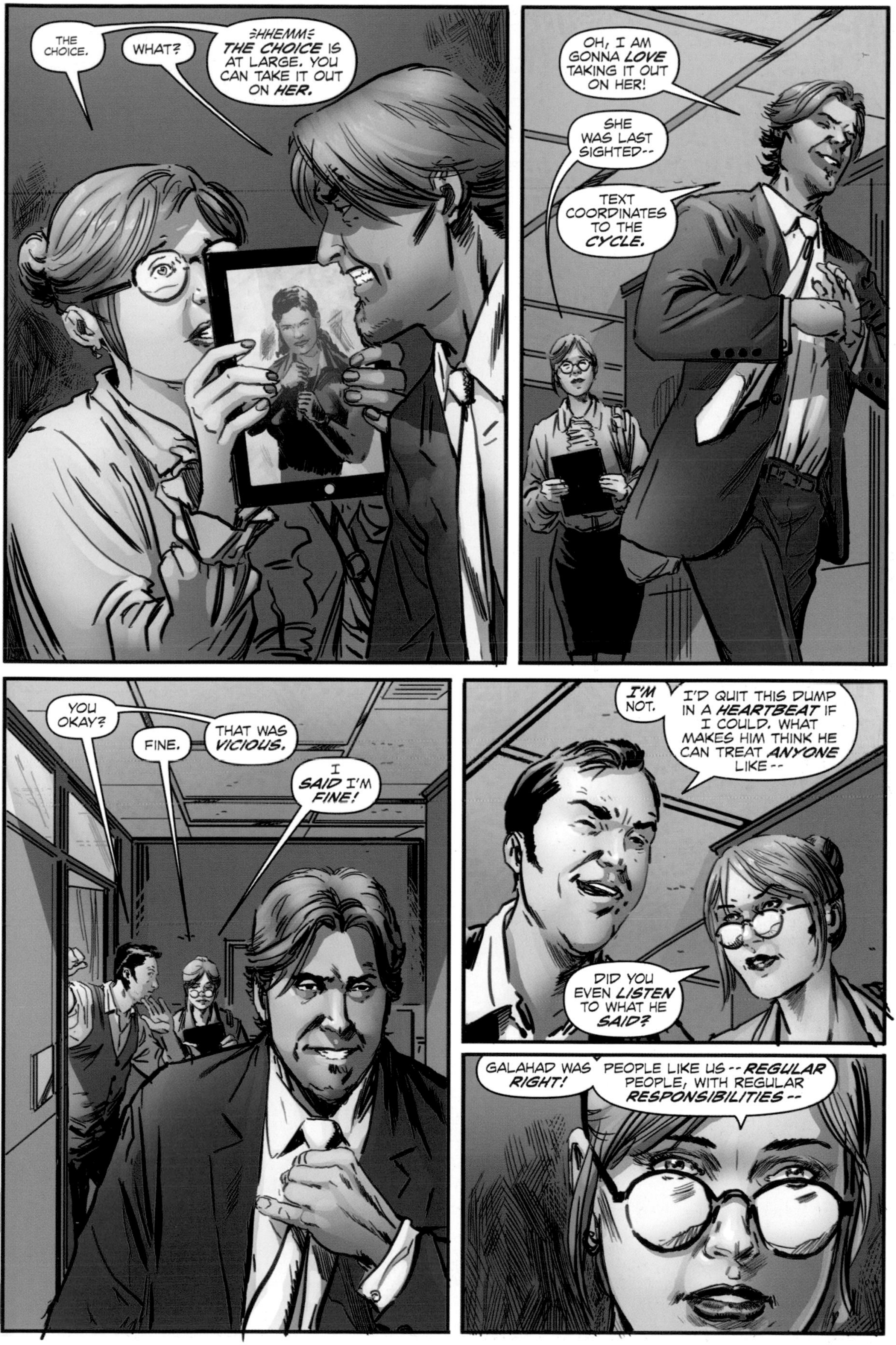
THE CHOICE.
WHAT?
HHEMM THE CHOICE IS AT LARGE. YOU CAN TAKE IT OUT ON HER.
OH, I AM GONNA LOVE TAKING IT OUT ON HER!
SHE WAS LAST SIGHTED--
TEXT COORDINATES TO THE CYCLE.
YOU OKAY?
FINE.
THAT WAS VICIOUS.
I SAID I'M FINE!
I'M NOT.
I'D QUIT THIS DUMP IN A HEARTBEAT IF I COULD. WHAT MAKES HIM THINK HE CAN TREAT ANYONE LIKE--
DID YOU EVEN LISTEN TO WHAT HE SAID?
GALAHAD WAS RIGHT!
PEOPLE LIKE US--REGULAR PEOPLE, WITH REGULAR RESPONSIBILITIES--

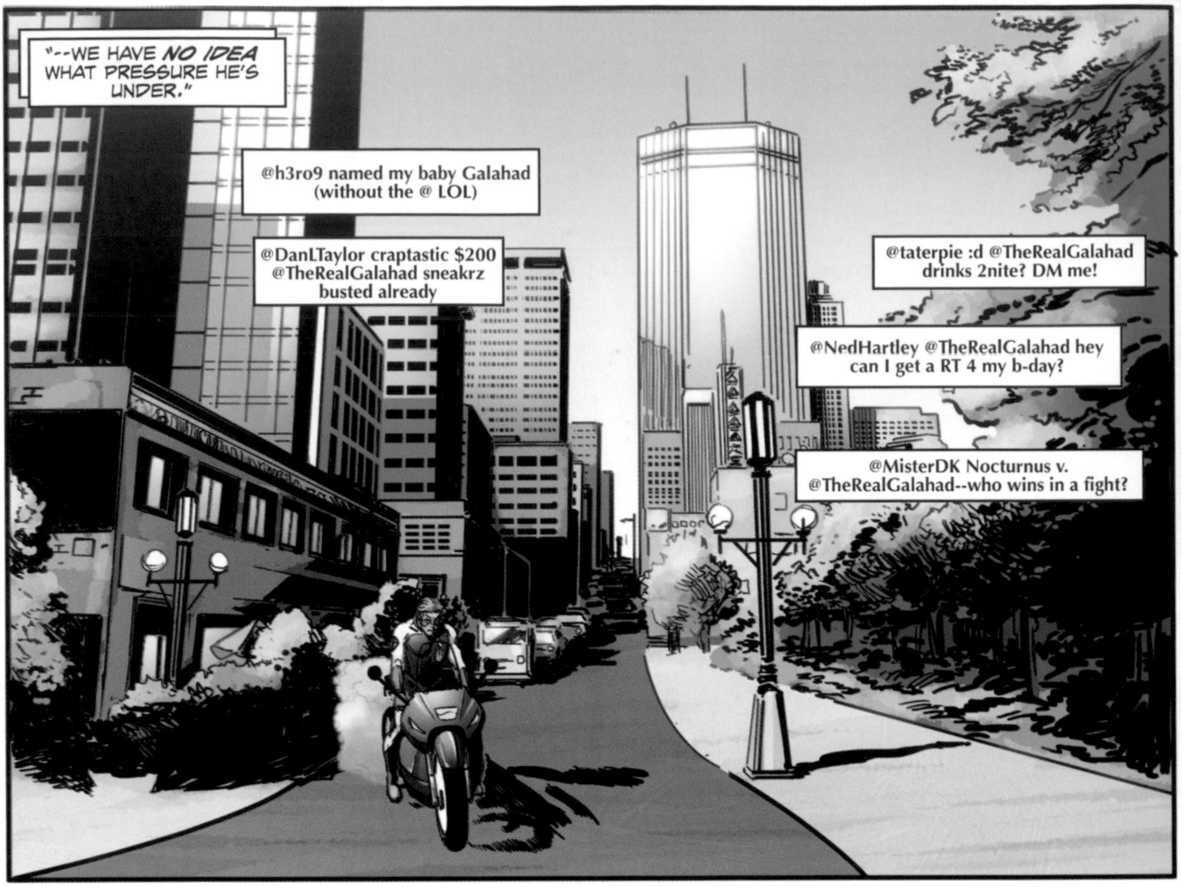
"--WE HAVE NO IDEA WHAT PRESSURE HE'S UNDER."
@h3ro9 named my baby Galahad (without the @ LOL)
@DanLTaylor craptastic $200 @TheRealGalahad sneakrz busted already
@taterpie :d @TheRealGalahad drinks 2nite? DM me!
@NedHartley @TheRealGalahad hey can I get a RT 4 my b-day?
@MisterDK Nocturnus v. @TheRealGalahad--who wins in a fight?

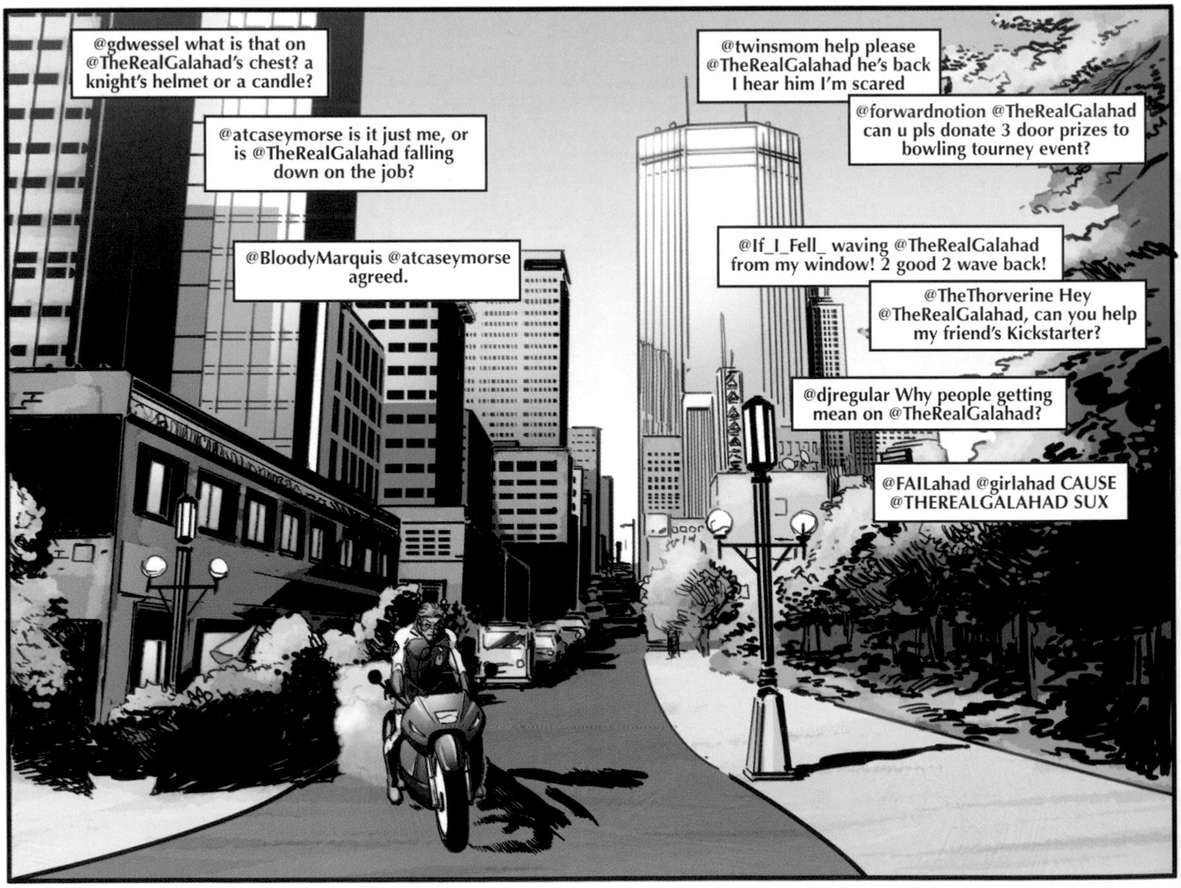
@gdwessel what is that on @TheRealGalahad's chest? a knight's helmet or a candle?
@atcaseymorse is it just me, or is @TheRealGalahad falling down on the job?
@BloodyMarquis @atcaseymorse agreed.
@twinsmom help please @TheRealGalahad he's back I hear him I'm scared
@forwardnotion @TheRealGalahad can u pls donate 3 door prizes to bowling tourney event?
@If_I_Fell_ waving @TheRealGalahad from my window! 2 good 2 wave back!
@TheThorverine Hey @TheRealGalahad, can you help my friend's Kickstarter?
@djregular Why people getting mean on @TheRealGalahad?
@FAILahad @girlahad CAUSE @THEREALGALAHAD SUX

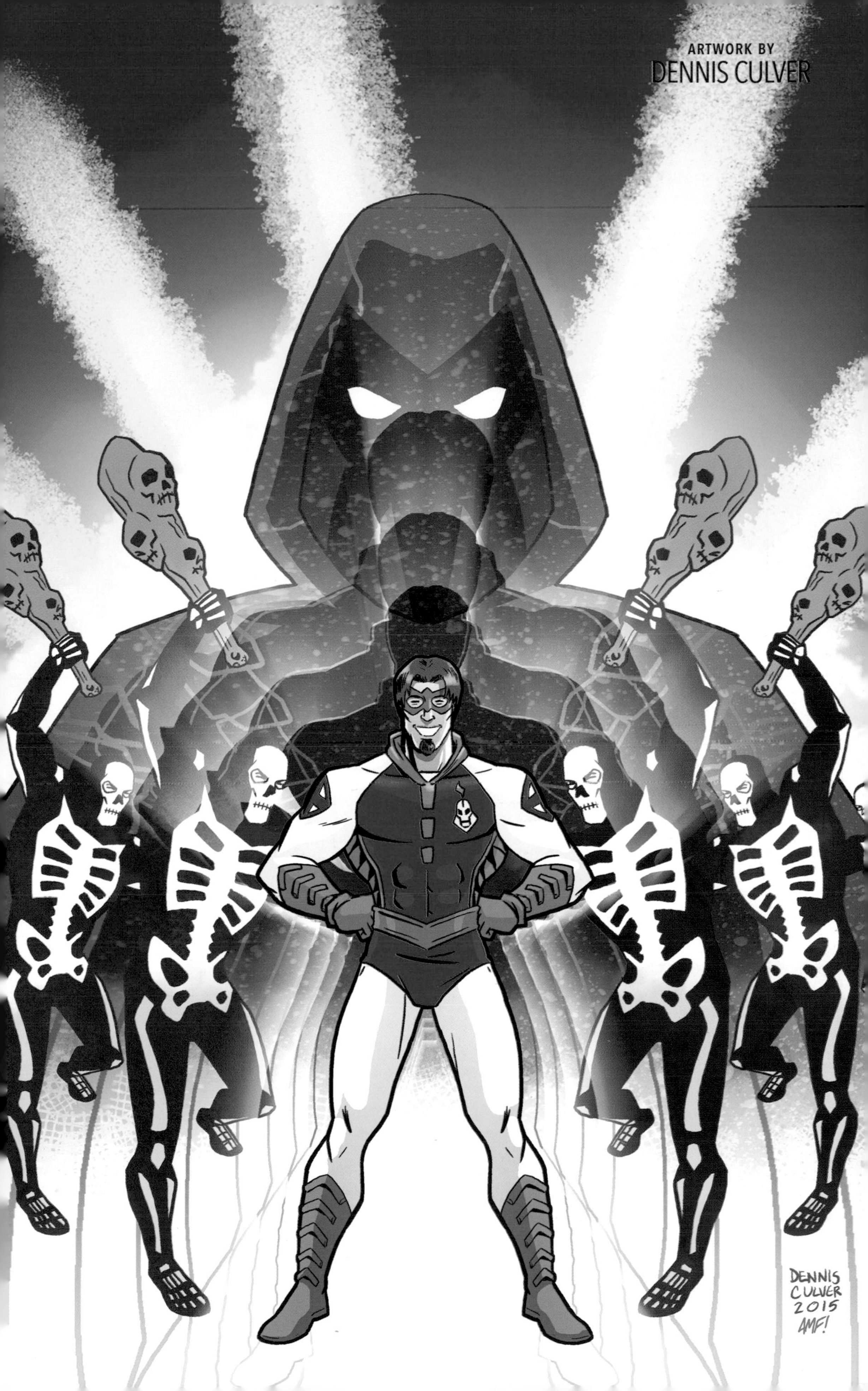
ARTWORK BY
DENNIS CULVER
DENNIS
CULVER
2015
AMF!

CHAPTER FOUR

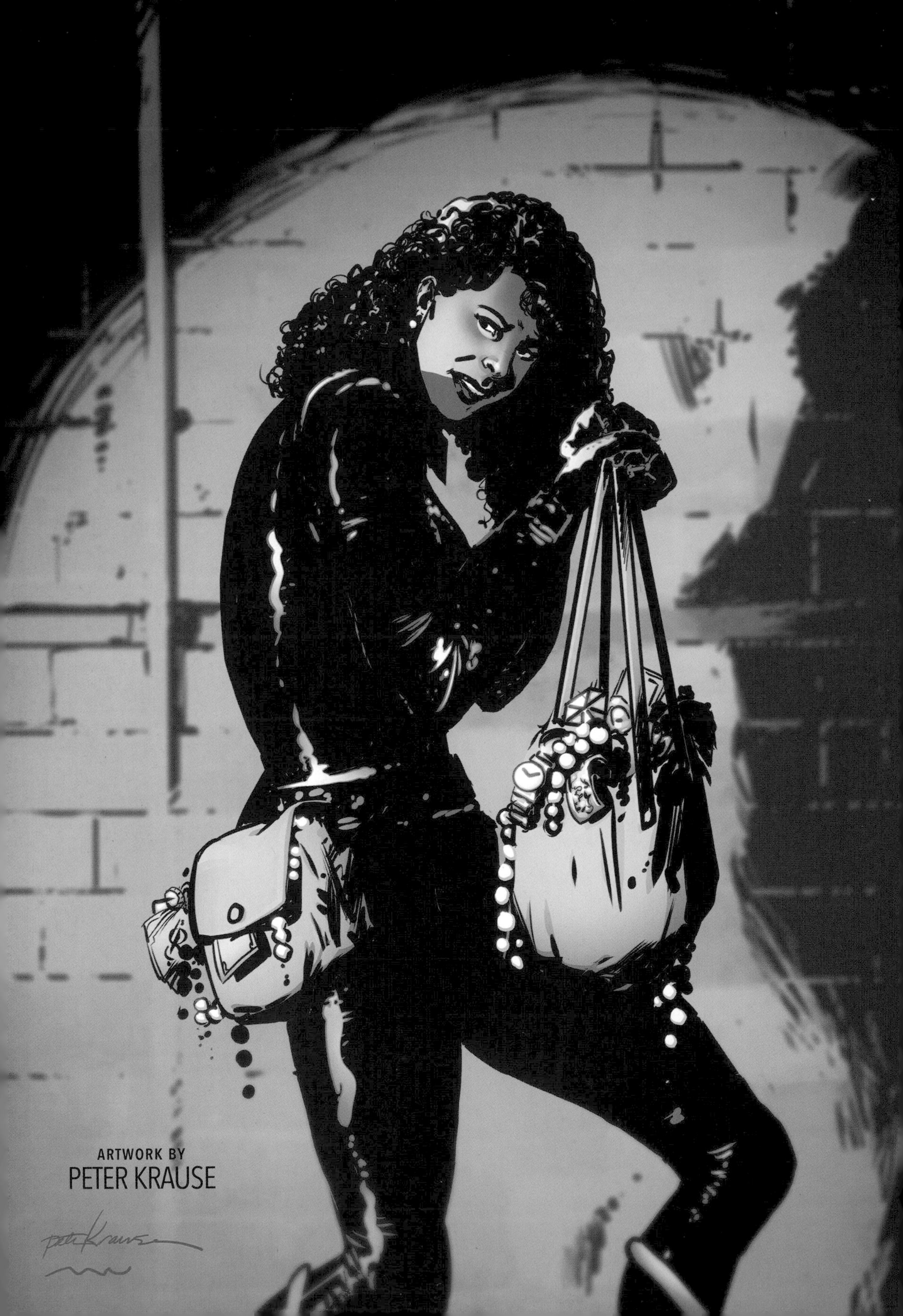

ARTWORK BY
PETER KRAUSE

MONDAY

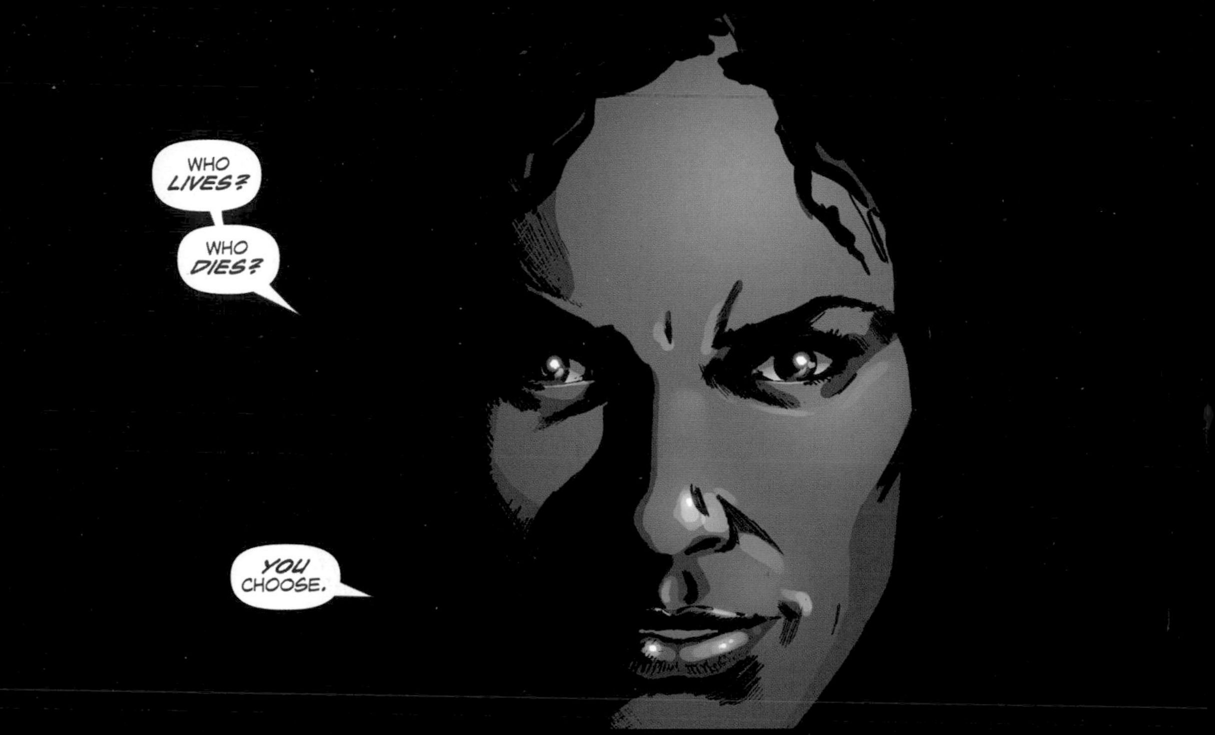
WHO LIVES?
WHO DIES?
YOU CHOOSE.

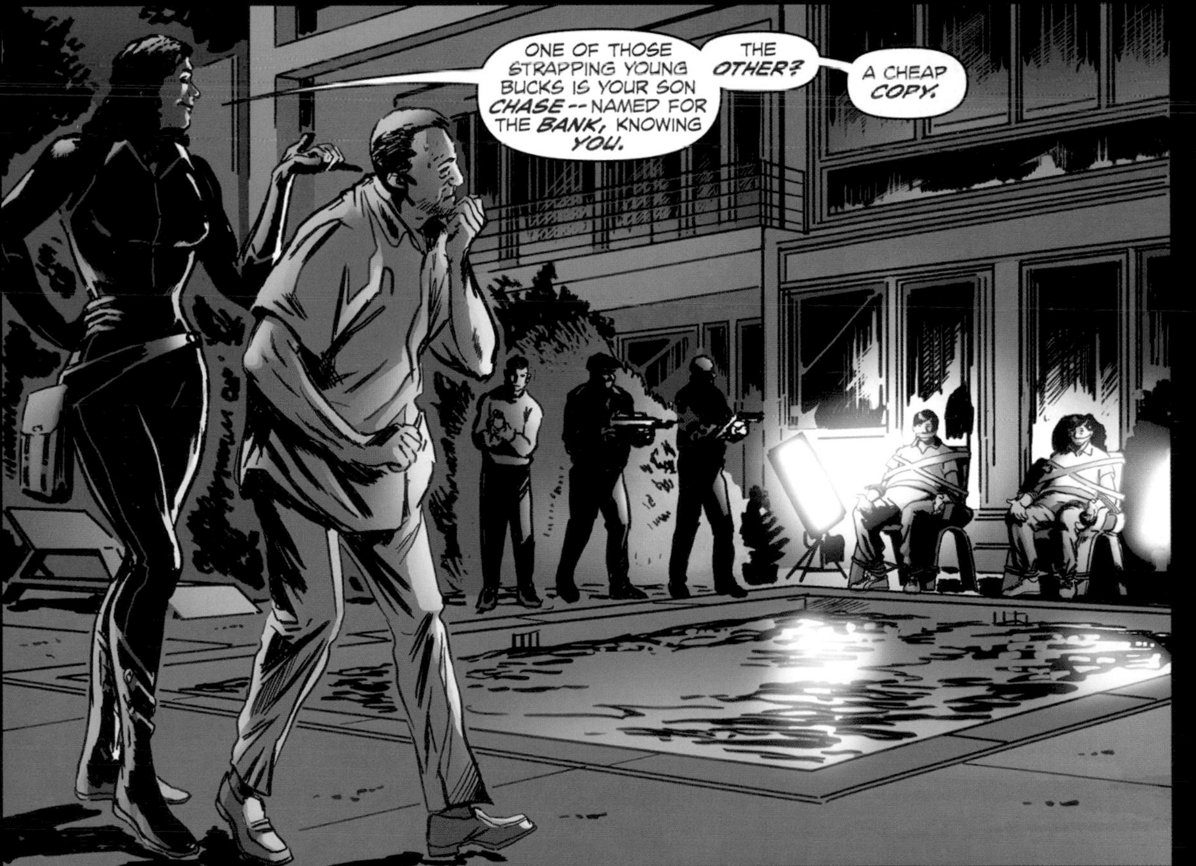
ONE OF THOSE STRAPPING YOUNG BUCKS IS YOUR SON CHASE-- NAMED FOR THE BANK, KNOWING YOU.
THE OTHER?
A CHEAP COPY.

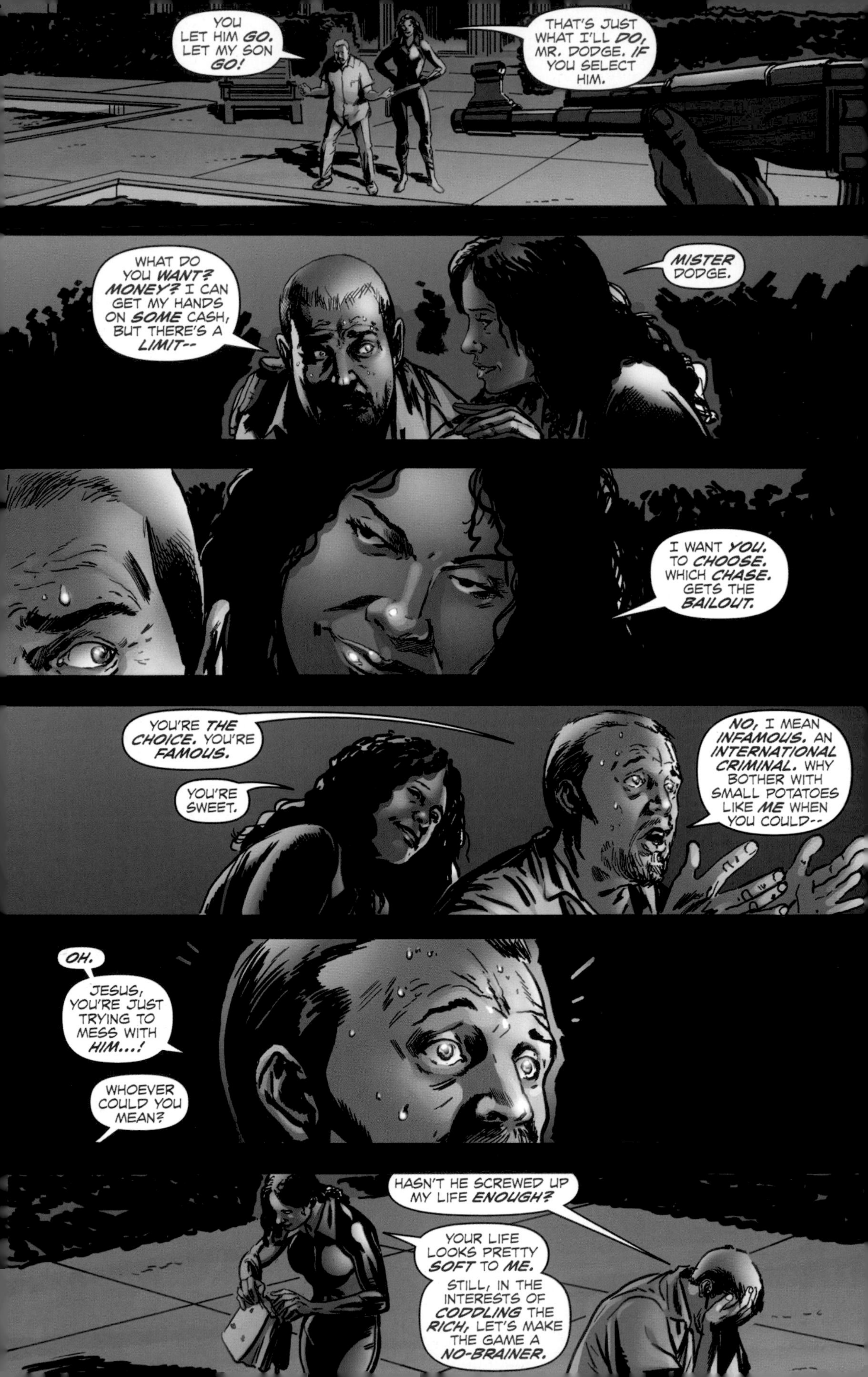
YOU LET HIM GO. LET MY SON GO!
THAT'S JUST WHAT I'LL DO, MR. DODGE. IF YOU SELECT HIM.
WHAT DO YOU WANT? MONEY? I CAN GET MY HANDS ON SOME CASH, BUT THERE'S A LIMIT--
MISTER DODGE.
I WANT YOU. TO CHOOSE. WHICH CHASE. GETS THE BAILOUT.
YOU'RE THE CHOICE. YOU'RE FAMOUS.
NO, I MEAN INFAMOUS. AN INTERNATIONAL CRIMINAL. WHY BOTHER WITH SMALL POTATOES LIKE ME WHEN YOU COULD--
YOU'RE SWEET.
OH.
JESUS, YOU'RE JUST TRYING TO MESS WITH HIM...!
WHOEVER COULD YOU MEAN?
HASN'T HE SCREWED UP MY LIFE ENOUGH?
YOUR LIFE LOOKS PRETTY SOFT TO ME.
STILL, IN THE INTERESTS OF CODDLING THE RICH, LET'S MAKE THE GAME A NO-BRAINER.

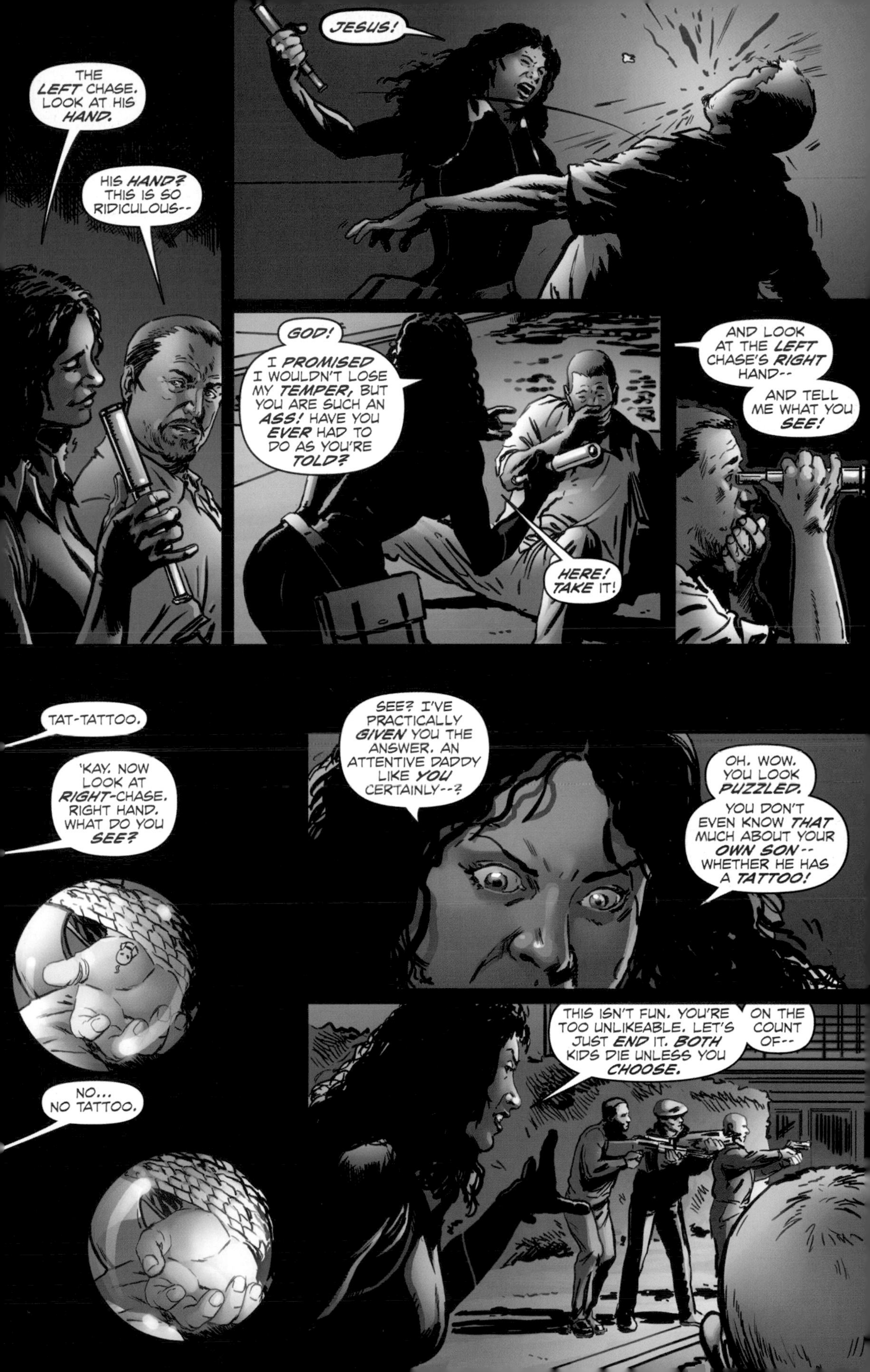

THE LEFT CHASE. LOOK AT HIS HAND.
HIS HAND? THIS IS SO RIDICULOUS--
JESUS!
GOD!
I PROMISED I WOULDN'T LOSE MY TEMPER, BUT YOU ARE SUCH AN ASS! HAVE YOU EVER HAD TO DO AS YOU'RE TOLD?
HERE! TAKE IT!
AND LOOK AT THE LEFT CHASE'S RIGHT HAND--
AND TELL ME WHAT YOU SEE!
TAT-TATTOO.
'KAY. NOW LOOK AT RIGHT-CHASE. RIGHT HAND. WHAT DO YOU SEE?
NO... NO TATTOO.
SEE? I'VE PRACTICALLY GIVEN YOU THE ANSWER. AN ATTENTIVE DADDY LIKE YOU CERTAINLY--?
OH. WOW. YOU LOOK PUZZLED.
YOU DON'T EVEN KNOW THAT MUCH ABOUT YOUR OWN SON -- WHETHER HE HAS A TATTOO!
THIS ISN'T FUN. YOU'RE TOO UNLIKEABLE. LET'S JUST END IT. BOTH KIDS DIE UNLESS YOU CHOOSE.
ON THE COUNT OF--

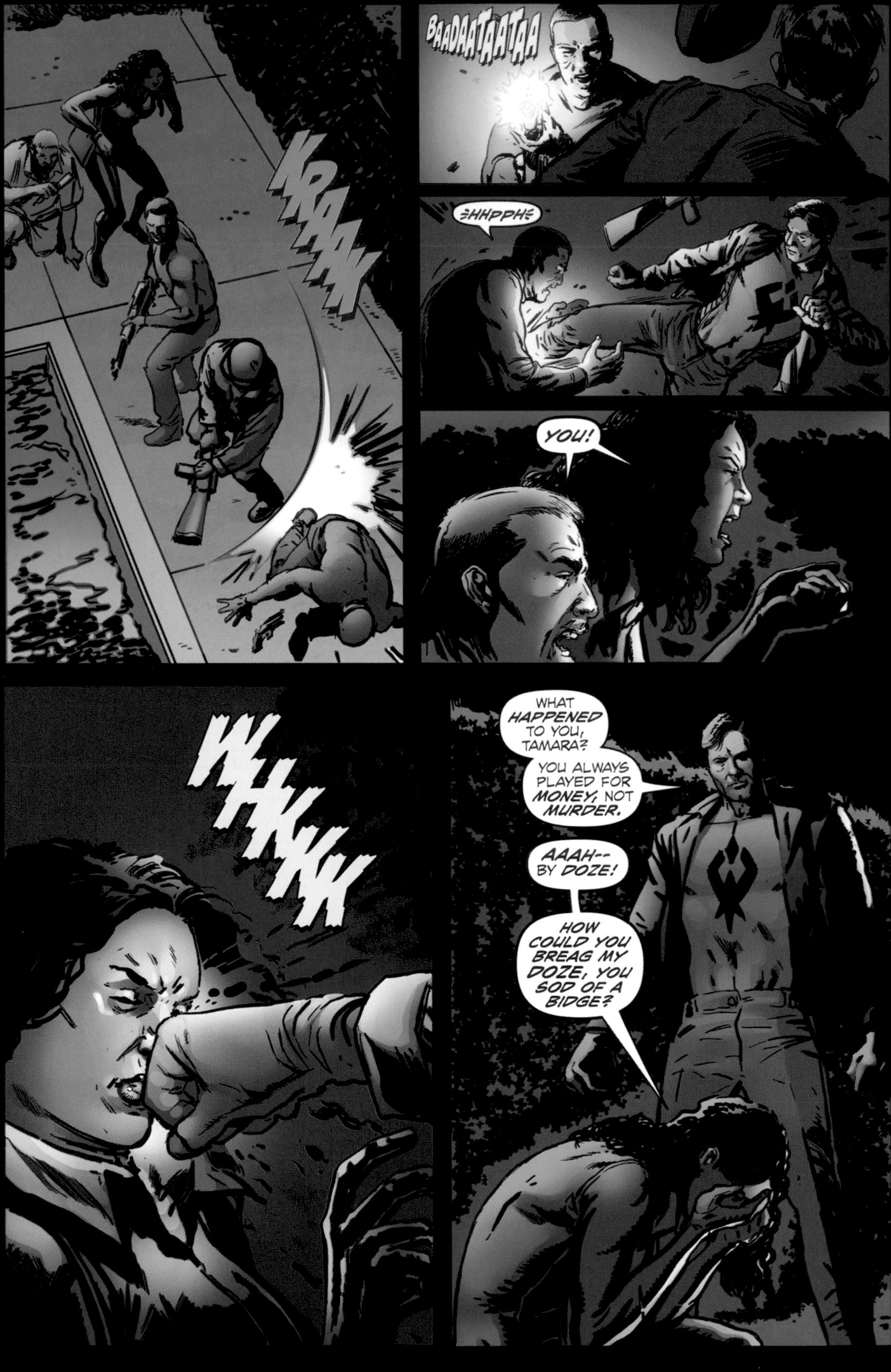
KRAAAK
BAADAATAATAA
HHPPH
YOU!
WHKKK
WHAT HAPPENED TO YOU, TAMARA?
YOU ALWAYS PLAYED FOR MONEY, NOT MURDER.
AAAH-- BY DOZE!
HOW COULD YOU BREAG MY DOZE, YOU SOD OF A BIDGE?

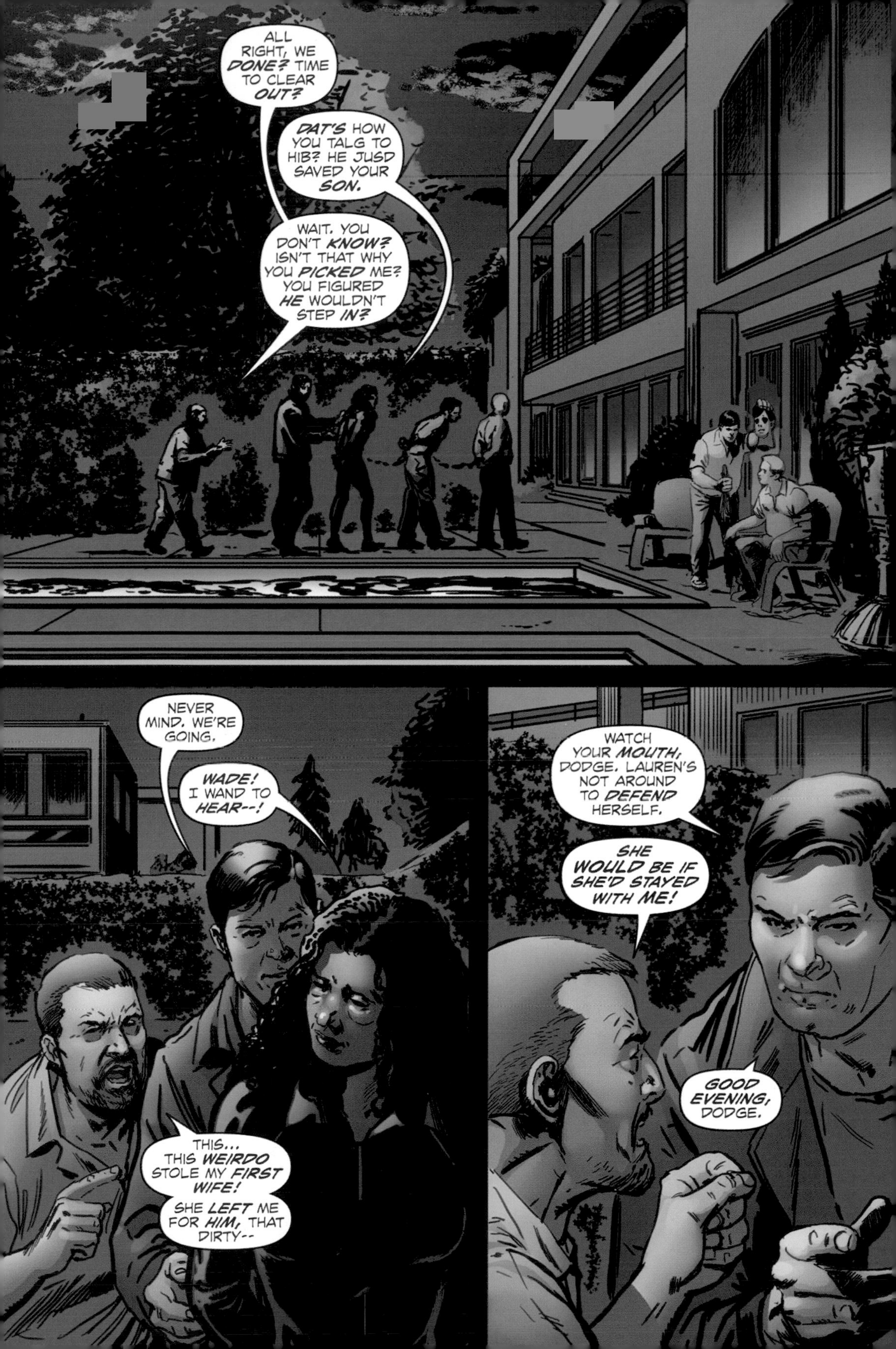
ALL RIGHT, WE DONE? TIME TO CLEAR OUT?
DAT'S HOW YOU TALG TO HIB? HE JUSD SAVED YOUR SON.
WAIT. YOU DON'T KNOW? ISN'T THAT WHY YOU PICKED ME? YOU FIGURED HE WOULDN'T STEP IN?
NEVER MIND. WE'RE GOING.
WADE! I WAND TO HEAR--!
THIS... THIS WEIRDO STOLE MY FIRST WIFE!
SHE LEFT ME FOR HIM, THAT DIRTY--
WATCH YOUR MOUTH, DODGE. LAUREN'S NOT AROUND TO DEFEND HERSELF.
SHE WOULD BE IF SHE'D STAYED WITH ME!
GOOD EVENING, DODGE.

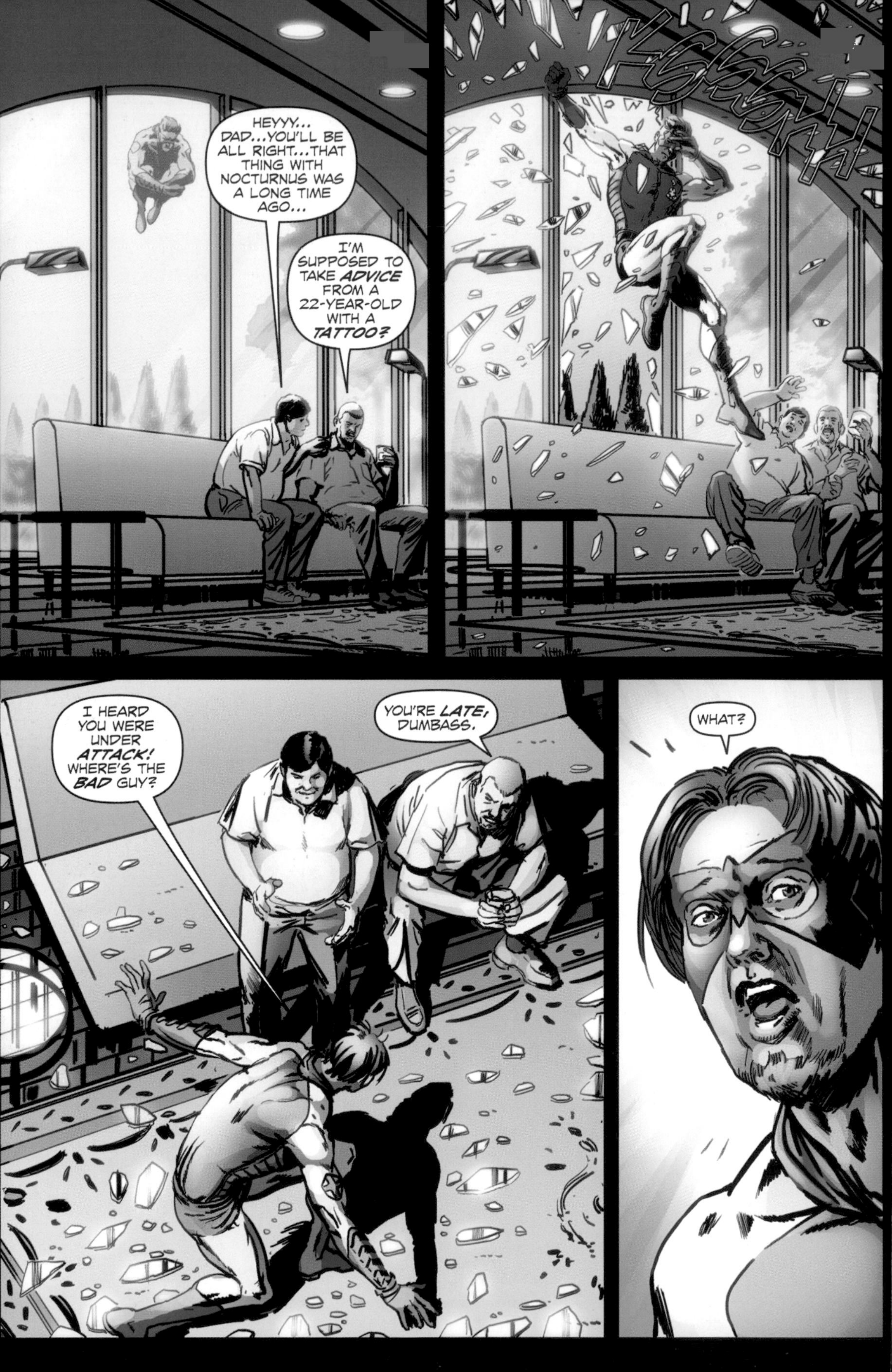
HEYYY... DAD...YOU'LL BE ALL RIGHT...THAT THING WITH NOCTURNUS WAS A LONG TIME AGO...
I'M SUPPOSED TO TAKE ADVICE FROM A 22-YEAR-OLD WITH A TATTOO?
I HEARD YOU WERE UNDER ATTACK! WHERE'S THE BAD GUY?
YOU'RE LATE, DUMBASS.
WHAT?

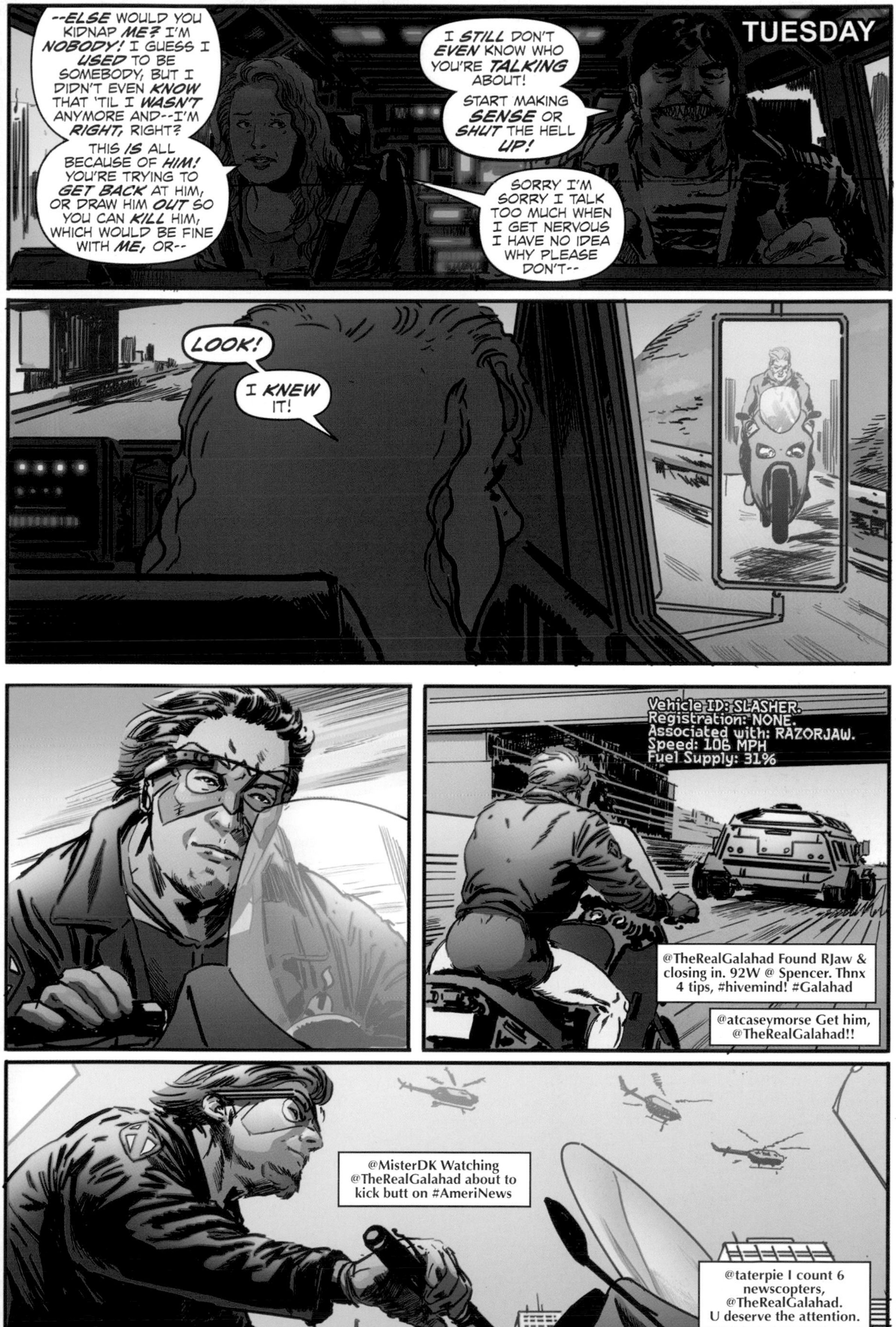
TUESDAY
--ELSE WOULD YOU KIDNAP ME? I'M NOBODY! I GUESS I USED TO BE SOMEBODY, BUT I DIDN'T EVEN KNOW THAT 'TIL I WASN'T ANYMORE AND--I'M RIGHT, RIGHT?
THIS IS ALL BECAUSE OF HIM! YOU'RE TRYING TO GET BACK AT HIM, OR DRAW HIM OUT SO YOU CAN KILL HIM, WHICH WOULD BE FINE WITH ME, OR--
I STILL DON'T EVEN KNOW WHO YOU'RE TALKING ABOUT!
START MAKING SENSE OR SHUT THE HELL UP!
SORRY I'M SORRY I TALK TOO MUCH WHEN I GET NERVOUS I HAVE NO IDEA WHY PLEASE DON'T--
LOOK!
I KNEW IT!
Vehicle ID: SLASHER.
Registration: NONE.
Associated with: RAZORJAW.
Speed: 106 MPH
Fuel Supply: 31%
@TheRealGalahad Found RJaw & closing in. 92W @ Spencer. Thnx 4 tips, #hivemind! #Galahad
@atcaseymorse Get him, @TheRealGalahad!!
@MisterDK Watching @TheRealGalahad about to kick butt on #AmeriNews
@taterpie I count 6 newscopters, @TheRealGalahad. U deserve the attention.

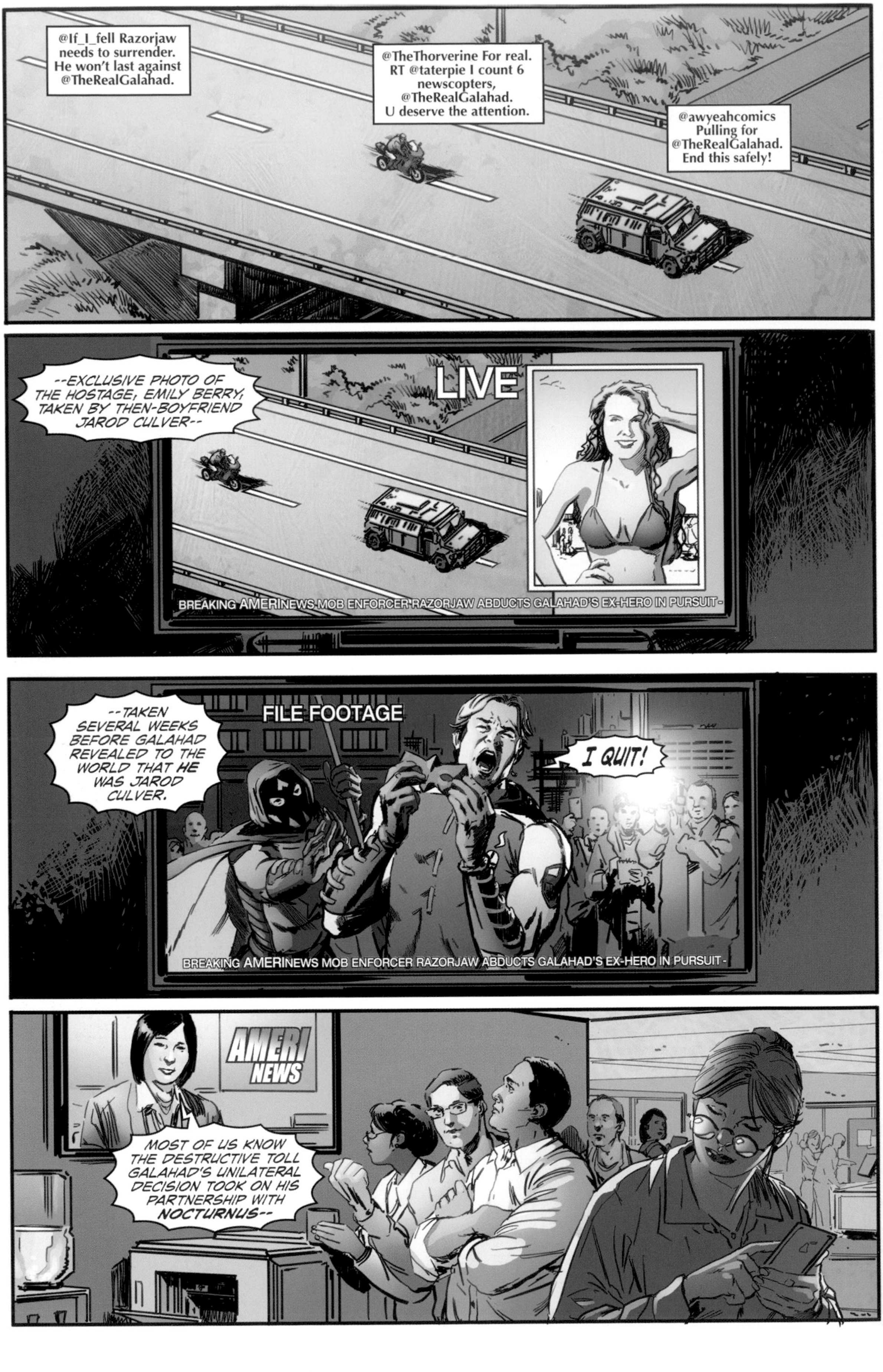

@If_I_fell Razorjaw needs to surrender. He won't last against @TheRealGalahad.
@TheThorverine For real. RT @taterpie I count 6 newscopters, @TheRealGalahad. U deserve the attention.
@awyeahcomics Pulling for @TheRealGalahad. End this safely!
--EXCLUSIVE PHOTO OF THE HOSTAGE, EMILY BERRY, TAKEN BY THEN-BOYFRIEND JAROD CULVER--
LIVE
BREAKING AMERINEWS MOB ENFORCER RAZORJAW ABDUCTS GALAHAD'S EX-HERO IN PURSUIT-
--TAKEN SEVERAL WEEKS BEFORE GALAHAD REVEALED TO THE WORLD THAT HE WAS JAROD CULVER.
FILE FOOTAGE
I QUIT!
BREAKING AMERINEWS MOB ENFORCER RAZORJAW ABDUCTS GALAHAD'S EX-HERO IN PURSUIT-
AMERI NEWS
MOST OF US KNOW THE DESTRUCTIVE TOLL GALAHAD'S UNILATERAL DECISION TOOK ON HIS PARTNERSHIP WITH NOCTURNUS--

FILE FOOTAGE

--BUT EMILY'S LIFE CHANGED EVERY BIT AS DRASTICALLY.

CLAIMING SHE HADN'T **KNOWN** CULVER'S SECRET, EMILY'S PARENTS MOVED HER TO AN UNDISCLOSED LOCATION. THE FAMILY WASN'T SEEN AGAIN--

BREAKING AMERINEWS REPORT: EMILY, FAMILY DIDN'T KNOW BOYFRIEND WAS GALAHAD-HERO IN PURSUIT-

--UNTIL *TODAY.*

@FAILahad g/f dumped you, @TheRealGalahad. U saving her or stalking her?

WHAT?

@fortresskey lol RT @FAILahad: g/f dumped you, @TheRealGalahad. U saving her or stalking her?

@MisterDK Creepy! RT @FAILahad: g/f dumped you, @TheRealGalahad. U saving her or stalking her?

@taterpie RT @FAILahad: g/f dumped you, @TheRealGalahad. U saving her or stalking her?

@jonrog1 Stalking! RT @FAILahad: g/f dumped you, @TheRealGalahad. U saving her or stalking her?

*FAIL*AHAD?

@TheRealGalahad @FAILahad watch this, loser #Galahad #heroism

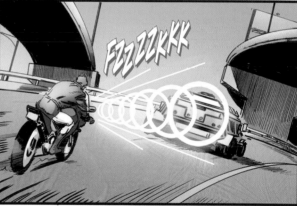

FZZZZKKK

WE'RE! DEAD!

YOUR *BOYFRIEND* JUST BLASTED US WITH AN *ELECTROMAGNETIC* PULSE!

WHAT? WAIT A MINUTE, I KNOW THIS STUFF. IF IT WERE AN *EMP,* NONE OF YOUR DEVICES WOULD BE WORKING AT *ALL,* NOT EVEN--

@TheRealGalahad That was for you, @FAILahad! #greatness #youaresowelcome #Galahad

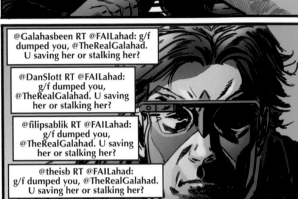

@Galahasbeen RT @FAILahad: g/f dumped you, @TheRealGalahad. U saving her or stalking her?

@DanSlott RT @FAILahad: g/f dumped you, @TheRealGalahad. U saving her or stalking her?

@filipsablik RT @FAILahad: g/f dumped you, @TheRealGalahad. U saving her or stalking her?

@theisb RT @FAILahad: g/f dumped you, @TheRealGalahad. U saving her or stalking her?

@DanLTaylor RT @FAILahad: g/f dumped you, @TheRealGalahad. U saving her or stalking her?

@pvponline RT @FAILahad: g/f dumped you, @TheRealGalahad. U saving her or stalking her?

@SotoColor RT @FAILahad: g/f dumped you, @TheRealGalahad. U saving her or stalking her?

@StephenWacker RT @FAILahad: g/f dumped you, @TheRealGalahad. U saving her or stalking her?

@SterlingGates RT @FAILahad: g/f dumped you, @TheRealGalahad. U saving her or stalking her?

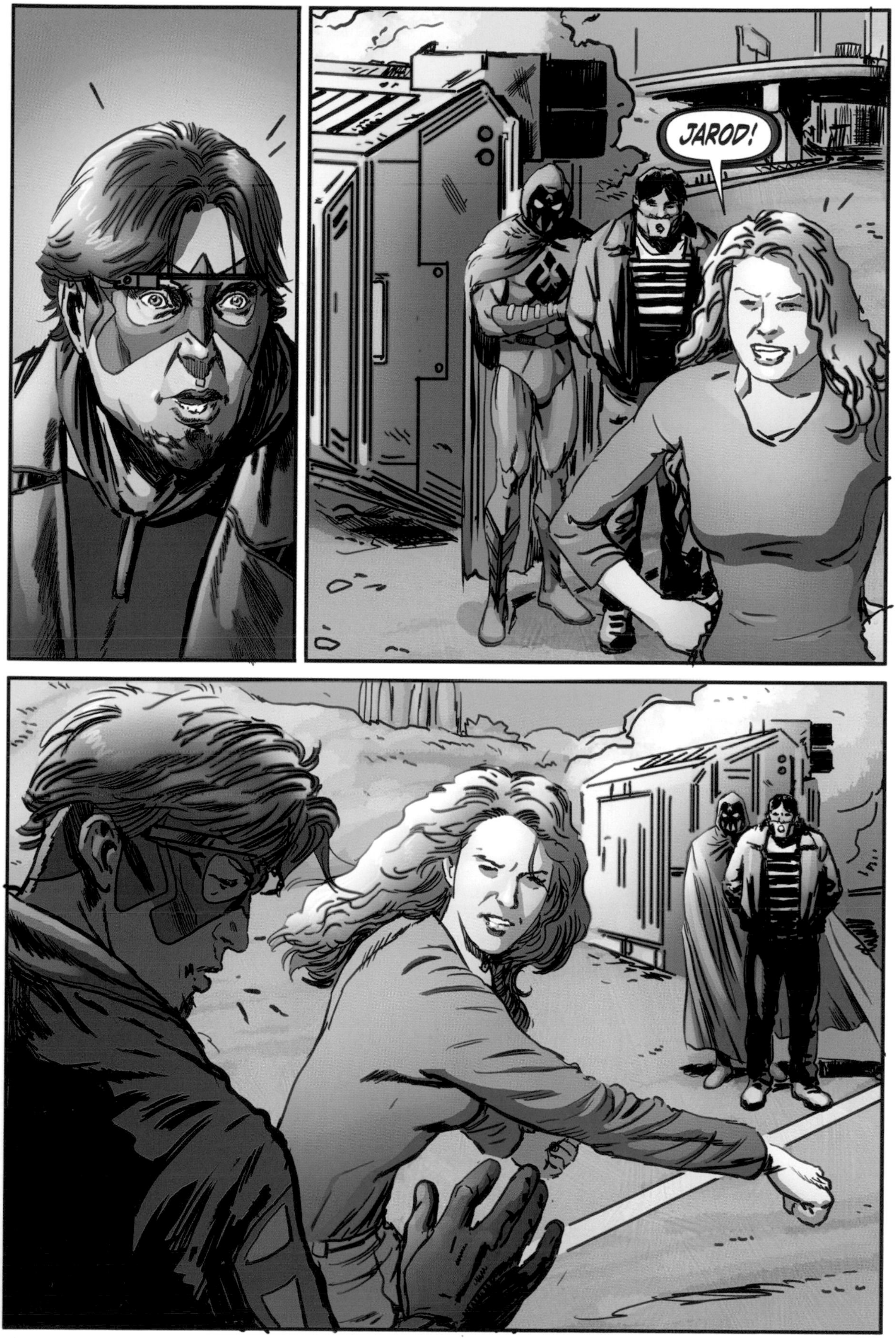
JAROD!

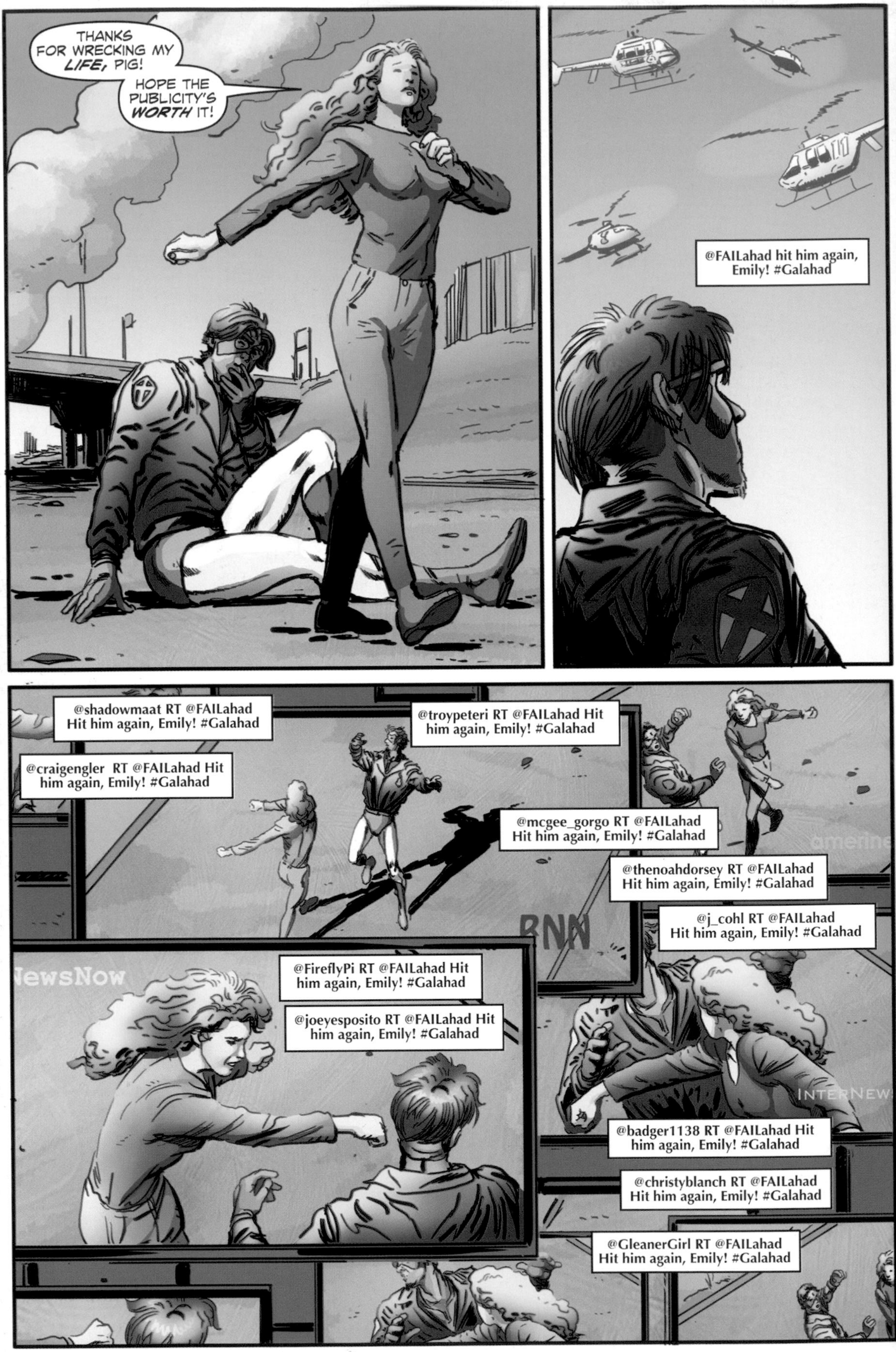
THANKS FOR WRECKING MY *LIFE,* PIG!
HOPE THE PUBLICITY'S *WORTH* IT!
@FAILahad hit him again, Emily! #Galahad
@shadowmaat RT @FAILahad Hit him again, Emily! #Galahad
@troypeteri RT @FAILahad Hit him again, Emily! #Galahad
@craigengler RT @FAILahad Hit him again, Emily! #Galahad
@mcgee_gorgo RT @FAILahad Hit him again, Emily! #Galahad
@thenoahdorsey RT @FAILahad Hit him again, Emily! #Galahad
@j_cohl RT @FAILahad Hit him again, Emily! #Galahad
BNN
NewsNow
@FireflyPi RT @FAILahad Hit him again, Emily! #Galahad
@joeyesposito RT @FAILahad Hit him again, Emily! #Galahad
@badger1138 RT @FAILahad Hit him again, Emily! #Galahad
@christyblanch RT @FAILahad Hit him again, Emily! #Galahad
@GleanerGirl RT @FAILahad Hit him again, Emily! #Galahad

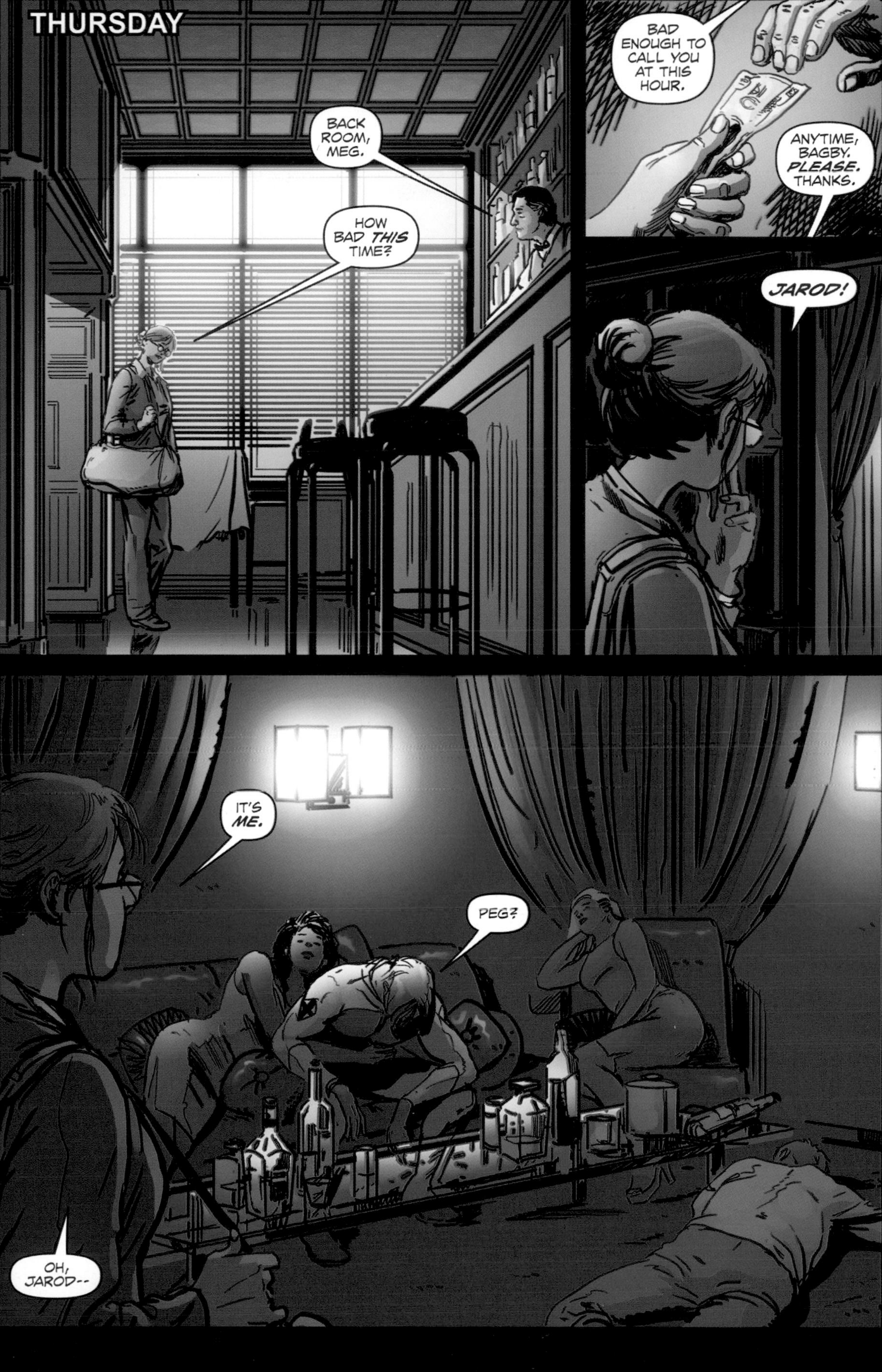
THURSDAY
BACK ROOM, MEG.
HOW BAD *THIS* TIME?
BAD ENOUGH TO CALL YOU AT THIS HOUR.
ANYTIME, BAGBY. *PLEASE.* THANKS.
JAROD!
IT'S *ME.*
PEG?
OH, JAROD--

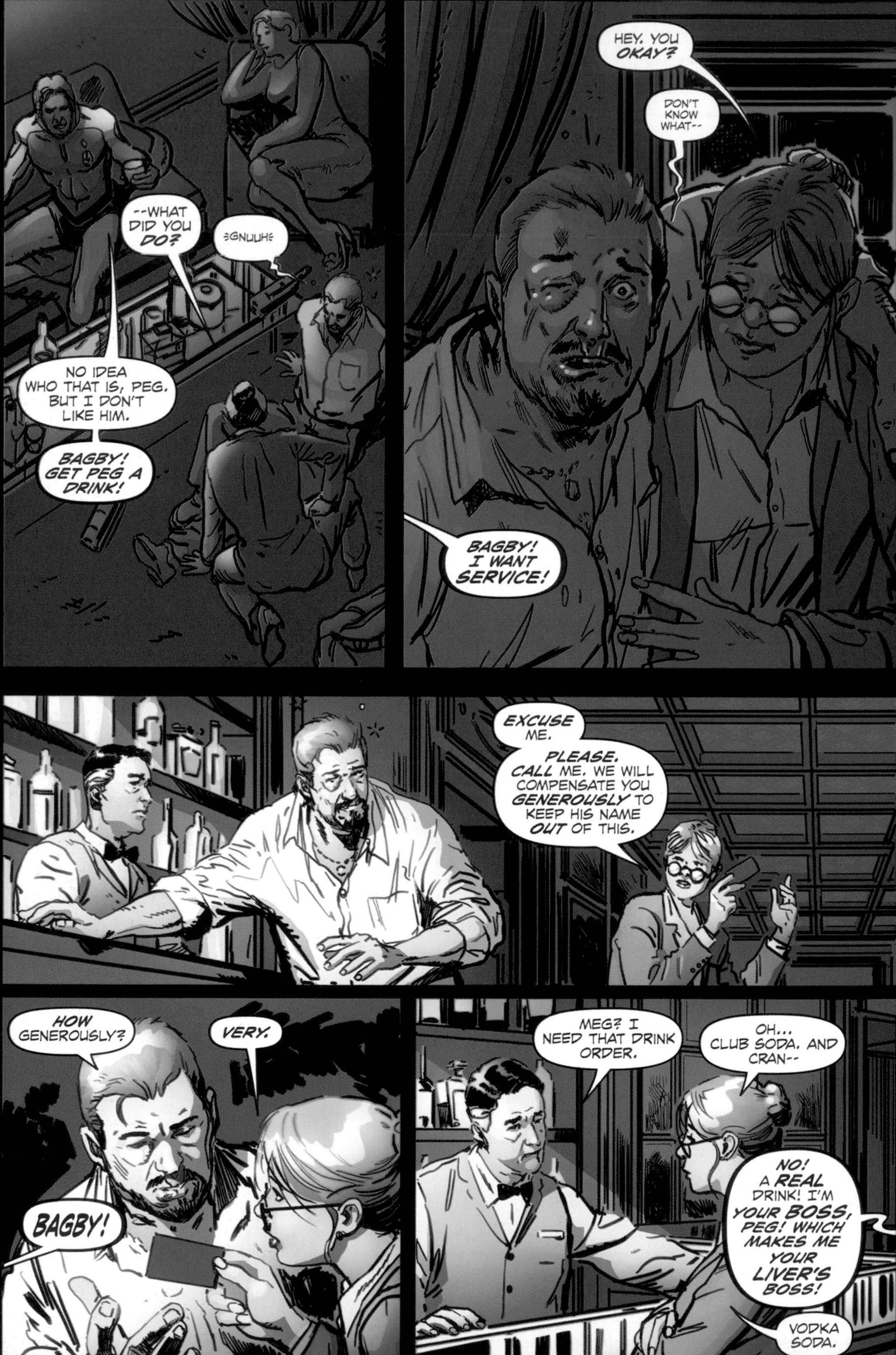
--WHAT DID YOU DO?
≡GNUUH≡
NO IDEA WHO THAT IS, PEG. BUT I DON'T LIKE HIM.
BAGBY! GET PEG A DRINK!
HEY. YOU OKAY?
DON'T KNOW WHAT--
BAGBY! I WANT SERVICE!
EXCUSE ME.
PLEASE. CALL ME. WE WILL COMPENSATE YOU GENEROUSLY TO KEEP HIS NAME OUT OF THIS.
HOW GENEROUSLY?
VERY.
BAGBY!
MEG? I NEED THAT DRINK ORDER.
OH... CLUB SODA. AND CRAN--
NO! A REAL DRINK! I'M YOUR BOSS, PEG! WHICH MAKES ME YOUR LIVER'S BOSS!
VODKA SODA.

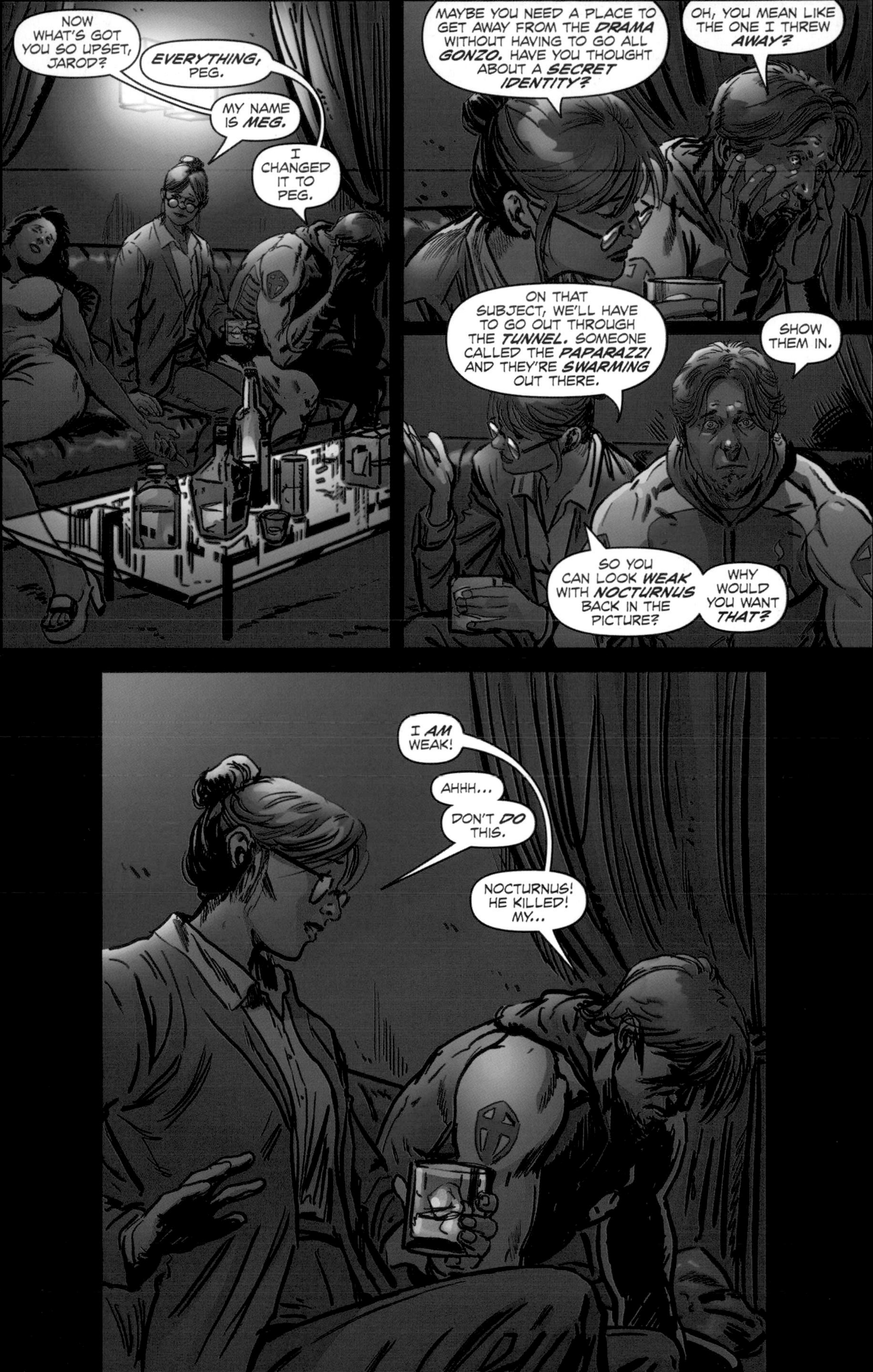
NOW WHAT'S GOT YOU SO UPSET, JAROD?
EVERYTHING, PEG.
MY NAME IS MEG.
I CHANGED IT TO PEG.
MAYBE YOU NEED A PLACE TO GET AWAY FROM THE DRAMA WITHOUT HAVING TO GO ALL GONZO. HAVE YOU THOUGHT ABOUT A SECRET IDENTITY?
OH, YOU MEAN LIKE THE ONE I THREW AWAY?
ON THAT SUBJECT, WE'LL HAVE TO GO OUT THROUGH THE TUNNEL. SOMEONE CALLED THE PAPARAZZI AND THEY'RE SWARMING OUT THERE.
SHOW THEM IN.
WHY WOULD YOU WANT THAT?
SO YOU CAN LOOK WEAK WITH NOCTURNUS BACK IN THE PICTURE?
I AM WEAK!
AHHH...
DON'T DO THIS.
NOCTURNUS! HE KILLED! MY...

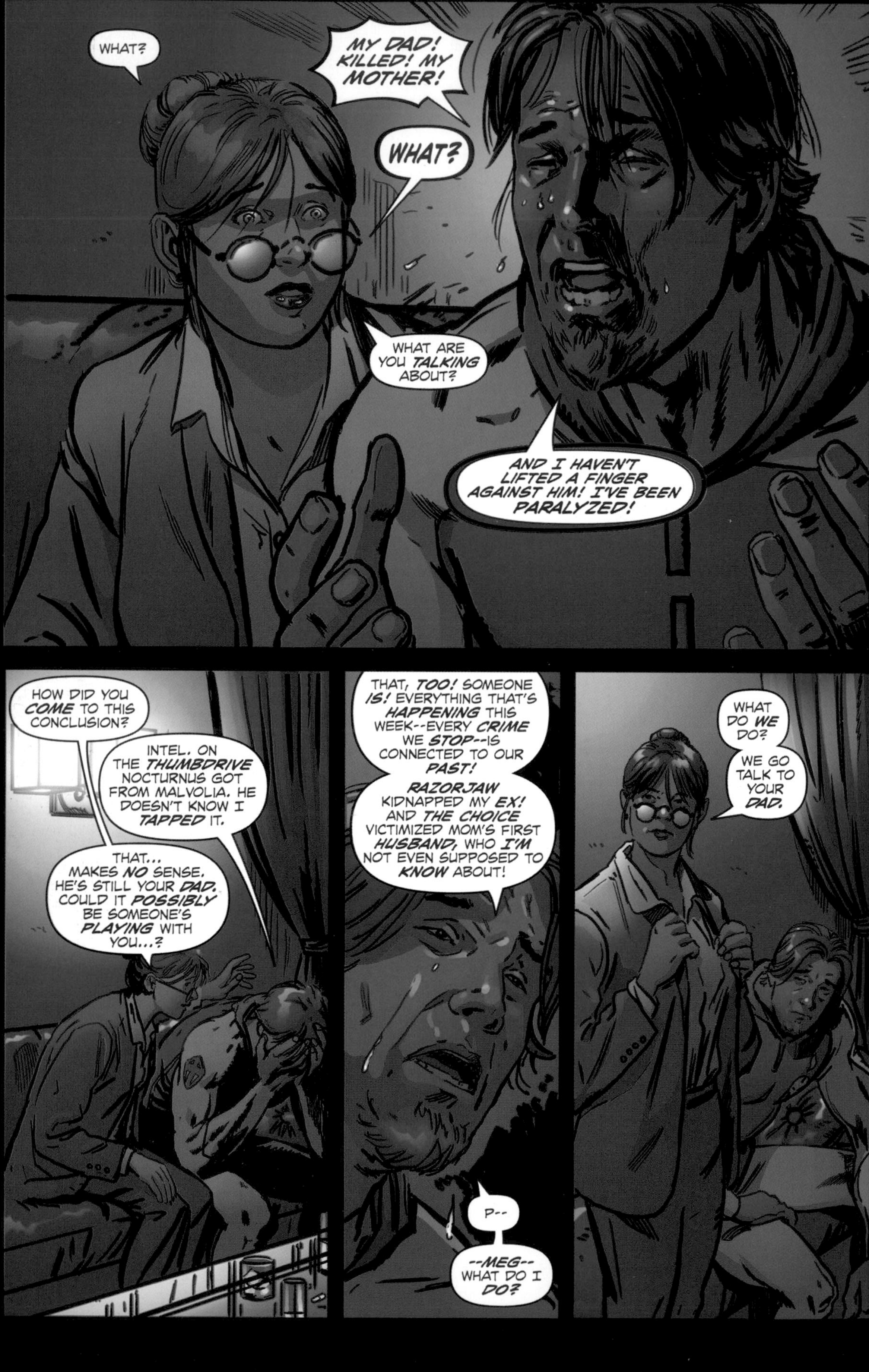
WHAT?
MY DAD! KILLED! MY MOTHER!
WHAT?
WHAT ARE YOU TALKING ABOUT?
AND I HAVEN'T LIFTED A FINGER AGAINST HIM! I'VE BEEN PARALYZED!
HOW DID YOU COME TO THIS CONCLUSION?
INTEL. ON THE THUMBDRIVE NOCTURNUS GOT FROM MALVOLIA. HE DOESN'T KNOW I TAPPED IT.
THAT... MAKES NO SENSE. HE'S STILL YOUR DAD. COULD IT POSSIBLY BE SOMEONE'S PLAYING WITH YOU...?
THAT, TOO! SOMEONE IS! EVERYTHING THAT'S HAPPENING THIS WEEK--EVERY CRIME WE STOP--IS CONNECTED TO OUR PAST!
RAZORJAW KIDNAPPED MY EX! AND THE CHOICE VICTIMIZED MOM'S FIRST HUSBAND, WHO I'M NOT EVEN SUPPOSED TO KNOW ABOUT!
P--
--MEG-- WHAT DO I DO?
WHAT DO WE DO?
WE GO TALK TO YOUR DAD.

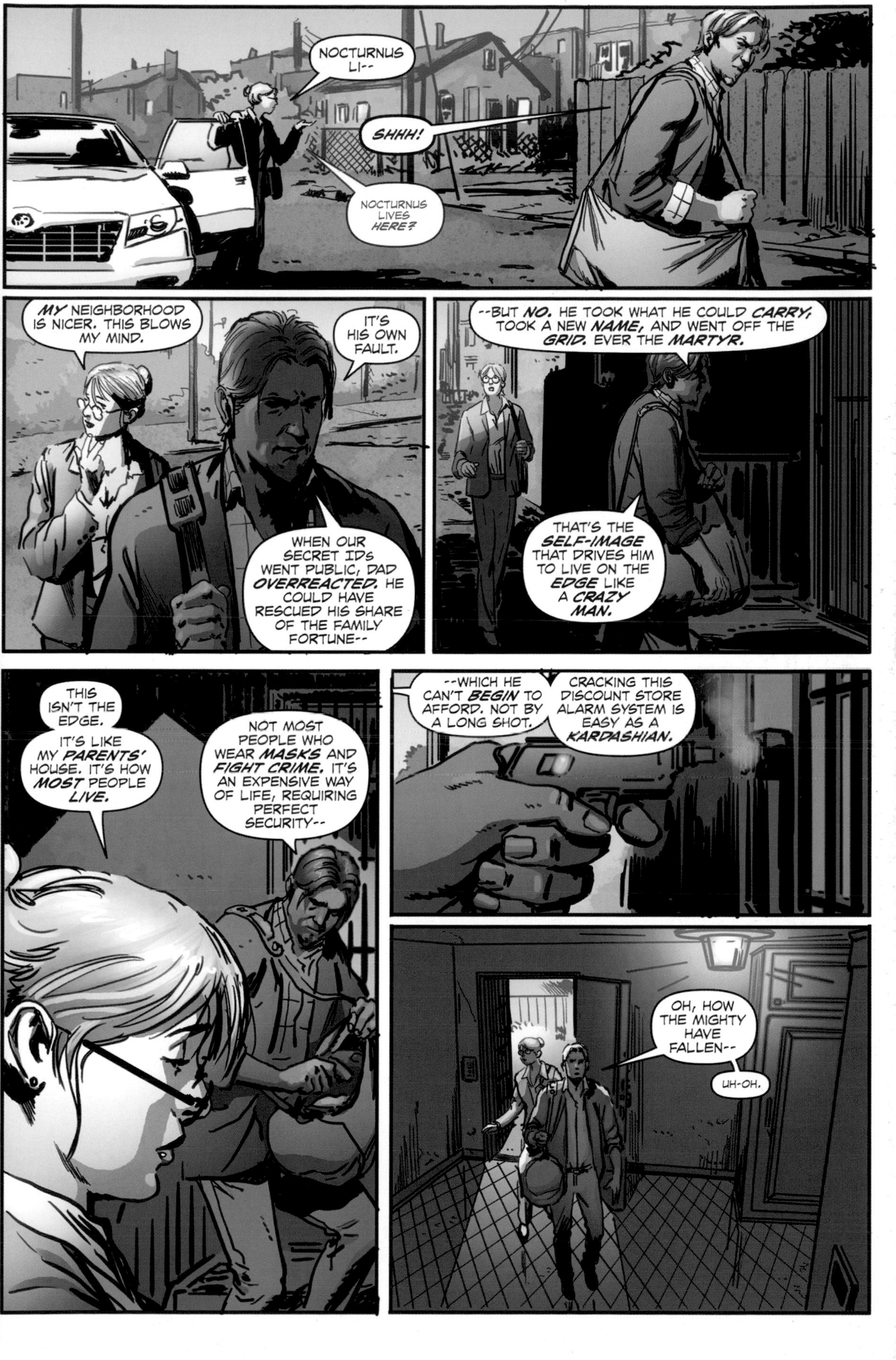
NOCTURNUS LI--
SHHH!
NOCTURNUS LIVES HERE?
MY NEIGHBORHOOD IS NICER. THIS BLOWS MY MIND.
IT'S HIS OWN FAULT.
WHEN OUR SECRET IDs WENT PUBLIC, DAD OVERREACTED. HE COULD HAVE RESCUED HIS SHARE OF THE FAMILY FORTUNE--
--BUT NO. HE TOOK WHAT HE COULD CARRY, TOOK A NEW NAME, AND WENT OFF THE GRID. EVER THE MARTYR.
THAT'S THE SELF-IMAGE THAT DRIVES HIM TO LIVE ON THE EDGE LIKE A CRAZY MAN.
THIS ISN'T THE EDGE.
IT'S LIKE MY PARENTS' HOUSE. IT'S HOW MOST PEOPLE LIVE.
NOT MOST PEOPLE WHO WEAR MASKS AND FIGHT CRIME. IT'S AN EXPENSIVE WAY OF LIFE, REQUIRING PERFECT SECURITY--
--WHICH HE CAN'T BEGIN TO AFFORD. NOT BY A LONG SHOT.
CRACKING THIS DISCOUNT STORE ALARM SYSTEM IS EASY AS A KARDASHIAN.
OH, HOW THE MIGHTY HAVE FALLEN--
UH-OH.

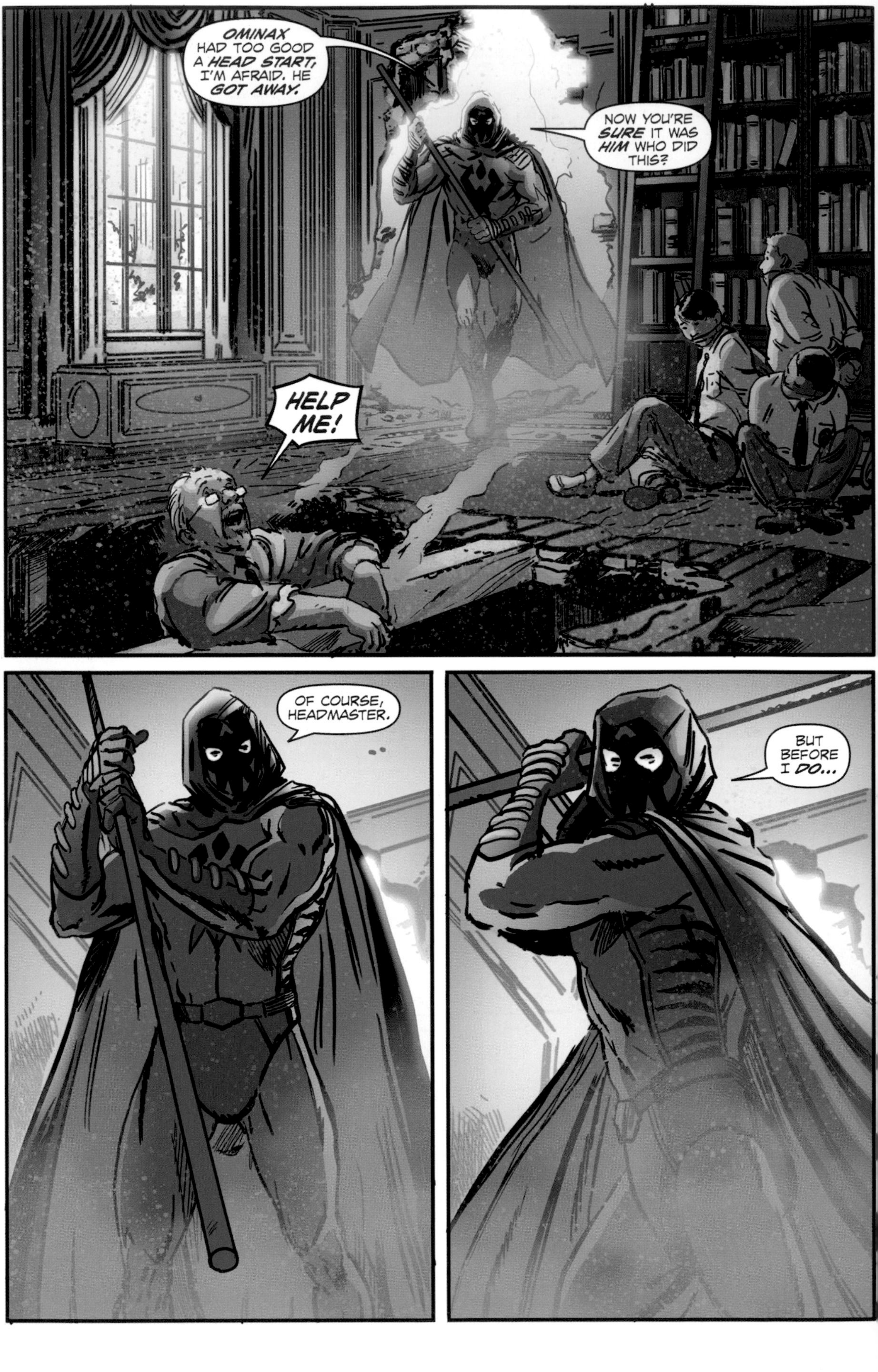
OMINAX HAD TOO GOOD A HEAD START, I'M AFRAID. HE GOT AWAY.
NOW YOU'RE SURE IT WAS HIM WHO DID THIS?
HELP ME!
OF COURSE, HEADMASTER.
BUT BEFORE I DO...

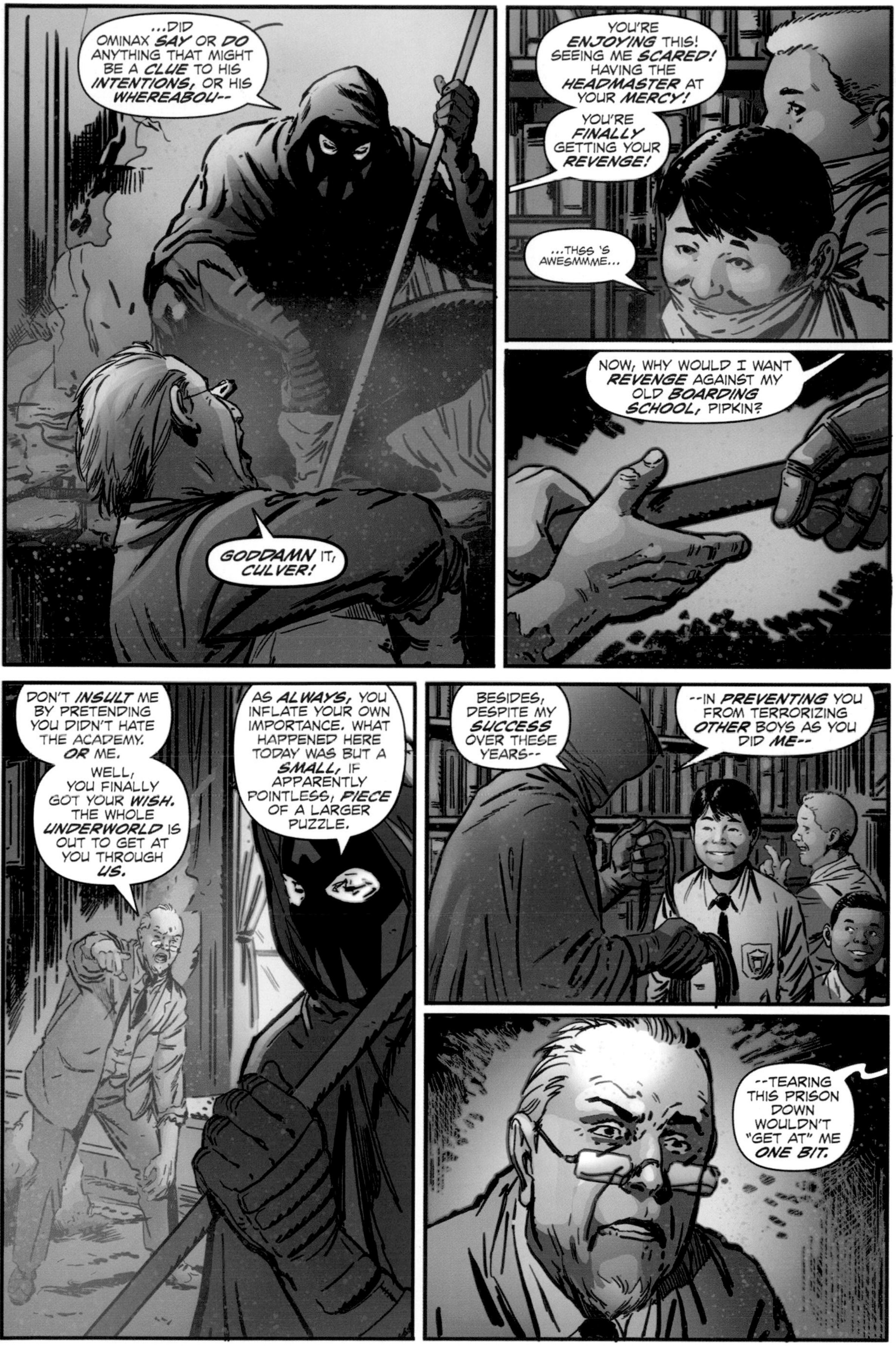
...DID OMINAX SAY OR DO ANYTHING THAT MIGHT BE A CLUE TO HIS INTENTIONS, OR HIS WHEREABOU--
GODDAMN IT, CULVER!
YOU'RE ENJOYING THIS! SEEING ME SCARED! HAVING THE HEADMASTER AT YOUR MERCY!
YOU'RE FINALLY GETTING YOUR REVENGE!
...THSS 'S AWESMMME...
NOW, WHY WOULD I WANT REVENGE AGAINST MY OLD BOARDING SCHOOL, PIPKIN?
DON'T INSULT ME BY PRETENDING YOU DIDN'T HATE THE ACADEMY. OR ME.
WELL, YOU FINALLY GOT YOUR WISH. THE WHOLE UNDERWORLD IS OUT TO GET AT YOU THROUGH US.
AS ALWAYS, YOU INFLATE YOUR OWN IMPORTANCE. WHAT HAPPENED HERE TODAY WAS BUT A SMALL, IF APPARENTLY POINTLESS, PIECE OF A LARGER PUZZLE.
BESIDES, DESPITE MY SUCCESS OVER THESE YEARS--
--IN PREVENTING YOU FROM TERRORIZING OTHER BOYS AS YOU DID ME--
--TEARING THIS PRISON DOWN WOULDN'T "GET AT" ME ONE BIT.

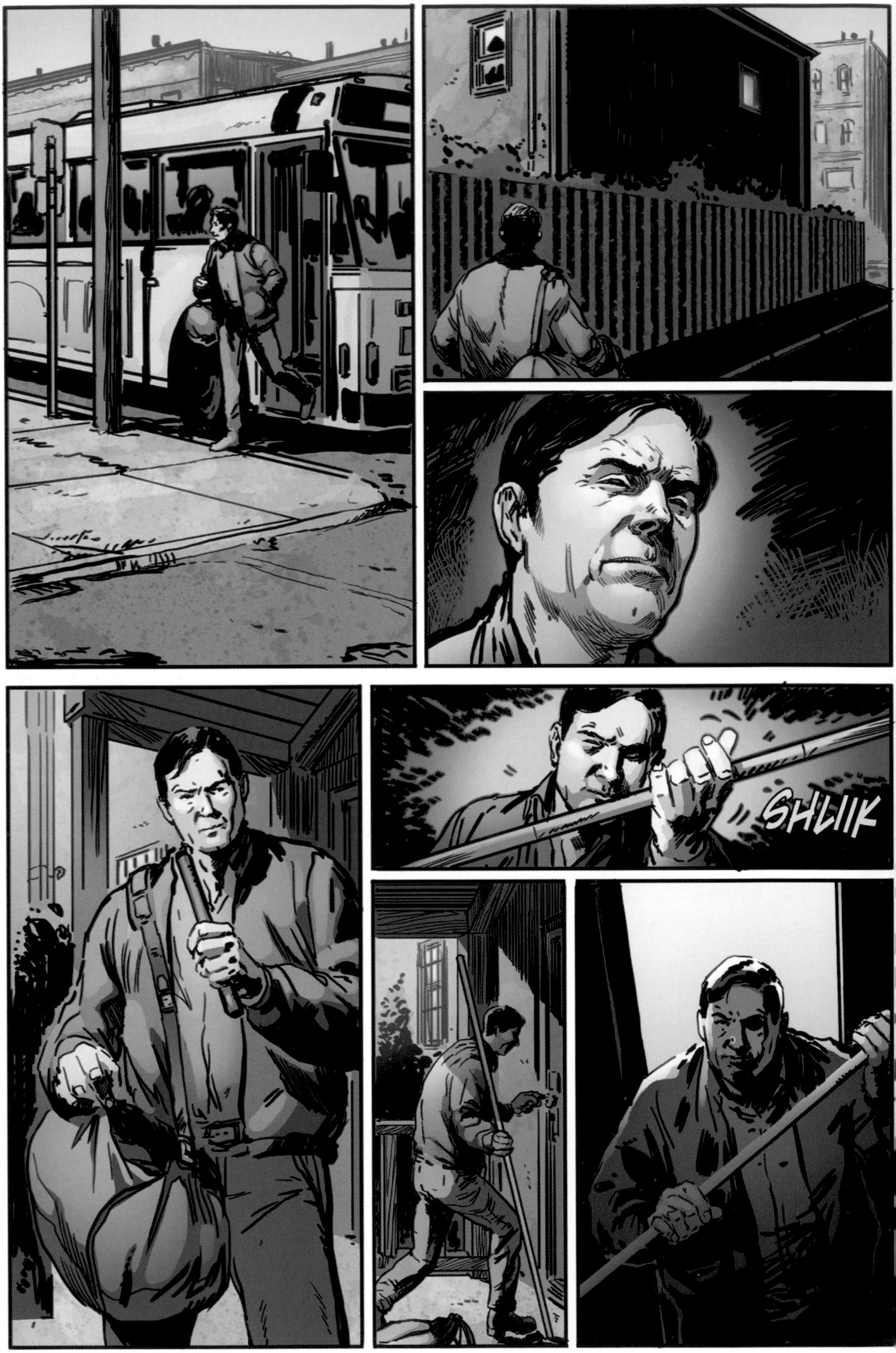
SHLIIK

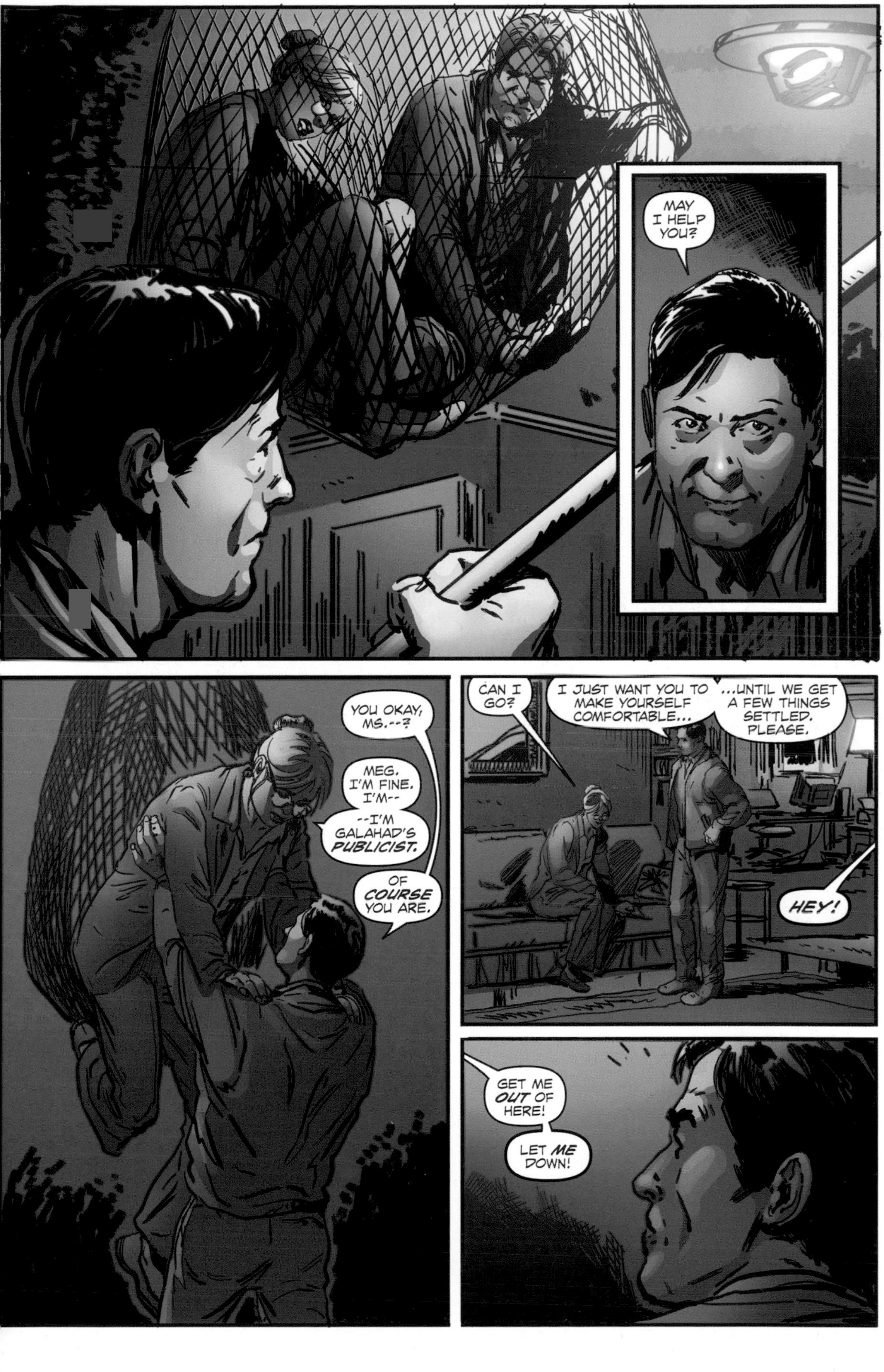
MAY I HELP YOU?
YOU OKAY, MS.--?
MEG. I'M FINE. I'M--
--I'M GALAHAD'S PUBLICIST.
OF COURSE YOU ARE.
CAN I GO?
I JUST WANT YOU TO MAKE YOURSELF COMFORTABLE...
...UNTIL WE GET A FEW THINGS SETTLED. PLEASE.
HEY!
GET ME OUT OF HERE!
LET ME DOWN!

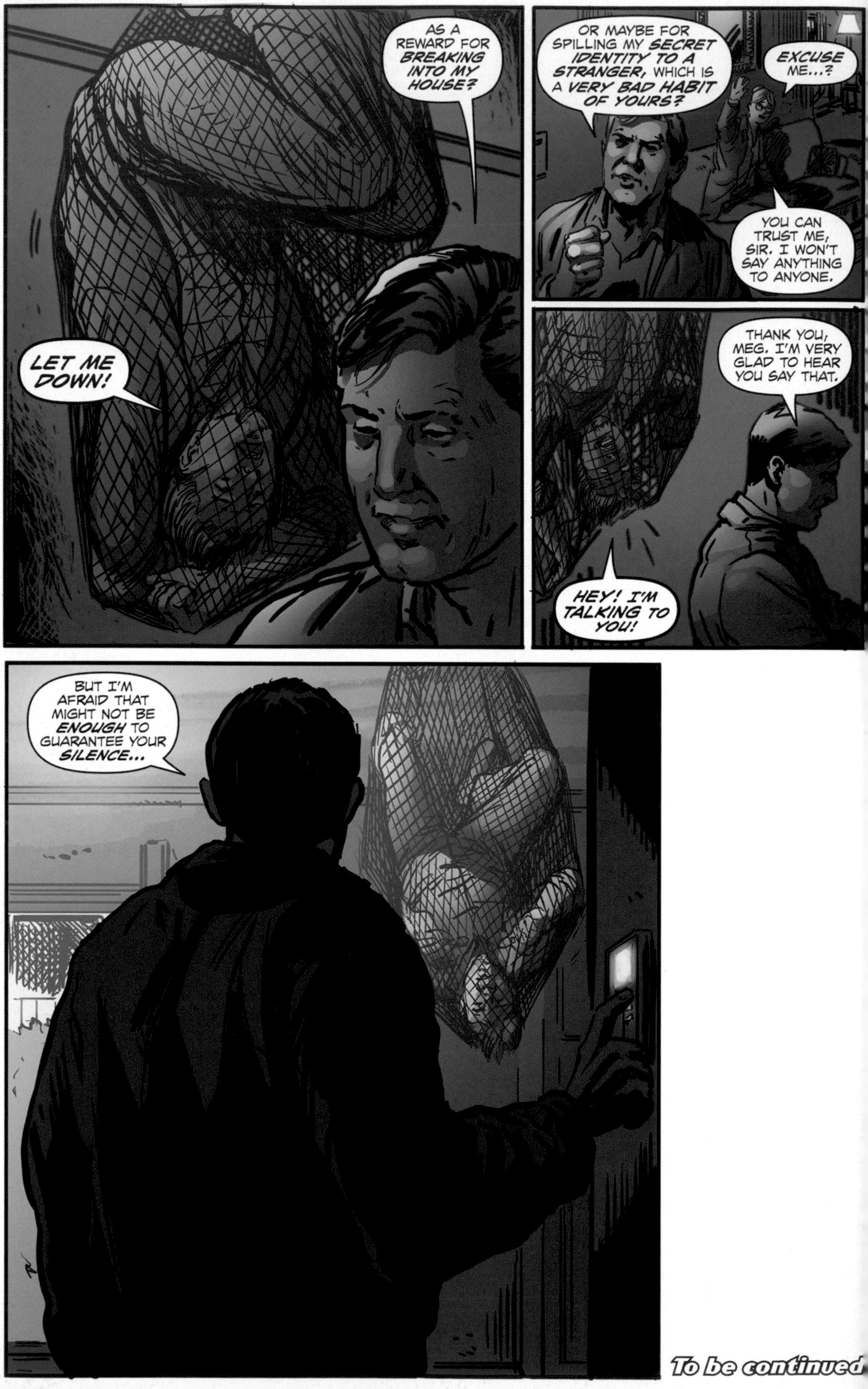
AS A REWARD FOR BREAKING INTO MY HOUSE?
LET ME DOWN!
OR MAYBE FOR SPILLING MY SECRET IDENTITY TO A STRANGER, WHICH IS A VERY BAD HABIT OF YOURS?
EXCUSE ME...?
YOU CAN TRUST ME, SIR. I WON'T SAY ANYTHING TO ANYONE.
THANK YOU, MEG. I'M VERY GLAD TO HEAR YOU SAY THAT.
HEY! I'M TALKING TO YOU!
BUT I'M AFRAID THAT MIGHT NOT BE ENOUGH TO GUARANTEE YOUR SILENCE...
To be continued

ARTWORK BY
RON SALAS

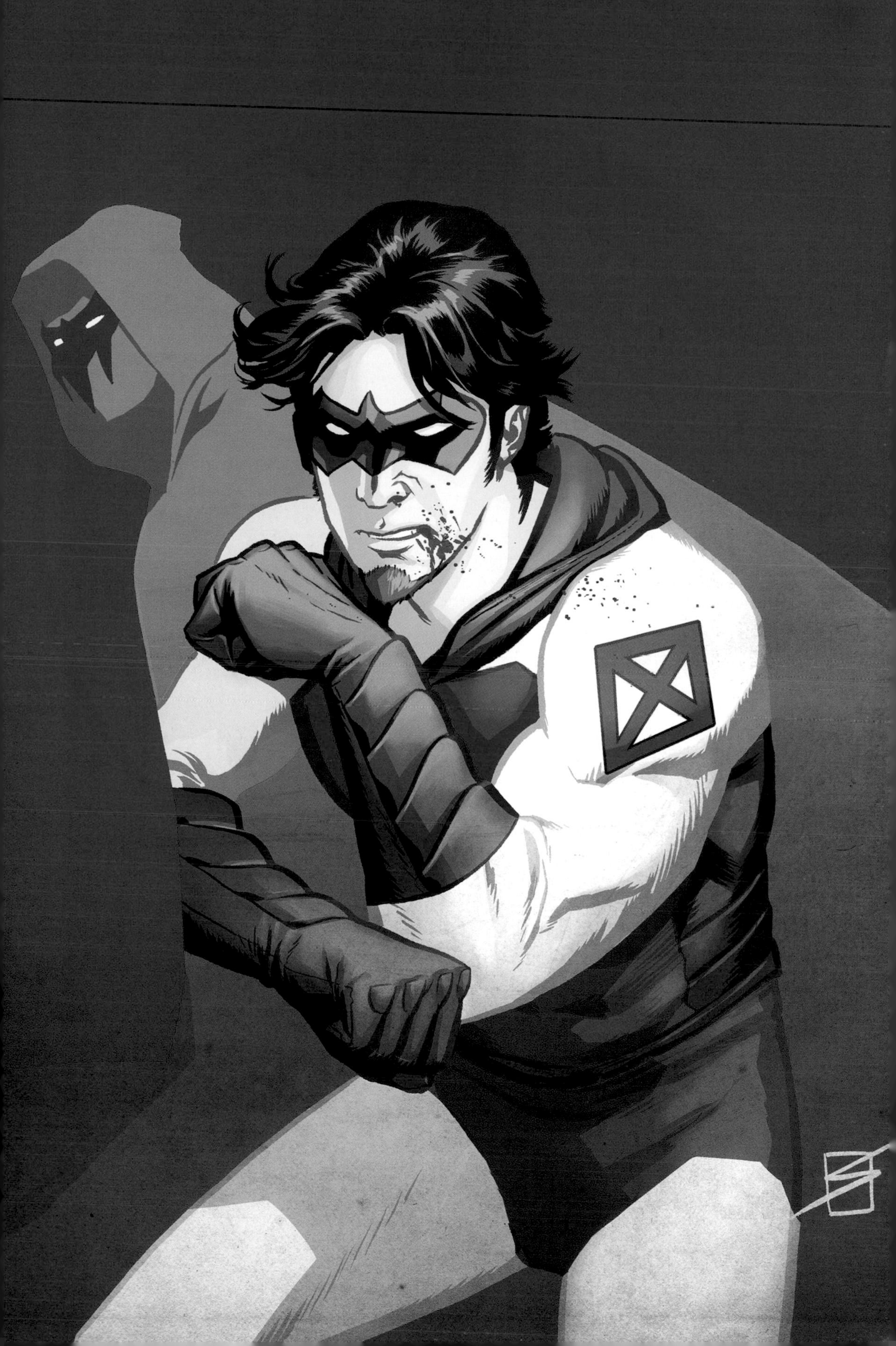

ART GALLERY

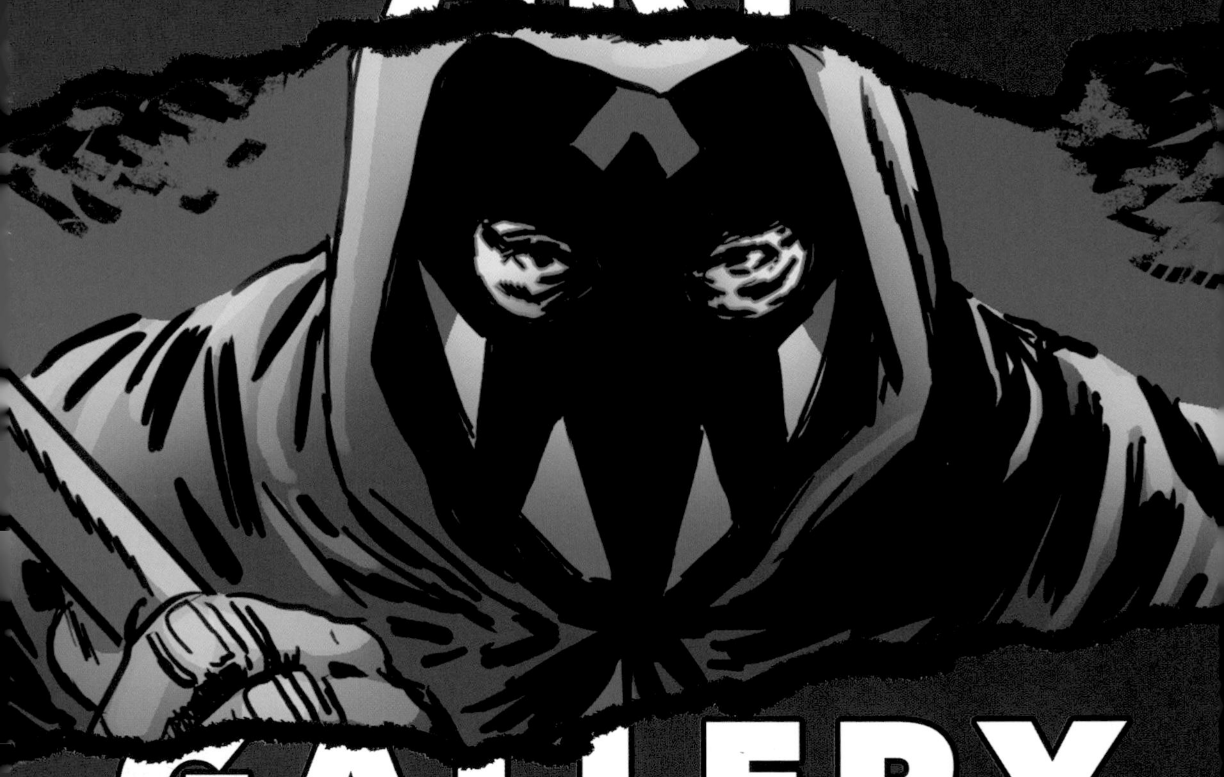

ARTWORK BY
PETER KRAUSE

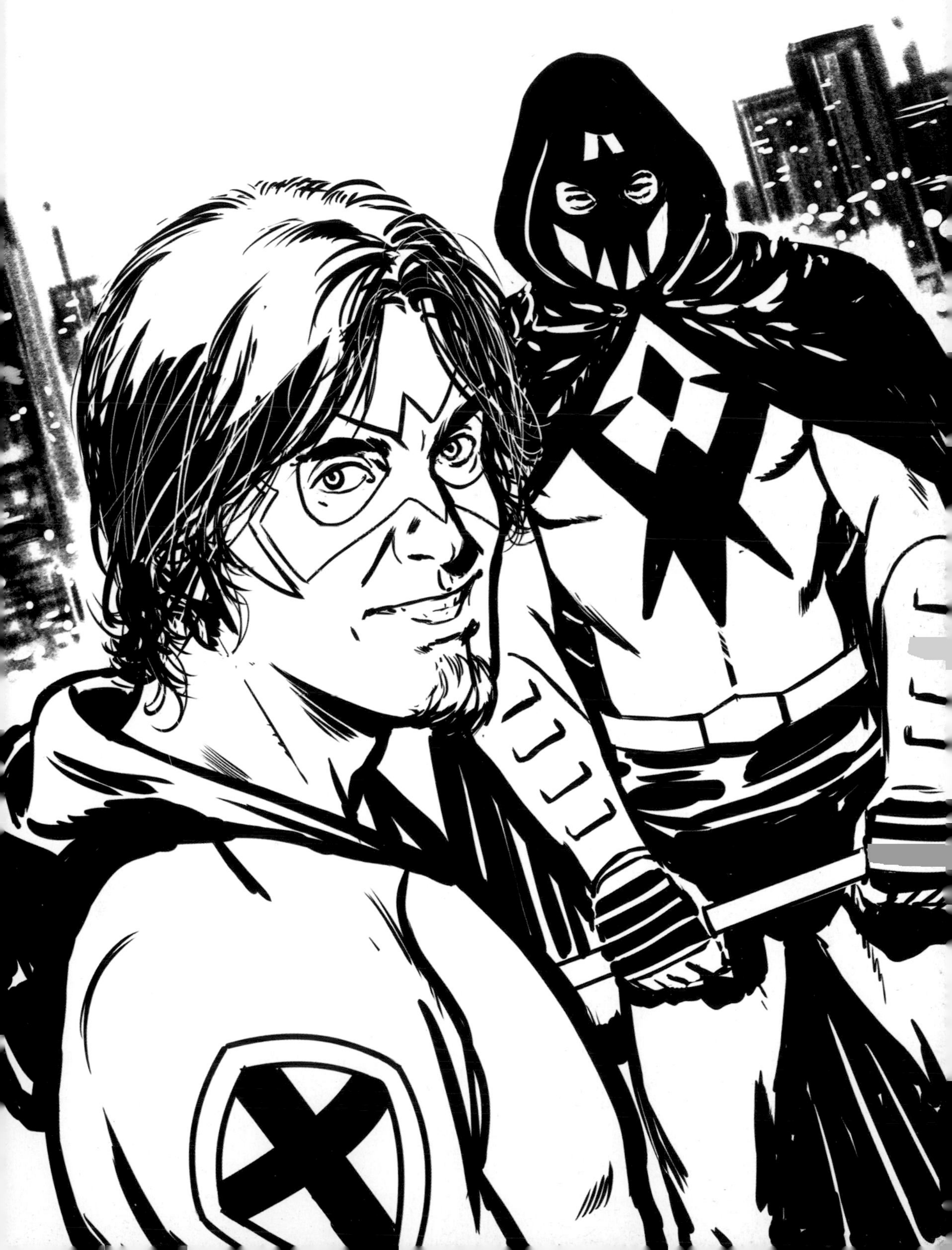

In the summer of 1974, Marvel Comics publisher Martin Goodman—by all accounts, a grandmaster at the game of cutting costs—tried a gambit that was at once fiendishly clever and ethically deplorable. Art pages, then and largely still, were drawn about one-and-a-half times printed size (so the artists could have room to do detailed line work), then sized down for final printing. Goodman wanted to trim budgets without trimming page counts—so all Marvel artists were ordered that summer to, once per issue, draw two consecutive pages on the same piece of art board, turned sideways, so it could be printed as a two-page spread, same size as drawn (actually, a little larger). Voila. Goodman wrung two pages of art from his freelancers, paid them for only one, and no one knew the difference except any kid with eyes in his head because we were all wondering why there was artwork in the middle of *Captain America* and *Marvel Team-Up* that was jarringly, inexplicably gigantic and sloppy looking.

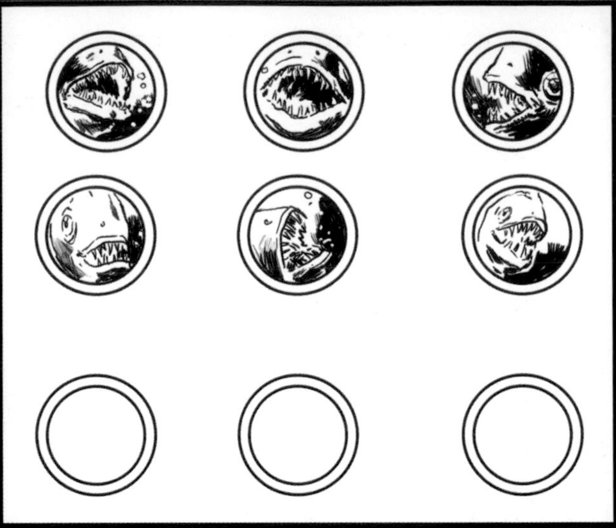

I bring up this little tidbit of comics history because I pulled the same crap on Peter Krause.

As you probably but don't necessarily know, before it's collected into print editions like this one, *Insufferable* runs free in weekly installments on Thrillbent.com. And at about the point where this issue begins, because everyone at Thrillbent Central was prepping for Comic-Con San Diego 2012, we were (read: I was) falling behind schedule. I desperately, desperately needed us to produce a chapter of *Insufferable* that Pete could do extra-quickly. I didn't, however, want to cheat the weekly Thrillbent.com visitors who'd come to expect eight to ten pages a week.

I found the solution using, once more, one of the tools that serves digital comics well and uniquely: the rack focus. This is what Pete drew (this and the piranha above). Compare it to what colorist Nolan Woodard used his wizardry to turn it into.

(To his credit, Pete hasn't started referring to me as "Mr. Goodman." He thought it was clever.)

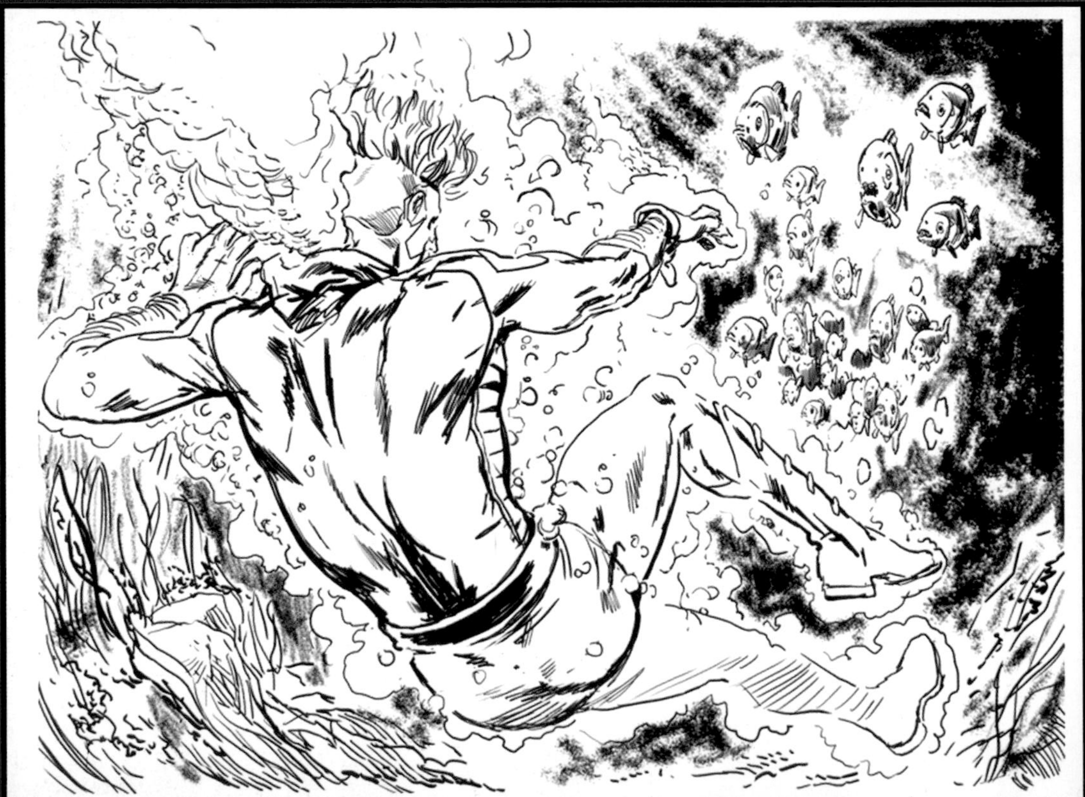

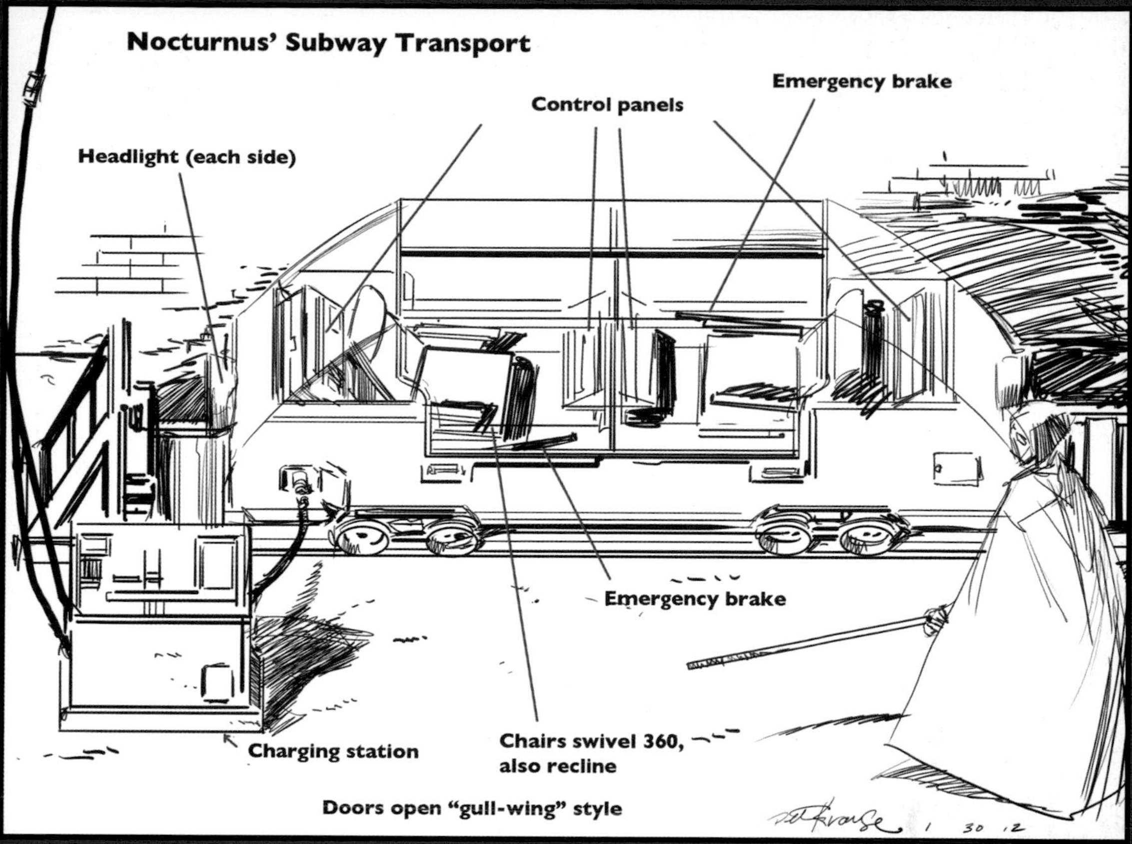
Nocturnus' Subway Transport
Emergency brake
Control panels
Headlight (each side)
Emergency brake
Charging station
Chairs swivel 360, also recline
Doors open "gull-wing" style
1 30 12

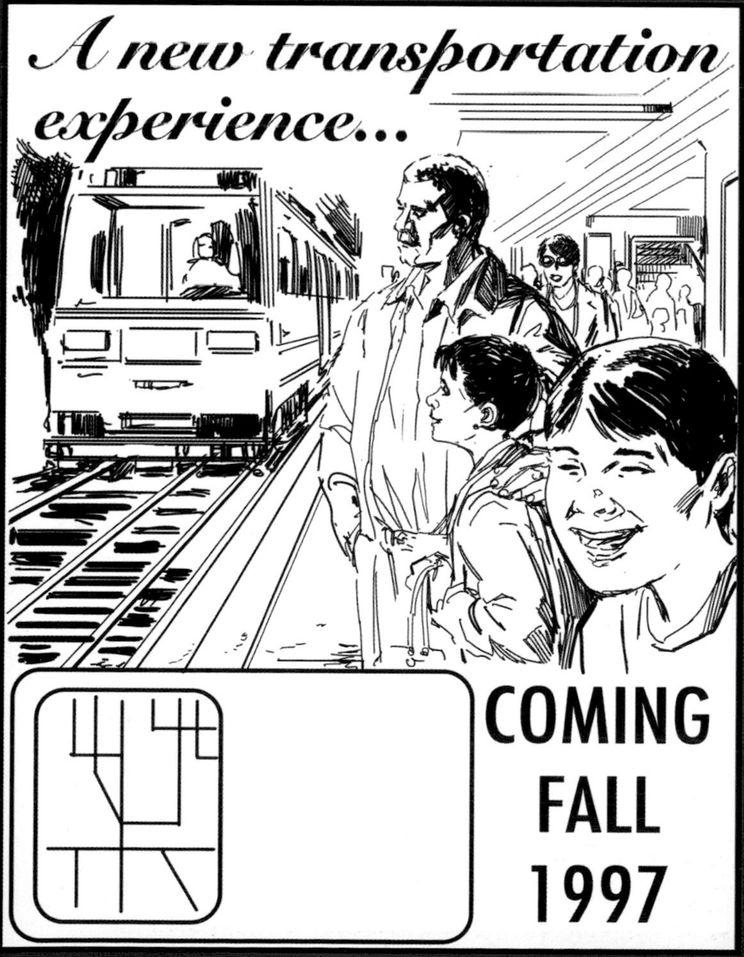
A new transportation experience...
COMING FALL 1997

Unbelievably, *Insufferable* isn't Peter Krause's only full-time job. He takes a lot of advertising and storyboard work on the side, and he is very, very good at designing things.

For example, here's a poster for the (never-completed) St. Barrington subway system, a display piece I'd asked him to whip up so I could, in the end, oh, never actually use it because my idea for the scene changed.

Pete now knows to ask me, "are you sure we're going to use this piece of art?" before he goes to this much trouble. But it's a beauty. Pete excels at capturing ordinary people. If you're some power publisher looking to produce licensed *Mad Men* comics, call Pete.

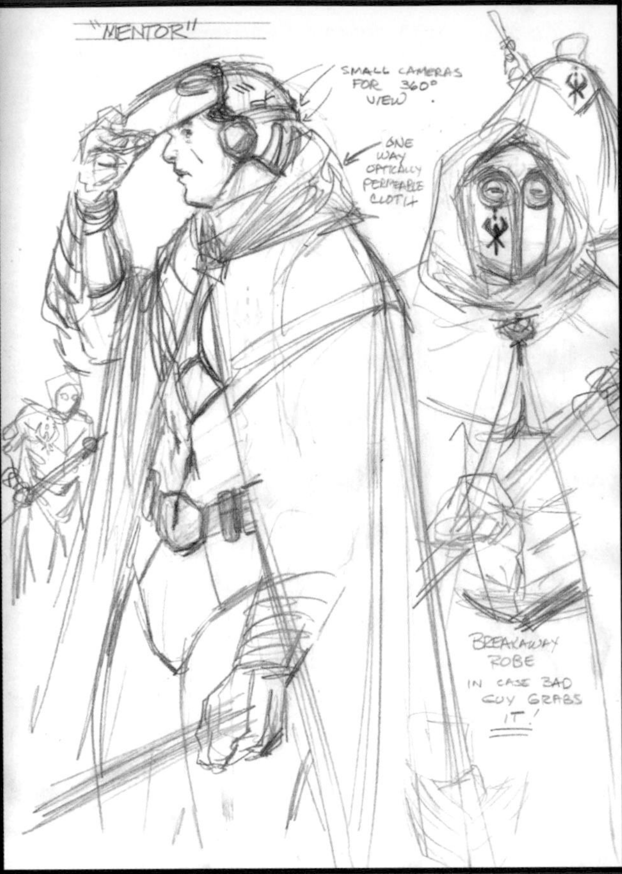
"MENTOR"
SMALL CAMERAS FOR 360° VIEW.
ONE WAY OPTICALLY PERMEABLE CLOTH
BREAKAWAY ROBE IN CASE BAD GUY GRABS IT!

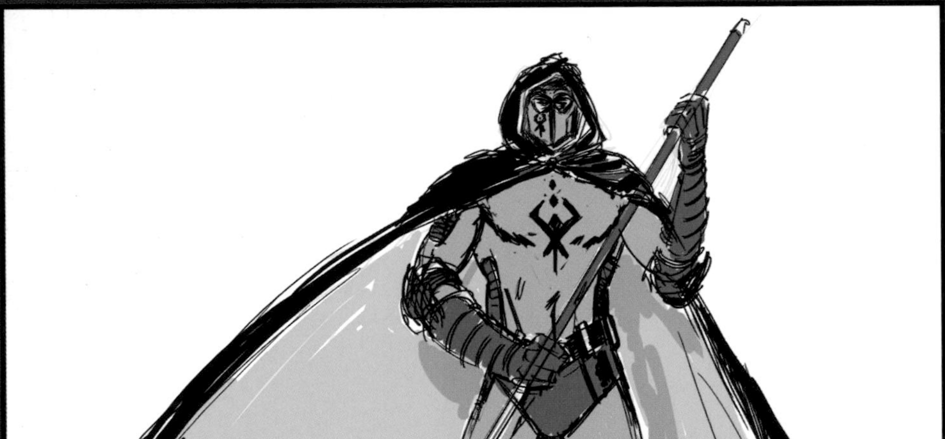

Peter Krause's preliminary sketches and costume designs for Nocturnus and Galahad.

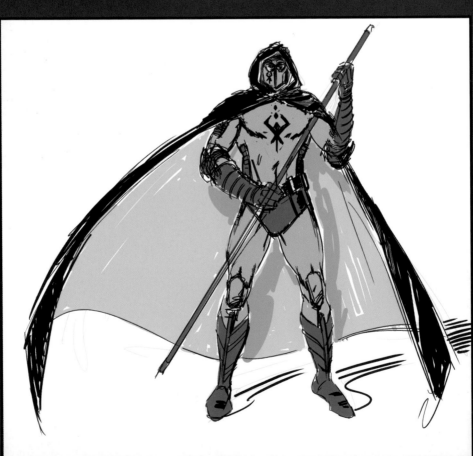

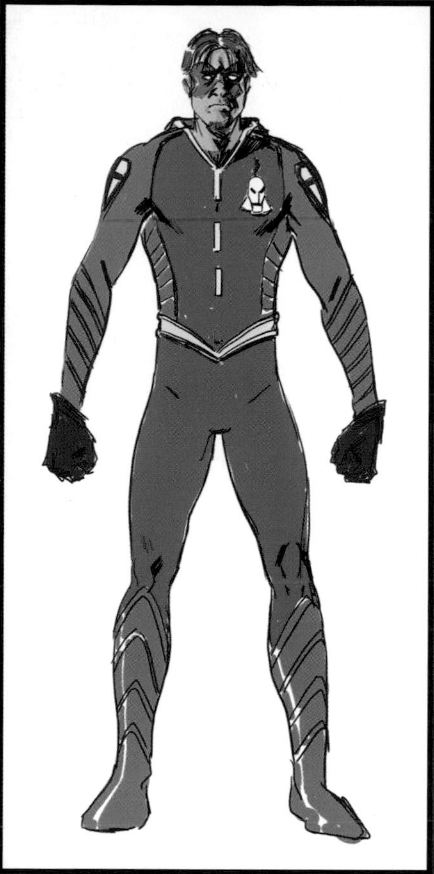

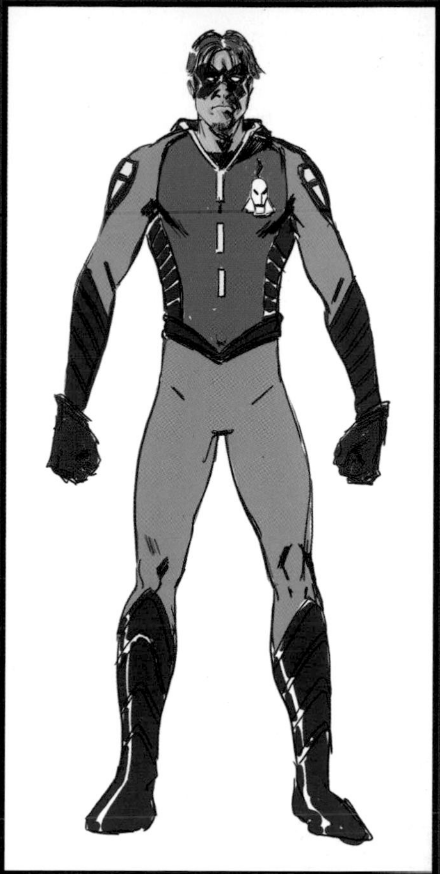

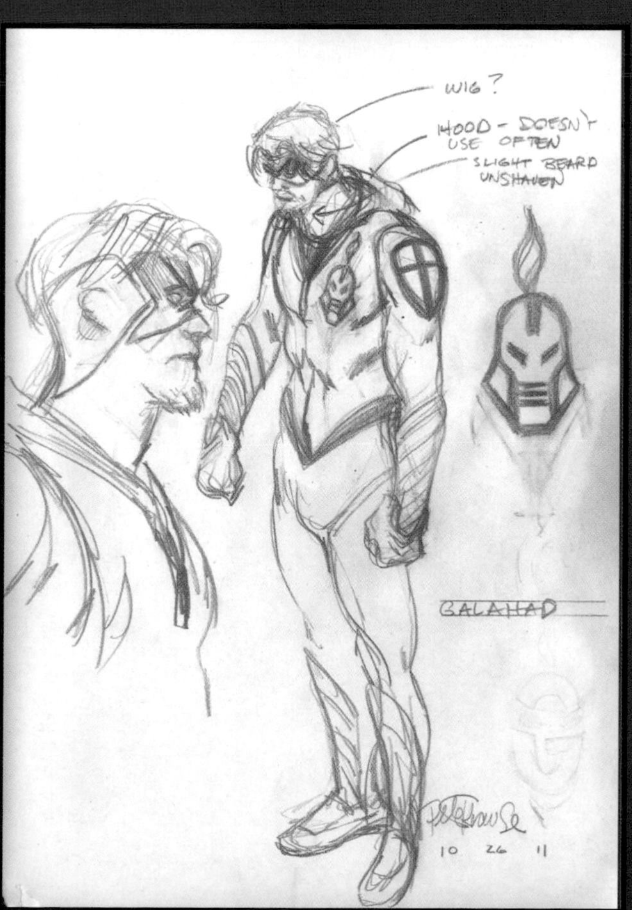
WIG?
HOOD - DOESN'T USE OFTEN
SLIGHT BEARD UNSHAVEN
GALAHAD
10 26 11

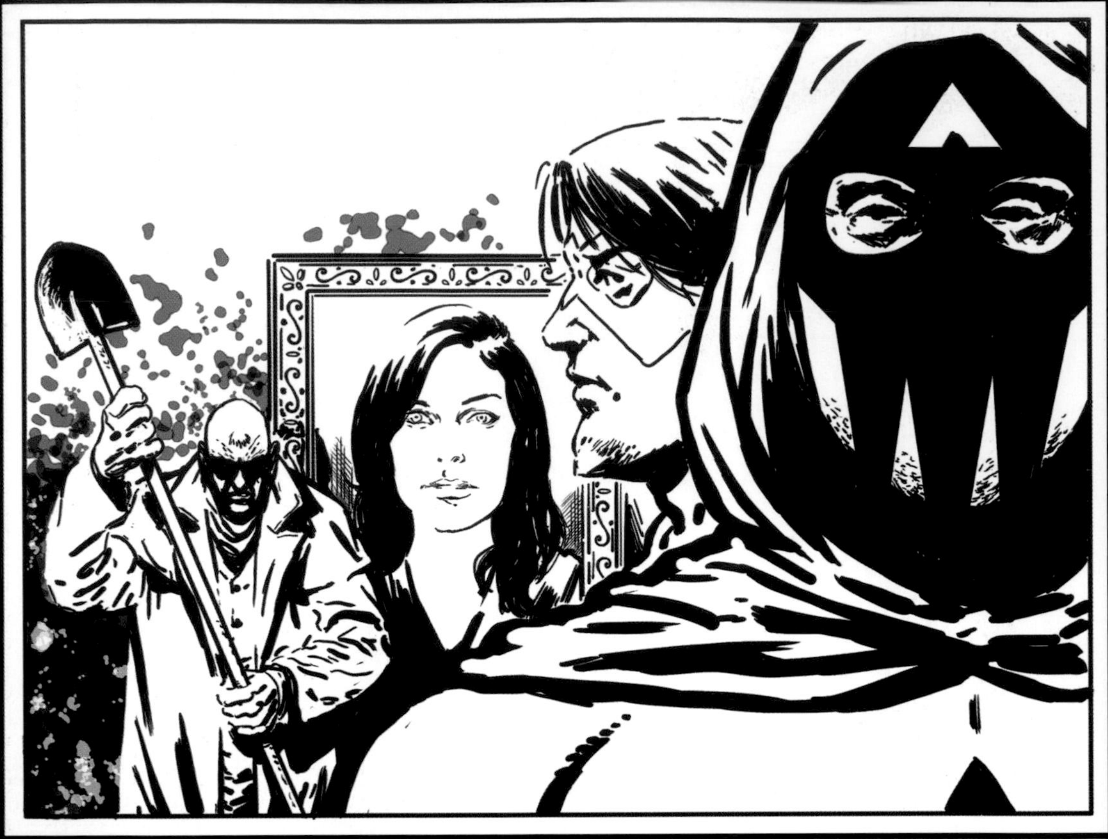

Thrillbent cover for *Insufferable* issues #1-4

Pencils and Inks: Peter Krause

Colors: Nolan Woodard

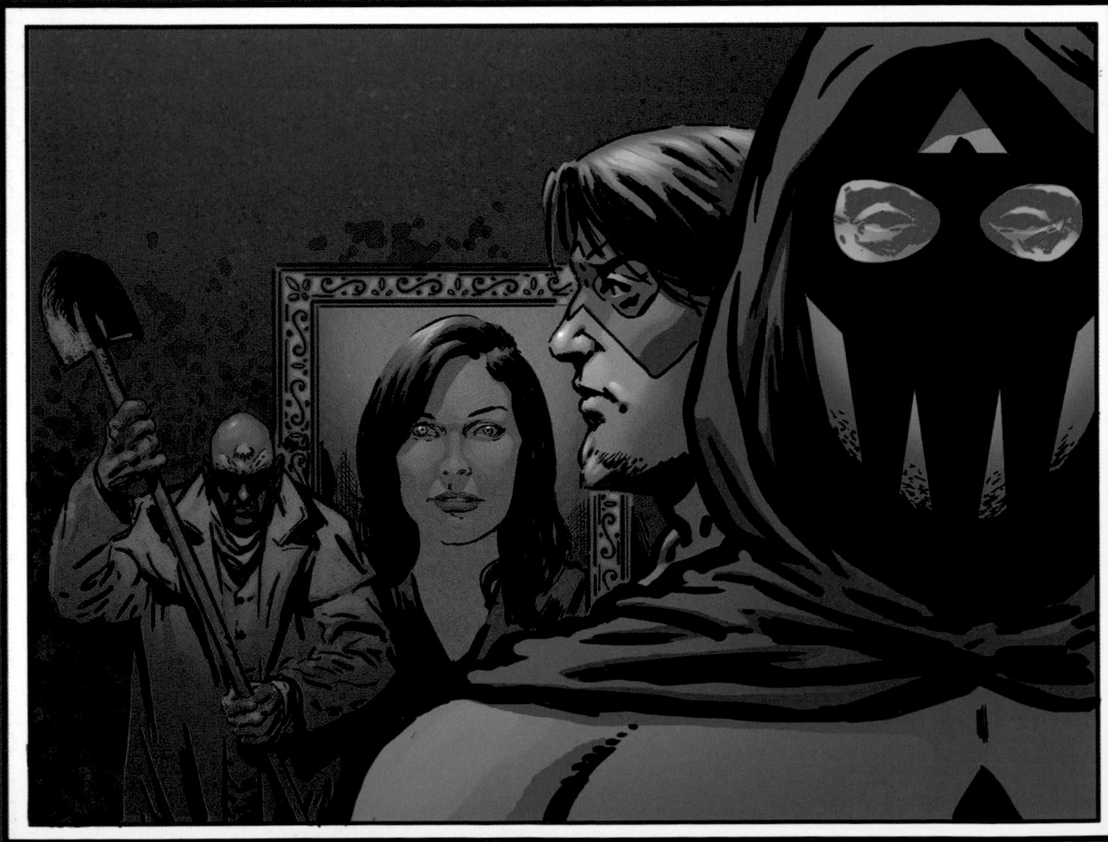

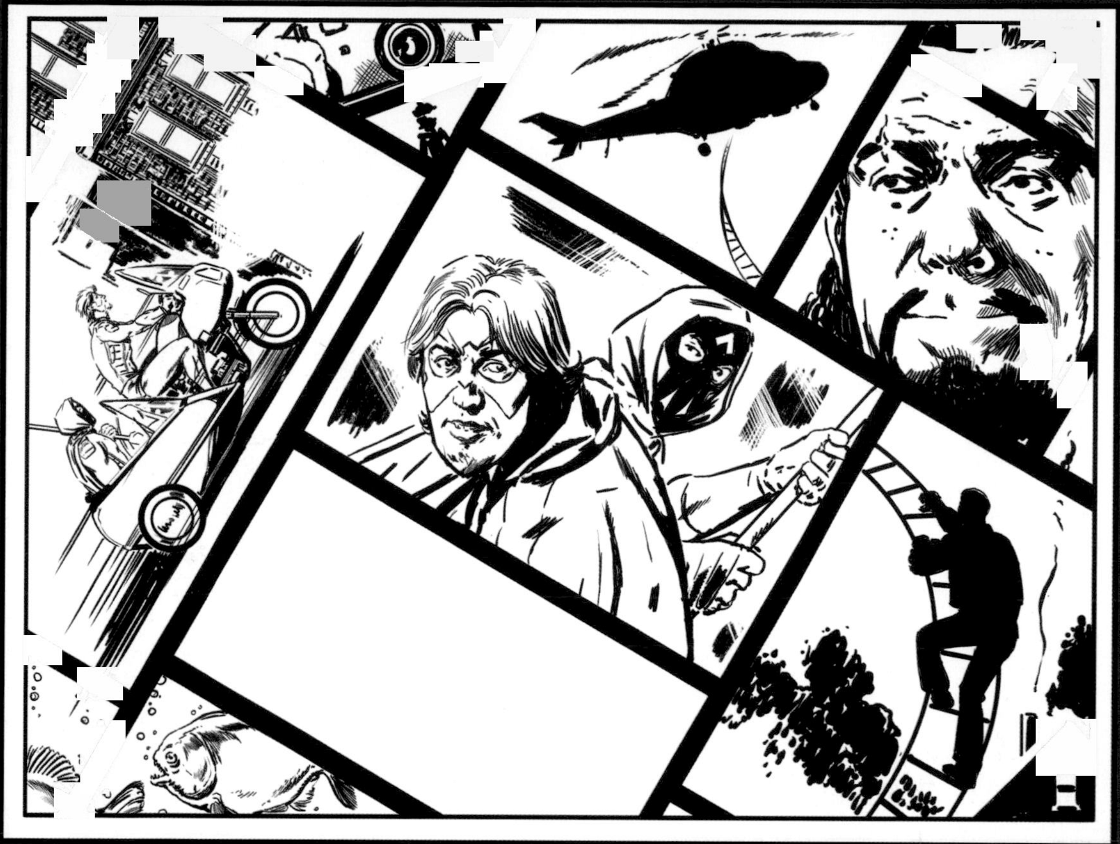

Thrillbent cover for *Insufferable* issues #5–8

Pencils and Inks: Peter Krause

Colors: Nolan Woodard

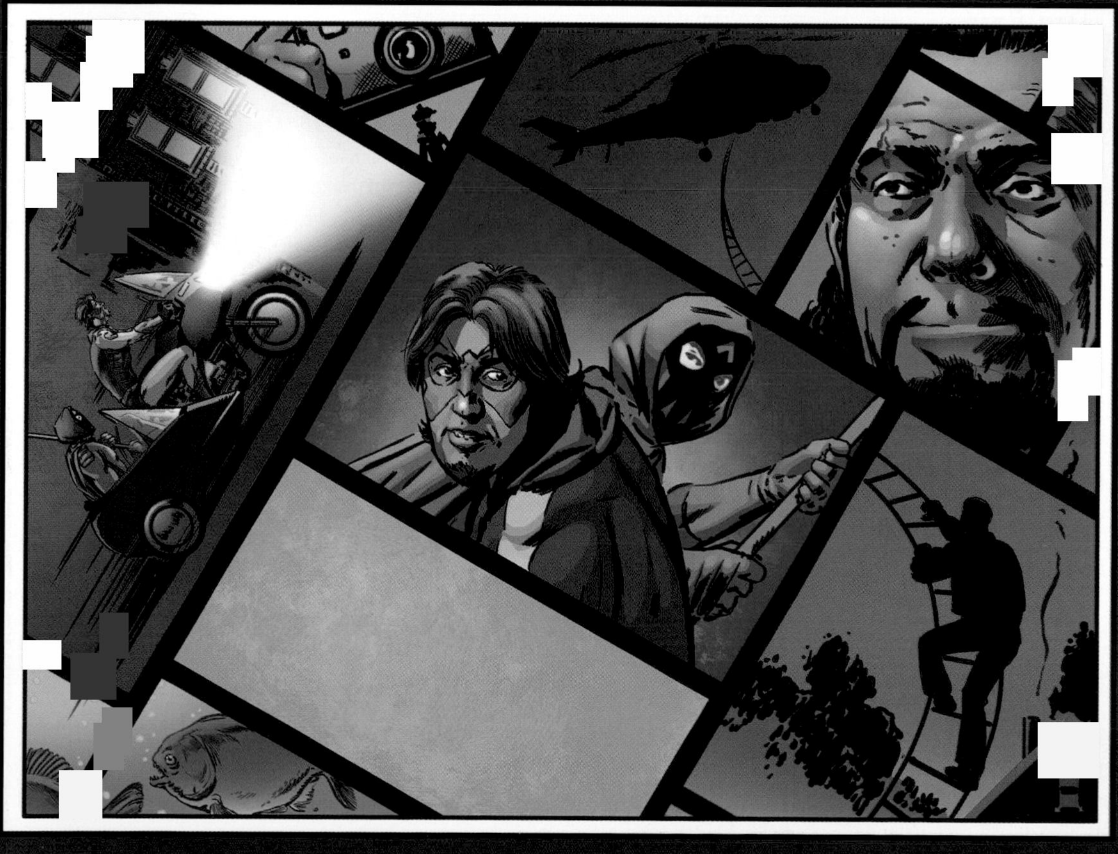

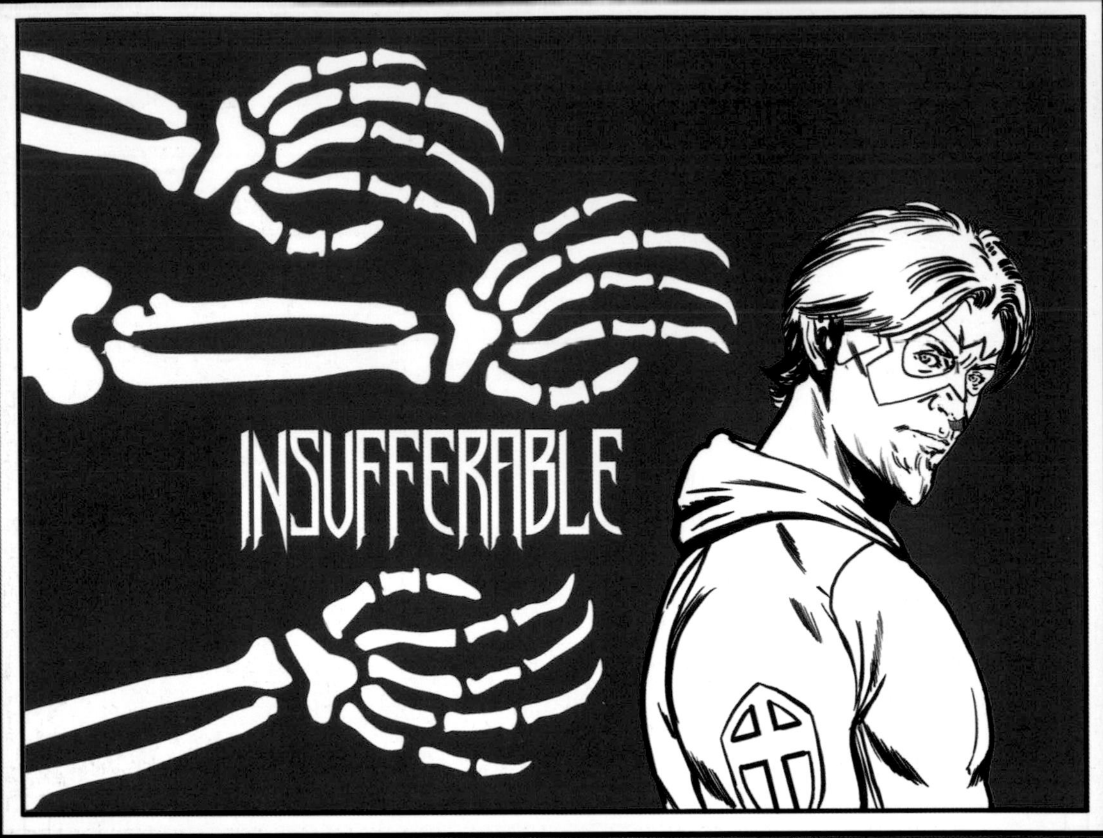
INSUFFERABLE

Thrillbent cover for *Insufferable* issues #9-12

Pencils and Inks: Peter Krause

Colors: Nolan Woodard

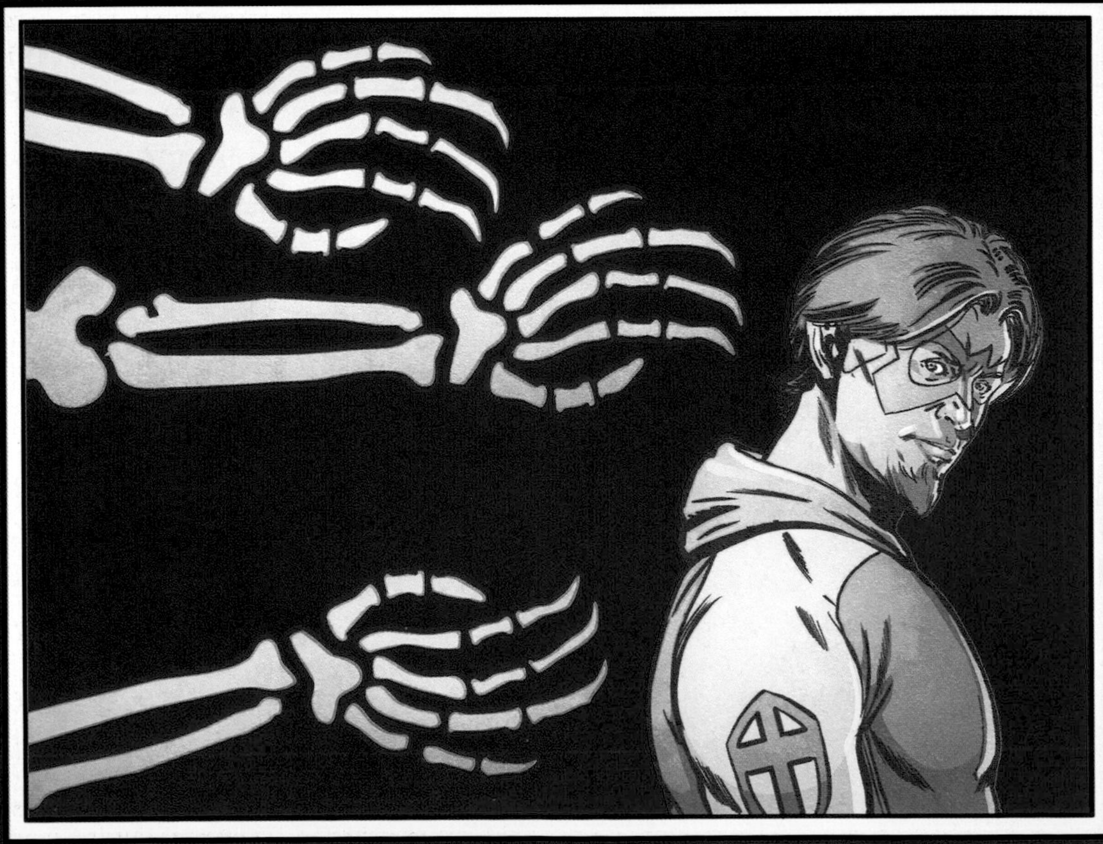

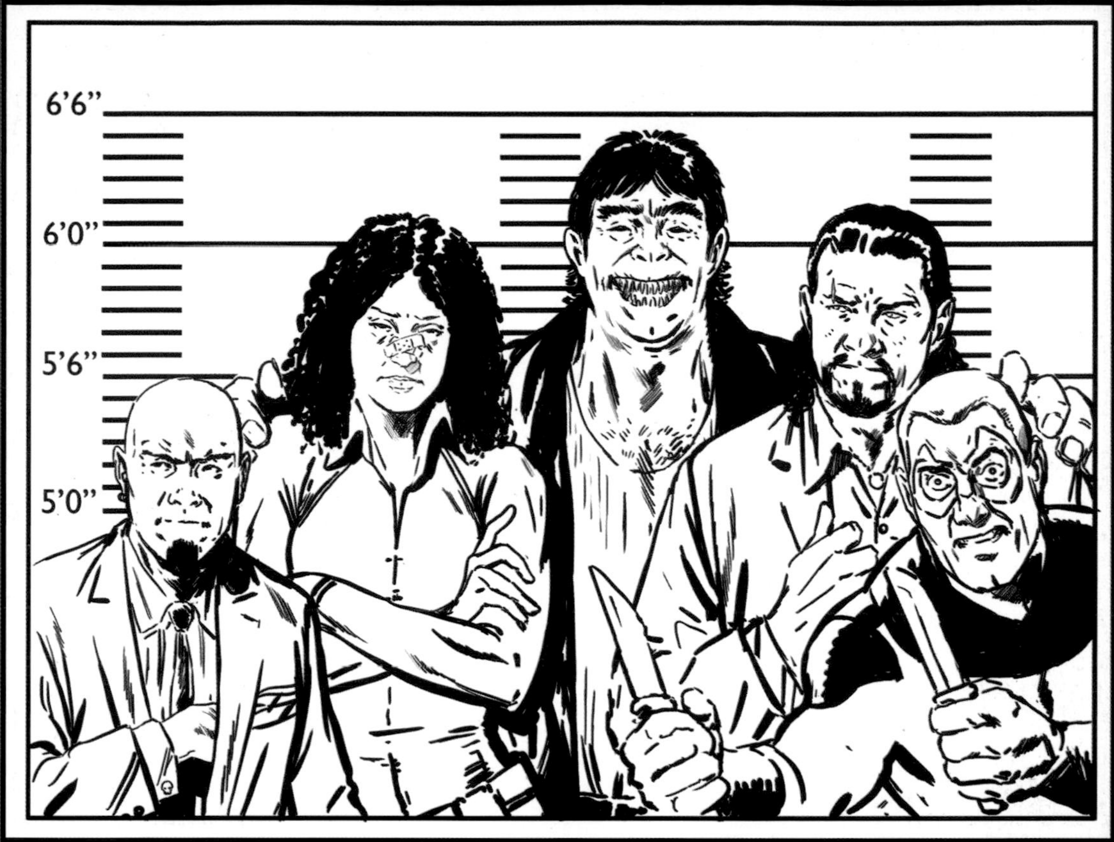

6'6"
6'0"
5'6"
5'0"

Thrillbent cover for *Insufferable* issues #13–16

Pencils and Inks: Peter Krause

Colors: Nolan Woodard

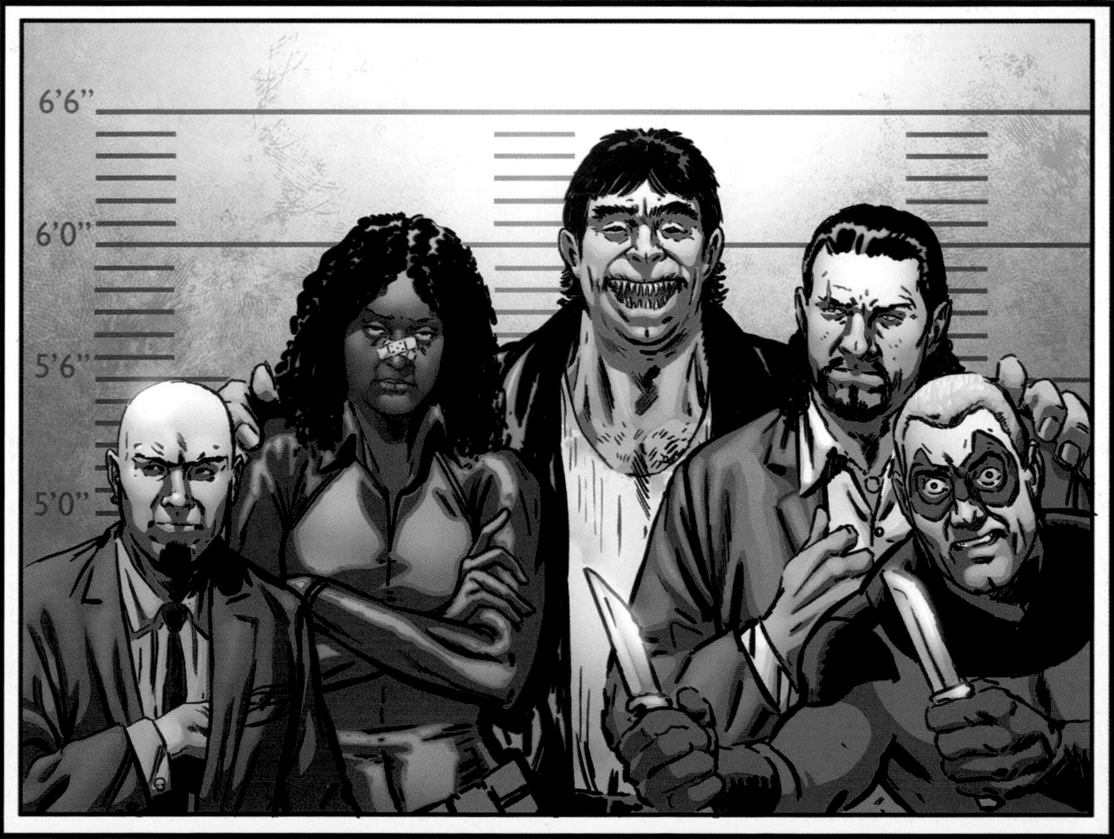

6'6"
6'0"
5'6"
5'0"

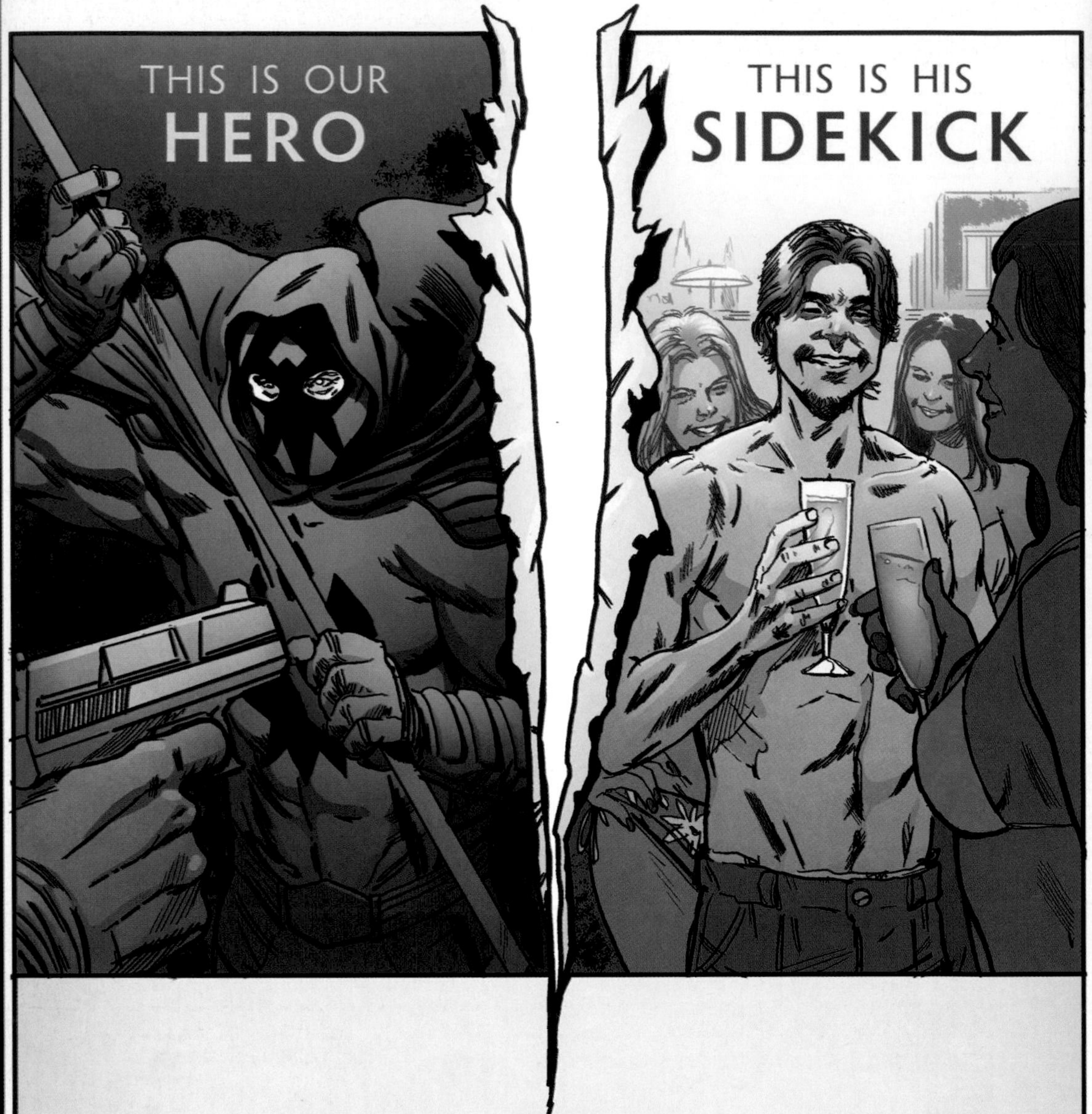
THIS IS OUR HERO
THIS IS HIS SIDEKICK
INSUFFERABLE
WAID • KRAUSE • WOODARD
MAY 2012

THESE ARE OUR VILLAINS

OMINAX

PRAETOREAN

THE CHOICE

RAZORJAW

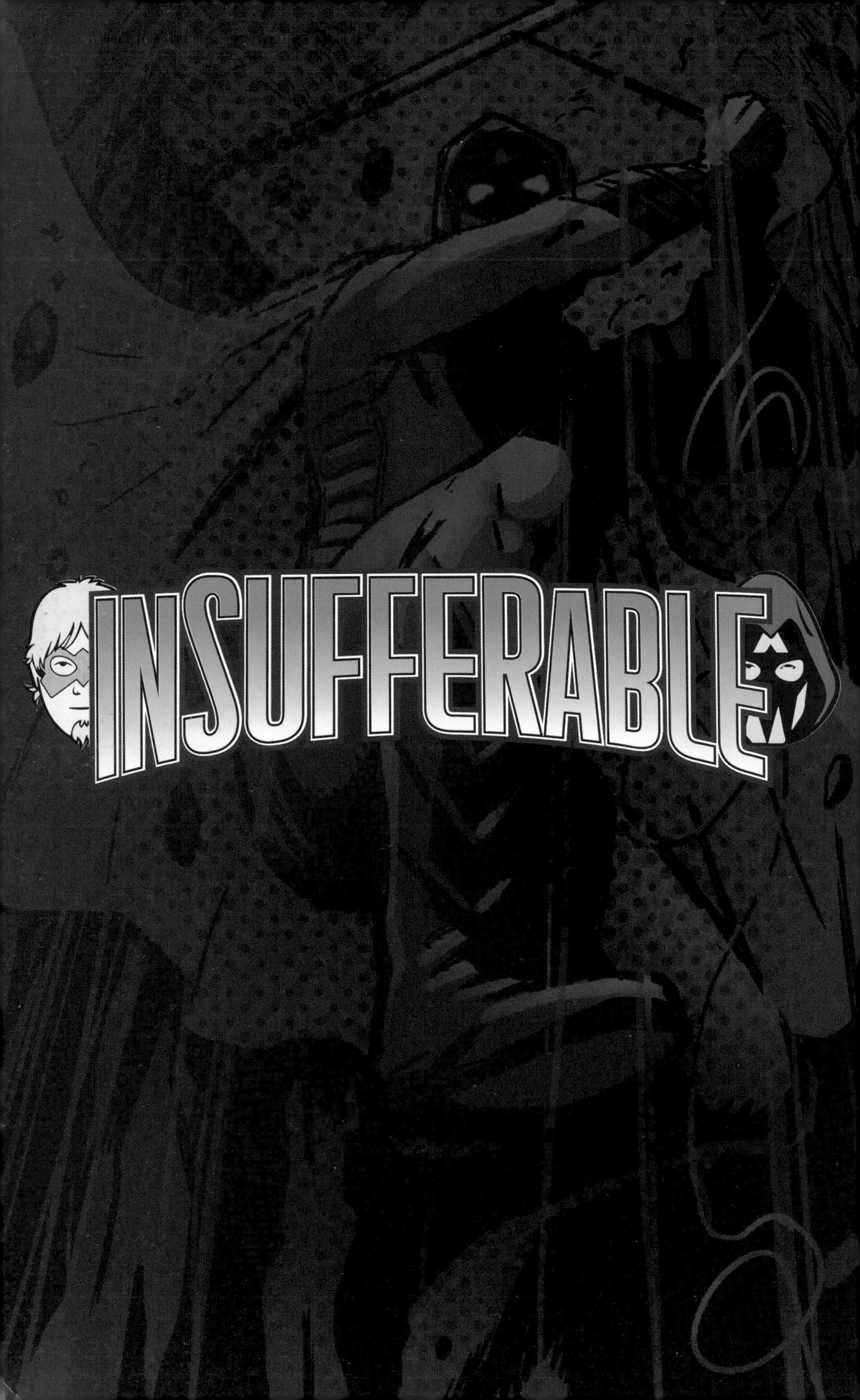
INSUFFERABLE